Extension Generally used to describe a payment plan that provides an extended period of time for *full* payment of creditors' claims.

Former-business bankrupt A bankrupt who is not engaged in a business venture at the time the bankruptcy petition is filed but whose financial problems result from earlier involvement in business.

Garnishment Withholding by employers of a percentage or dollar amount of an employee's wages for payment directly to a creditor or creditors according to a court order. Procedures for effecting garnishment are matters of state law and vary widely.

Insolvency Generally understood to mean inability to pay debts as they become due. For most purposes of the Bankruptcy Act, it means that the fair value of a debtor's property is less than his obligations.

Involuntary petition A petition filed by creditors alleging that the debtor has committed an "act of bankruptcy" as defined by the statute.

Lien A creditor's interest, created by statute, judicial process, or agreement, in property which can then be used for the repayment of an obligation if the debtor defaults.

No-asset case A case in which all of the bankrupt's property, if any, is exempt by virtue of state or federal laws applying to bankruptcy proceedings.

Nominal-asset case A case in which proceeds of nonexempt assets are consumed by payment of administrative expenses, leaving nothing to be distributed to creditors.

Nonbusiness bankrupt A bankrupt whose financial problems are unrelated to involvement in a business operation.

Priority creditor A creditor whose claim is among categories specified by the Bankruptcy Act to be paid first after secured claims and expenses of administering the case have been paid.

Proof of claim A document filed by creditors with the bankruptcy court. It provides details of amounts allegedly owed by the bankrupt and of the transaction on which the claim is based. In case of objections, its validity is decided by the referee.

Receiver An official appointed by the referee in straight bankruptcy proceedings to look

after the asse... tion and the ... trustee. A re... Chapter X c... and in Chapte... ... not to leave the debtor in charge of his own affairs while the proceeding is pending.

Referee A federal official appointed for a term of six years to preside over bankruptcy cases.

Restraining order An order obtained either by the petitioner or by other creditors to prevent a creditor or creditors from proceeding with individual collection efforts after the bankruptcy petition has been filed.

Schedules The petitioner's lists of debts and assets, which are required to be filed either with the bankruptcy petition or shortly thereafter. Items on these lists are referred to as "scheduled."

Secured creditor A creditor who holds an interest in collateral as security for the payment of its debt. Typical security agreements include mortgages on real estate and automobiles.

Straight bankruptcy A colloquialism not found in the Bankruptcy Act, but referring to the type of proceeding in which the bankrupt's distributable assets (if any) are divided among creditors who have proved claims and the bankrupt may receive a discharge.

Trustee An official either elected by creditors at a meeting held before the referee or appointed by the referee if the creditors fail to elect. The trustee is responsible for the collection and distribution of the bankrupt's property.

Turnover order An order by the referee or district judge requiring that property or the proceeds from the sale of property be turned over to the receiver or trustee for administration as part of the bankruptcy estate.

Unsecured creditor A creditor whose claim is neither secured by collateral nor given priority under the Bankruptcy Act. (This designation, employed almost universally, is technically imprecise because priority creditors also are not secured.)

Writ of execution A document issued to a court officer (usually a sheriff or constable) after judgment, authorizing the officer to pick up and liquidate assets for the purpose of satisfying the judgment.

DAVID T. STANLEY *and* MARJORIE GIRTH
with the collaboration of
Vern Countryman, Gerald R. Jantscher, Warren A. Law,
Victor G. Rosenblum, and Melvin G. Shimm

BANKRUPTCY

PROBLEM, PROCESS, REFORM

THE BROOKINGS INSTITUTION
Washington, D.C.

Copyright © 1971 by
THE BROOKINGS INSTITUTION
1775 Massachusetts Avenue, N.W., Washington, D.C. 20036

ISBN 0–8157–8098–2

Library of Congress Catalog Card Number 79–161592

1 2 3 4 5 6 7 8 9

THE BROOKINGS INSTITUTION is an independent organization devoted to nonpartisan research, education, and publication in economics, government, foreign policy, and the social sciences generally. Its principal purposes are to aid in the development of sound public policies and to promote public understanding of issues of national importance.

The Institution was founded on December 8, 1927, to merge the activities of the Institute for Government Research, founded in 1916, the Institute of Economics, founded in 1922, and the Robert Brookings Graduate School of Economics and Government, founded in 1924.

The general administration of the Institution is the responsibility of a Board of Trustees charged with maintaining the independence of the staff and fostering the most favorable conditions for creative research and education. The immediate direction of the policies, program, and staff of the Institution is vested in the President, assisted by an advisory committee of the officers and staff.

In publishing a study, the Institution presents it as a competent treatment of a subject worthy of public consideration. The interpretations and conclusions in such publications are those of the author or authors and do not necessarily reflect the views of the other staff members, officers, or trustees of the Brookings Institution.

Foreword

Although the quarter-century since the end of the Second World War has been characterized by general prosperity and rising incomes, it has also been a period in which the number of bankruptcies has increased dramatically—some twentyfold. The growth of a phenomenon regarded by many Americans with apprehension or distaste leads to several kinds of questions. What sorts of persons and businesses go bankrupt? Why do they do so? How are bankruptcies related to other economic events? How does the bankruptcy process work—and how well? What does it cost and who pays? What happens to bankrupts? Should the bankruptcy laws and procedures be changed? Such questions gain importance from two other trends in the postwar period: mounting public interest in the plight of the consumer (most bankruptcies are personal, or consumer, bankruptcies) and growing discontent with the effectiveness of judicial administration (bankruptcies are administered in federal courts).

Such questions and problems lay behind the request by representatives of the federal judiciary that Brookings undertake research in this field, for there had been no major study of bankruptcy administration in two decades and none of bankruptcy policy in three. This book, the product of that research, deals with the economic, legal, and personal aspects of the subject, but its main emphasis is on bankruptcy as a governmental process—on its institutions, personnel, procedures, and financing.

This study was directed by David T. Stanley, a senior fellow in the Brookings Governmental Studies Program, following a proposal developed by Victor G. Rosenblum of Northwestern University and Franklin P. Kilpatrick, now of The Ohio State University, after exploratory research by Mr. Rosenblum. Mr. Stanley was assisted full time by Marjorie Girth, now of the State University of New York at Buffalo Law School, and part time by Vern Countryman of Harvard Law School, Warren A. Law of Harvard Business School, Melvin G. Shimm of Duke University Law School, Mr. Rosenblum, and Gerald R. Jantscher of the Brookings Economic Studies staff. Jeanne B. Walker and Sara Sklar served successively as administrative secretaries. The project was under the general supervision of George A. Graham, director of Governmental Studies, and his successor, Gilbert Y. Steiner. The manuscript was edited for publication by Elizabeth H. Cross, statistics were checked for accuracy by Evelyn P. Fisher, and the index was prepared by Joan C. Culver.

This study was supported by grants from the Ford Foundation and the Walter E. Meyer Research Institute of Law.

The statements, conclusions, and recommendations are those of the authors and do not necessarily reflect the views of the trustees, officers, or staff members of the Ford Foundation, the Meyer Institute, or the Brookings Institution.

KERMIT GORDON
President

September 1971
Washington, D.C.

Acknowledgments

Many persons and organizations helped us in preparing this study. We were assisted in evaluating our findings and recommendations and in a review of the manuscript by an advisory committee consisting of Samuel Ballin of Milbank, Tweed, Hadley and McCloy, New York City; Clark Byse, Harvard Law School; David Caplovitz, Sociology Department, Columbia University; Judge Phillip Forman, Trenton, New Jersey; Charles Horsky of Covington & Burling, Washington, D.C.; Esther Peterson, former assistant secretary of labor; John Vogel, executive vice president, National Bank of North America, West Hempstead, New York; and J. Wilson White, assistant general credit manager, E. I. du Pont de Nemours & Company. These persons served as individuals, not as representatives of their organizations. We are grateful for their frank and knowledgeable comments.

We also appreciate the cooperation and assistance of Warren Olney III, director, Administrative Office of the United States Courts; his successor, Ernest C. Friesen, Jr., and the staff of the Office, particularly Royal E. Jackson, chief of the Bankruptcy Division, and his associates Berkeley Wright, H. Kent Presson, Thomas A. Beitelman, Jr., Ernest Geeslin, and the late William Miller; Edwin L. Covey, retired chief of the Bankruptcy Division; and the district judges, referees in bankruptcy, and others who aided our research in the eight federal court districts studied. Also Fountain Meadows and his associates at Chilton Research Services, Philadelphia; Georges Biro of Market Probe International, New York City; John Davies of the Gallup Organization, Inc.; Alan D,

Carey of Associated Credit Bureaus of America, Inc.; Harold T. Redding of Dun and Bradstreet, Inc.; Stefan A. Riesenfeld of the University of California (Berkeley) School of Law; James A. Bayton of Howard University; and Peter G. Fish of Duke University. Our thanks, too, for aid from officers of the National Bankruptcy Conference, the National Conference of Referees in Bankruptcy, the National Association of Credit Management, the National Consumer Finance Association, and the Consumer Bankruptcy Committee of the American Bar Association.

The following persons effectively conducted field research in specific districts: John A. Spanogle of the University of Maine Law School; Charles E. Corker of the University of Washington Law School; C. Thomas Dienes and Charles M. Steinberg of Northwestern University Law School; Robert S. Summers and Laird C. Kilpatrick of the University of Oregon Law School; Pierre R. Loiseaux, Ellen Hendrick, and William Huie, Jr., of the University of Texas Law School; and Martin Levine, Ronald W. Stovitz, Sally Hart Lohr-Schmidt, Thomas S. Loo, Martin L. Mandel, Larry Sandel, and Neil McCarroll, Jr., of the University of Southern California Law School.

Valuable criticism of the draft manuscript was received from Mr. Jackson and members of his staff, from Geoffrey C. Hazard, Jr., of the American Bar Foundation, Howard Schnoor of the Bureau of the Budget, Herbert Jacob of Northwestern University, Mr. Spanogle, and several anonymous readers.

We are particularly grateful to Jeanne Walker and Sara Sklar for their patience and skill in coordinating administrative and secretarial details, and to Elizabeth Cross for expert handling of difficult editorial problems.

DAVID T. STANLEY

MARJORIE GIRTH

Contents

TEXT TABLES

APPENDIX TABLES

What Is Happening and What Needs to Be Done

Over the last quarter-century, in good times as well as bad, Americans have been going bankrupt in greatly increasing numbers. One citizen out of every five either has been involved in a bankruptcy proceeding, as a bankrupt or a creditor, or is acquainted with someone who has become bankrupt. Each year nearly one American in a thousand files a petition in bankruptcy, and nearly $2 billion in debts are canceled in the bankruptcy courts. It is a rare businessman who has never known a bankrupt among his associates, his suppliers, or his customers. And no matter what the monetary costs of bankruptcy are, there are also human costs—frustration, controversy, and wasted effort. Yet bankruptcy has received only sporadic attention from scholars and is ignored by the news media except when some movie star or business tycoon appears in bankruptcy court.

This book presents the results of the most comprehensive review of the operation of bankruptcy in the United States that has been undertaken in the past thirty years. Bankruptcy—the law, the institutions, and the procedures established to deal with persons and businesses that are unable to pay their debts—is studied primarily as a governmental process, although the discussion deals also with points of finance, economics, and law. In the course of the study hundreds of bankruptcy cases were analyzed and hundreds of persons interviewed in eight judicial districts. Most of this first chapter is devoted to a summary of our findings and recommendations and to an explanation of the methods used to study bankruptcy problems. In Chapter 2 we explain what bankruptcy is all about, and in Chapter 3 present statistics that describe bankruptcy in the United States and discuss its impact on the functioning of our economy. In Chapters 4–9, the operation of the bankruptcy system is described in detail: what happens to the bankrupt not only while he is in bankruptcy court but before he gets there and after he leaves. The final chapter recommends steps to improve the whole process.

The specialist will find it convenient to have this summary chapter at the outset. Others are urged to use it for reference after considering the main body of our work. Throughout the book the reader may find it helpful to consult the glossary of technical terms (inside the front and back covers) whenever he needs to refresh his memory.

FINDINGS OF THIS STUDY

1. The annual number of personal bankruptcies increased by a factor of twenty during the first two decades after World War II, reaching a peak of 191,729 in 1967. The rate then declined for two years but rose again in 1970. Many overburdened debtors go bankrupt when their creditors threaten to collect their debts through legal action, particularly when the threat is to garnishee their wages and put their jobs in jeopardy.

2. Business bankruptcies have also increased in number, though at a much slower rate than personal bankruptcies, and now represent fewer than one out of twelve bankruptcies. Most of them are small businesses, typically going bankrupt with $12,000 in assets and $40,000 in liabilities; but there are a few large-scale failures every year. Business bankruptcies usually result from a combination of poor business management and unfavorable market conditions.

3. Bankrupts are not destitute. The typical personal bankrupt is a blue-collar worker with an eleventh-grade education who is earning more than $100 a week.

4. Although the American people in general disapprove of bankruptcy, the bankrupts themselves show a wide range of attitudes about their experience—some are ashamed, some are angry, some are relieved, some are numb, and some are even happy.

5. There are wide variations in how bankruptcy is administered

from one district to another and from one state to another, despite
the uniform federal law and court structure. State laws vary enormously, particularly concerning what property the bankrupt may
keep (called exempt assets) and what efforts creditors may make to
collect their debts. Even among the federal bankruptcy courts there
are striking differences in policies.

6. Little rehabilitation takes place under the special provisions
of the rehabilitative chapters of the Bankruptcy Act. A majority of
these cases end in failure, and are either dismissed or converted into
straight bankruptcy proceedings.

7. Despite the stigma of bankruptcy and the evidence it gives of
financial failure, debtors find it really no harder to get credit after
bankruptcy than they did before. Creditors take the risk of losses on
bad debts in order to do business.

8. The remarkable increase in the rate of bankruptcies since
World War II is probably attributable above all else to the rapid
growth in the volume of personal indebtedness that took place during these years. The rate of bankruptcies was also sensitive in the
short run to changes in the level of unemployment.

9. The effect of bankruptcy on the general economy is not substantial or detrimental.

10. Creditors get so little out of bankruptcy proceedings that
they have almost no incentive to be interested. They do not bother
to prove their claims or to exercise their rights to "creditor control"
of the proceedings. In any event, their losses are passed along to
other customers in the form of higher prices or to the taxpayer.

11. Except in the largest and most lucrative cases, bankrupts are
typically represented by attorneys who handle their cases routinely,
unimaginatively, and often inexpertly.

12. Administratively, the bankruptcy system as it is managed
through the courts violates most principles of sound organization
and management. The system provides inadequate supervision,
audit, and investigation, leading to opportunities for error and
fraud. Procedures are slow and archaic; records are incomplete and
sloppy.

13. The personnel system meets literally no accepted standards
of effective personnel administration: there are no merit system
policies, systematic employee relations procedures, or adequate
training programs.

14. Over 70 percent of all bankruptcy cases have no assets left after exempt property is set aside and pay neither administrative costs nor creditors. In just over half of the rest, administrative costs consume the excess assets. Thus creditors receive payment in approximately 15 percent of the cases. In this last group, administrative costs consume an average of one-quarter of the assets.

15. Bankruptcy is the only federal legal proceeding that is self-supporting—that is, one in which the parties are expected to pay all or a substantial part of the costs of administering their case and a share of the overhead costs of the system. There is no justification for such a policy.

16. Most of the priorities given to certain classes of creditors (such as taxes owed or rent due landlords) are based on dubious logic and indefensible social policy.

17. Although the debtor is discharged of the debts listed in his bankruptcy, he is sometimes harassed by his creditors about his discharged debts, and sometimes makes binding new agreements to pay them.

This assembly of administrative and fiscal error and confusion has become an accepted way of professional life for the personnel of the bankruptcy courts, their supervisors, the district court judges, and members of the bankruptcy bar. The problems are so pervasive and so interlocked that partial solutions are not acceptable. The mess is too bad to tinker with. We need a new bankruptcy act, a new organizational structure, a new personnel system, a new method of financing, and new records and procedures.

WHAT NEEDS TO BE DONE?

Under the new bankruptcy system that we recommend:

1. All bankruptcy cases except reorganizations of corporations would be handled by a newly established administrative agency using the most effective modern procedures. (Reorganizations would remain in district courts.) The personnel of this agency would be selected, promoted, and developed under an effective merit system. Its methods would be brisk but humane.

2. Deadlines would be shortened and procedures streamlined so that typical small no-asset bankruptcy cases would be processed in

a small fraction of the time now consumed. The total record-keeping, communication, recording, and filing processes would be redesigned in accordance with the latest principles of integrated data processing.

3. There would be effective appeals provisions within the bankruptcy agency, as well as ready access to the federal courts.

4. Financial counseling would be available to debtors as long as their cases were pending.

5. The bankruptcy system, like other federal adjudicative processes, would be financed out of general revenues, although modest filing fees might be charged.

6. Debtors in uncomplicated, uncontested cases could choose to dispense with the services of an attorney.

7. Bankruptcy officials would disallow or reduce debts which were clearly unconscionable or which resulted from improvident extension of credit.

8. Uniform, nationwide, more realistic exemption provisions would replace the present hodgepodge of allowances in state laws.

9. The number of grounds for objection to discharges would be reduced, as would the number of types of claims that could be excepted from discharges.

10. Tax authorities and landlords would no longer receive priority in the distribution of bankruptcy proceeds, but employees who were owed wages would be more generously provided for.

11. Salaried appraisers would promptly value each debtor's property so that he would be fairly treated with respect to his exempt property, his secured debts, and any deficiency judgments that had been obtained.

12. The business rehabilitative provisions of the Bankruptcy Act (Chapter XI) would be revised so that "feasibility" would be based on a finding that the business could survive after the plan had been completed.

13. Provisions for the rehabilitation of individual debtors (Chapter XIII) would be broadened to include persons other than wage earners, and administered so that objecting creditors would be compelled to accede to workable, generally beneficial plans.

14. Debtors would be more effectively protected by law from efforts to collect discharged debts.

15. The administrative agency responsible for bankruptcy would

be regularly and effectively appraised to ensure that it was operating with fairness, integrity, and speed.

Recommendations of such scope and force are necessary because of the many interrelated shortcomings of the bankruptcy process. We repeat that partial changes will not do the job. These recommendations will be opposed by organizations and persons with a stake in the present system. Yet sweeping reforms must be made if both debtors and creditors are to be treated fairly and efficiently.

METHOD OF STUDY

These findings and recommendations are based primarily on case analyses and interviews in eight federal judicial districts: Northern Ohio, Northern Alabama, Maine, Northern Illinois, Oregon, Western Texas, Southern New York, and Southern California.[1] These courts were chosen to reflect variations in geography, population, the economy of the area, type and volume of bankruptcy caseload, relative costs of bankruptcy proceedings, and extent to which rehabilitative proceedings were used. Within each district, the Brookings research staff observed court proceedings and interviewed referees in bankruptcy, district judges, and a variety of trustees, attorneys, creditors, business debtors, and other persons with a direct interest in bankruptcy proceedings.[2] With a few exceptions, all district judges, referees, and Chapter XIII trustees were interviewed.[3] An effort was made to see the more prominent and active trustees, attorneys, and others. They were selected on the basis of suggestions by referees, local law school faculties, and members of the bar. Many were interviewed because of the frequency with which their names appeared in the cases sampled.

1. In 1966, after our field research was completed, the Northern and Southern California districts were reconstituted as four districts. No combination of the new districts has boundaries coextensive with those of the district we studied, so more recent data are not strictly comparable.

2. See Appendix Table A-1 for the number of persons in each category interviewed in each district.

3. In Southern New York all referees in New York City and five of the judges were interviewed. The only other exceptions were instances where appointments could not be made because of illness or other compelling reasons.

CASE FILE ANALYSES

Several constraints were imposed on the number and kinds of bankruptcy cases studied. First, the sample was limited to cases closed in fiscal year 1964—recent enough that the data and some of the people would be available, yet old enough that information might be obtained about debtor rehabilitation. Second, two rare categories of cases were excluded because they are apart from the mainstream of bankruptcy processes and problems: railroad reorganizations and readjustments of debts of local government agencies. Third, the number of cases of each type to be studied was determined by judging the probable staff and time available, and the number needed to convey a reasonable understanding of the elements and factors involved. Thus it was considered necessary to study more asset cases than no-asset cases, for the latter, though more numerous, are simpler to analyze.[4]

Cases were sampled at random from records filed when cases were closed. In some instances a sample case led to a related case: the bankrupt's spouse; the bankrupt's partner(s); a personal bankruptcy tied to a corporate bankruptcy, or vice versa. The related case was then added to the sample so that the whole story would be there for study. The sample finally contained 1,675 cases, of which 1,120 were straight bankruptcies.[5] Personal, as opposed to business, cases accounted for 824 of the straight bankruptcies and 1,277 of the total cases studied.

The information in the cases (amounts of debts, length of time taken, administrative costs, payments to creditors, and much other information) was tabulated by computer.

OTHER STUDIES

Several supplementary studies supplied other needed data:
1. Interviews with 400 individual debtors and bankrupts in seven

4. Only business asset cases were sampled in Southern New York. This was done after research in the other seven districts showed that the business cases covered in the seven might be too few and too small to provide a sufficient basis for conclusions.
5. The numbers of cases abstracted and analyzed in each district are shown in Appendix Table A-2, with sampling rates and the multipliers used to correct for differences in sampling rates among districts.

of the eight districts provided details about their circumstances and reactions.[6]

2. The general public were interviewed as part of a Gallup poll to find out their knowledge and attitudes about bankruptcy.[7]

3. Credit bureau information was obtained about the bankrupts and debtors in our sample, both as of the time they filed petitions in bankruptcy court, and later.[8]

4. Dun and Bradstreet provided whatever information was available about businesses in the Brookings sample that had been through rehabilitative proceedings under the Bankruptcy Act.

5. The authors mailed a questionnaire to more than a thousand trial attorneys drawn from a professional mailing list to find out the extent to which negligence suits were deterred by a defendant's threatening to file in bankruptcy, or actually doing so.[9]

6. At the request of the authors the staff of the Administrative Office of the United States Courts obtained information on (a) professional backgrounds and tenure of referees in bankruptcy, (b) costs of operation of referees' offices, and (c) the nature and outcome of petitions for review (appeals).

7. In an effort to get cost figures to compare with those of the bankruptcy courts, costs of liquidating property in eight federal agencies were investigated.

8. Studies were made of the bankruptcy process in several other countries to find out what features, if any, might be applicable to the United States.[10]

The results of these studies are presented in more detail in subsequent sections of this book.

6. For methodological detail, see Appendix A, section 3.

7. For methodological detail, see Appendix A, section 4.

8. For methodological detail, see Appendix A, section 5.

9. See Appendix Table A-6 for the number of questionnaires sent out and returned for each district, the rates of return, sampling rates, and multipliers used to correct for differences in interdistrict comparisons.

10. See Appendix B, section 5.

2

The Meaning of Bankruptcy

The bankruptcy process[1] was established to resolve in a fair and orderly manner the conflicts in interest that arise among the creditors of a debtor who cannot pay his debts. Other legal remedies are available that enable creditors to attempt to recover their claims from the property of the debtor; but if that property is too meager to pay all claims in full, one creditor's success in satisfying his claim causes loss to another creditor.

In the absence of a bankruptcy law, the news that a debtor was unable to pay his debts could start a race among his creditors to press their claims against his assets before they were used up. In such a "race of diligence," chance and circumstance would decide the outcome: some creditors might satisfy their claims entirely, while others would be paid little or nothing. Only by luck would the debtor's property be distributed among his creditors in a manner generally felt to be equitable.

Unhealthy temptations to preferential treatment would also be created. An insolvent debtor might offer to pay something to only one or two of his creditors. If the offer were accepted, the other creditors would be deprived of a fair share of his property.

The object of the bankruptcy law is to ensure that all creditors

---

1. This chapter is a very simplified explanation of the various processes carried out under the Bankruptcy Act. It omits many exceptions to general practices and many other procedural and legal details.

are treated fairly. It does not require equal treatment for all but treats the claims of some creditors as superior to the claims of others and states that the former are to be paid ahead of the latter. So creditors are allocated to classes according to the nature of their claims before any distribution is made. Members of different classes are treated differently. But within each class all creditors are treated equally and no creditor's claim is given precedence.

For centuries bankruptcy law served this object above all others. At the end of the nineteenth century, however, another object became equally important in the United States. The bankruptcy process became also a method of granting relief to the honest but unfortunate debtor, who through ill luck or bad judgment was burdened with more debt than he could afford. The earliest bankruptcy law contained no provision for discharging the debts of a bankrupt debtor; if the proceeds from the sale of his estate fell short of meeting all his creditors' claims, the bankrupt remained in debt for the unpaid balance. Today, however, not only does bankruptcy law allow discharges to be granted, but they are granted practically as a matter of course. The bankrupt is relieved of all liability for any balances that will remain after his property has been sold and the proceeds applied against his creditors' claims. He is said to be "discharged from his debts." (The statute enumerates a few debts from which a bankrupt cannot be discharged. More will be said of them later.)

The examination of the bankrupt and of his accounts during the proceeding allows the court to investigate the way he managed his affairs in the period before he became bankrupt. Theoretically, this investigation affords an opportunity for uncovering evidence of illegal conduct. As a practical matter, criminal proceedings are very rarely instituted against business bankrupts and almost never against consumer bankrupts.

EARLY BANKRUPTCY LAWS

Since the founding of the Republic, the Constitution has given to Congress the power "to establish . . . uniform laws on the subject of bankruptcies throughout the United States." Congress exercises this power irregularly, however, and during the first century of the nation's history, federal bankruptcy laws, rather than state laws, were in force for a total of just fifteen years. Three times (1800, 1841,[2] and 1867) Congress enacted a law, and three times (1803, 1843, and 1878) Congress repealed it. Each time the law had been enacted in response to an economic crisis, and each time it failed to serve the needs of both creditors and debtors.

During the intervals between the repeal of one federal bankruptcy act and the passage of the next, state bankruptcy laws were controlling. Such laws were not satisfactory. They were not uniform, and some of them discriminated against out-of-state creditors.

Twenty years later another economic crisis produced the Bankruptcy Act of 1898, which has continued in force to the present day, and there is no reason now to doubt the permanency of federal control. The last serious attempts to repeal this law were made more than half a century ago. The act has been amended more than ninety times since its passage, most extensively in 1938 by the Chandler Act.

THE BANKRUPTCY ACT TODAY

The Bankruptcy Act currently consists of fourteen chapters. The first seven lay the foundations and build much of the structure of the bankruptcy system: they establish the federal district courts as the courts of bankruptcy, define the rights and duties of bankrupts and their creditors, spell out the procedural rules that must be followed in the proceedings, create the offices of referee and trustee, prescribe how the bankrupt's estate is to be administered and distributed, and in general do all that must be done to enable a straight bankruptcy proceeding to be started and carried to conclusion.

Chapters VIII through XIII authorize the special chapter proceedings. Much of the substance of these chapters was incorporated in the law in 1938, after the hard experience of the Great Depression. Chapter VIII has to do with the reorganization of interstate railroad corporations. Chapter IX concerns the composition of debts of certain public authorities. Few proceedings are conducted under either chapter, a dramatic exception being the reorganization of

2. The 1841 act took effect in 1842.

the Penn Central railroad under Chapter VIII. Chapter X is more important, for it contains the elaborate and lengthy rules for reorganizing corporations in the courts of bankruptcy. Chapters XI, XII, and XIII are about arrangements (discussed below). Chapter XI covers unsecured debts in business cases. Chapter XII, infrequently used, provides for noncorporate bankrupts' debts that are secured by liens on real property. Chapter XIII authorizes arrangements under which wage earners pay a part of their earnings to the courts, which in turn pay off creditors' claims. Chapter XIV covers treatment of maritime liens.

VOLUNTARY AND INVOLUNTARY STRAIGHT BANKRUPTCY

Bankruptcy proceedings begin with the filing of a petition in court asking that a debtor be declared a bankrupt. Usually the petition is filed by the debtor, who is seeking the benefit of a discharge from his debts; this is voluntary bankruptcy. An involuntary bankruptcy may be filed by creditors to force the liquidation of the debtor's estate and the application of the proceeds to the payment of their claims (by one creditor if there are fewer than twelve in all; otherwise by three).

It used to be that a bankruptcy proceeding could be instituted only by the second of these methods. The idea that a person might procure his own bankruptcy would have seemed preposterous in view of the suggestion of past misdeeds or irregular conduct that clung to the condition. But attitudes changed, and finally debtors were empowered to file their own petitions in bankruptcy. Today such voluntary bankruptcies outnumber involuntary bankruptcies by more than one hundred to one.

Almost any person or organization that can go into debt can become bankrupt. Persons, partnerships, unincorporated businesses, corporations—with some exceptions—all may become bankrupts. But no farmer can be put into involuntary bankruptcy, nor a wage earner whose earnings are less than $1,500 a year, nor anyone whose total debts are less than $1,000, nor a nonprofit corporation.

In discussions of bankruptcy, a distinction is often drawn between business and nonbusiness bankruptcies. This division is a convenient one, because business bankruptcies are often considerably more complicated than nonbusiness bankruptcies and may raise a much wider range of problems; so the division will be maintained in this book. But a different nomenclature will be used: nonbusiness bankruptcies will be called "personal" bankruptcies. And personal bankruptcies will be subdivided into two classes, one called "former business" bankruptcies, and the other, "nonbusiness" bankruptcies. The first class consists of cases in which some of the debtor's financial difficulties had their source in his conduct of a business that closed its doors before the bankruptcy proceedings began. The second class includes all other personal bankruptcy cases. The reader will be reminded of this distinction when the subject of personal bankruptcies is taken up in a later chapter.

For many years bankruptcy proceedings knew but one conclusion: the bankrupt surrendered his estate, if any, to the court, the estate was liquidated, the proceeds were distributed to the various classes of creditors, and the bankrupt was discharged from his debts. A proceeding that ends this way today, as about 85 percent of bankruptcy cases do, is known as "straight bankruptcy."

ARRANGEMENTS AND REORGANIZATIONS

Years ago it was realized that so drastic a remedy as straight bankruptcy might not be necessary to solve the problems of overburdened debtors. Thus there developed common-law *compositions*, under which creditors could agree to accept partial payment in satisfaction of their claims, and *extensions*, under which they could agree to longer times for repayment. Sometimes a combination of both could be used. These remedies suffered from the weakness that a minority of obstinate creditors might withhold their consent from a proposed payment plan and refuse to be bound by it.

Common-law compositions and extensions are still used in situations in which all or most creditors can agree. But under Chapters XI and XIII of the Bankruptcy Act, a composition or extension, or both, can be imposed on all unsecured creditors if a majority consent to the terms of the proposed payment plan. Such plans are called *arrangements*.

Chapter XI is used by business debtors and by persons who are not wage earners. Chapter XIII was added to the Bankruptcy Act in 1938 to help low-income debtors. Only wage earners may take advantage of its provisions. At one time eligibility was restricted to those whose annual earnings did not exceed a certain modest amount, but that restriction has been removed. The chapter was adopted in the belief that many debtors struggling under their burdens could avoid bankruptcy and pay their debts in full or in part over an extended period if the court would approve and supervise a plan for the repayment of their debts out of earnings, and would forbid their creditors to harass them while they carried it out. Once the debtor and a majority of his creditors accept the plan, the debtor is obliged to submit his earnings to the supervision of the court.

Even if a straight bankruptcy proceeding has been started, it can be converted to an arrangement proceeding if the debtor and creditors can agree on a proposal for payments. Such a proceeding may take longer, but the debtor avoids being stigmatized as a bankrupt, retains his assets, and the creditors may ultimately receive larger payments than the straight bankruptcy proceeding would have produced. If the debtor offers a plan for adjustment of his debts that is acceptable to a majority of his creditors, the court will usually confirm the arrangement and enforce it.

Like arrangements, *reorganizations* are also an alternative to straight bankruptcy. They are much less common and are normally resorted to only in the case of a large, publicly held corporation.

Bankruptcy proceedings providing for arrangements or reorganizations are sometimes called "chapter proceedings," in reference to the chapters of the Bankruptcy Act that set forth the procedures to be followed in each case. Chapter proceedings are also called "rehabilitative proceedings," although, as we shall see in later chapters, it is debatable whether many debtors are rehabilitated.

THE STRAIGHT BANKRUPTCY PROCESS IN BRIEF

We conclude by summarizing the course of an ordinary straight bankruptcy proceeding. This will help define terms used later in the book. The description is deliberately superficial since two later chapters contain a detailed description and critical discussion of the bankruptcy process, once for personal bankruptcies, and again for business bankruptcies.

The sketch presented here is of a voluntary personal bankruptcy proceeding. Along with his petition in bankruptcy, the debtor must also file with the court schedules that list his assets, debts, and exempt property. The last of these is property protected by the laws of the debtor's state against distribution to his creditors. So that he will not be left utterly destitute after passing through bankruptcy, a bankrupt may keep as much of his property as the laws of his state allow. These exemptions vary widely from state to state, being liberal in some and niggardly in others. They will be discussed in more detail in a later chapter.

It may seem surprising that state laws control any part of the bankruptcy process, when the power to enact bankruptcy laws is so plainly vested in Congress. The explanation is historical rather than logical: when Congress debated the bill that established the current bankruptcy system, some legislators demanded as the price of their support that the states be allowed to set exemptions for their residents; and the demand was granted. Earlier federal bankruptcy acts had provided for a uniform exemption throughout the country. Unquestionably, the present system of differing exemptions continues only on the sufferance of Congress; the power of Congress to enact a uniform exemption law for bankruptcy cases is disputed by no one.

REFEREES AND TRUSTEES

Bankruptcy proceedings are conducted before an official called a referee, who for most purposes is the "court of bankruptcy." His powers are similar to but not identical with or as extensive as those of a federal judge. It is he who calls and presides over meetings of the bankrupt's creditors, at which the bankrupt may be questioned about his debts and his property. If the bankrupt's estate amounts to anything, the creditors will elect a trustee to administer it; if they cannot agree on a choice or if no creditors are present at the meeting, the referee may appoint a trustee. It is the trustee's duty to collect the bankrupt's estate, liquidate it, and distribute the proceeds, called "dividends," to the creditors as directed by the referee.

Unlike the referee, who is paid a salary by the government, the trustee is paid a variable fee that depends in part on the size of the bankrupt's estate. The trustee receives ten dollars of the fifty-dollar fee the bankrupt paid when he filed his petition.[3] Many times this is all the trustee receives. Only when the bankrupt's estate exceeds his exemptions, leaving something to be paid to others, can the trustee be paid anything more. Then his fee is derived from the bankrupt's estate, and so ultimately comes from the creditors. If in the course of administering the estate he engaged the services of other personnel, such as an appraiser or an auctioneer, they too are paid from the nonexempt assets in the estate. If it is clear that the bankrupt's assets are negligible, it may be uneconomical as well as unnecessary to appoint a trustee.

SECURED DEBTS

It would be well to take notice here of an important class of debts, called secured debts, that require special treatment during the bankruptcy proceeding. A secured debt is one for which the creditor holds property that secures the fulfillment of the debtor's obligation and that may be applied to satisfaction of the debt in the event of default. Examples of secured debts are legion. Much consumer installment debt is of this kind, in which the security is the article of sale itself—an automobile, for instance, or a refrigerator. The seller does not keep the article, of course, but he can repossess it if the buyer defaults on his payments.

The treatment of secured debts in the bankruptcy process is highly complicated, and only the barest outline of the subject can be offered here. Let us assume that a creditor has filed a secured claim in bankruptcy court and that the court has taken possession of his security. If the value of the security is *less* than the amount of the debt, the court will turn the security over to the creditor. His claim will then be allowed only to the extent that the debtor's liability exceeds the value of the security. This excess liability will be treated as an unsecured debt and will be subject to discharge if it cannot be paid from the estate. If the value of the security is *more* than the amount of the debt, the court will sell it and pay the secured debt out of the proceeds.

3. Except when the bankrupt defaults on an undertaking to pay the fee in installments.

If the creditor took possession of and liquidated his security before the debtor entered bankruptcy, and if its value was insufficient to discharge the debtor's liability, the creditor may have gone to a state court to obtain a "deficiency judgment" ordering the debtor to pay off his indebtedness. But now the debt is an unsecured debt, because the creditor has reclaimed his security. When the debtor enters bankruptcy, his creditor may file an unsecured claim for the amount of the debt that remains, and the claim will be treated no differently than the claims of other unsecured creditors.

CLOSING STEPS

After the trustee has liquidated the bankrupt's estate, the proceeds are distributed as dividends to the bankrupt's creditors according to the priority of their claims. The Bankruptcy Act establishes an order in which claims are to be paid: the costs of administering the estate in bankruptcy are to be paid first; then wages and commissions that are owed to the bankrupt's employees, up to a limit of $600 a claimant; followed by other classes of claims, which include many federal, state, and local taxes the bankrupt owes, rent due his landlord, if the landlord is entitled to priority by state law, and federal claims other than taxes. Not until all the claims of the "priority creditors" are satisfied can any proceeds of the estate be paid to other unsecured creditors.

Meanwhile the court ordinarily will have discharged the bankrupt from those of his debts that are dischargeable. Some debts are not dischargeable. Debts the bankrupt omitted from the schedule he filed are not discharged unless the creditor had notice or actual knowledge of the bankruptcy. The Bankruptcy Act lists a number of assorted debts that a bankrupt cannot be discharged from, apparently on the ground that to permit their discharge would be contrary to the public interest. Examples of these are the bankrupt's liability for many federal, state, or local taxes, for credit obtained by fraud, for alimony or child support, and for "the seduction of an unmarried female."

After all expenses and dividends have been paid, the referee discharges the trustee, approves the accounts, and closes the case, and the records are turned over to the clerk of the district court.

3

The Economics of
Bankruptcy

Much of this book is concerned with details of the bankruptcy
process because we want to consider how well the process is doing
what is expected of it. First, however, we will examine the scale of
operations of the bankruptcy system in the United States, sketch
some of its features, inquire into the recent growth in the number of
bankruptcies, and consider briefly some of the effects of bankruptcy
on the economy.

GROWTH AND PRESENT SCALE OF BANKRUPTCIES

Figure 3-1 shows how many bankruptcy cases were filed in the
United States in each fiscal year from 1899 through 1970. A note-
worthy feature is the highly irregular growth in the rate of filings.
During several intervals, as from 1906 to 1915 and 1922 to 1932,
growth was slow but steady; at other times the annual number of
bankruptcy filings declined several years in a row, notably during
the two World Wars. But the most prominent feature is the record
of explosive growth in the rate of bankruptcy filings since the end
of World War II. In 1946, only 10,196 bankruptcy cases were filed,
fewer than in any other year of this century; in 1967, 208,329 cases
were filed, the highest number. Between those years, annual filings
increased almost continuously, though not at a uniform rate: in

FIGURE 3-1. *Number of Personal, Business, and Total Bankruptcy Cases Filed, by Fiscal Year*[a]

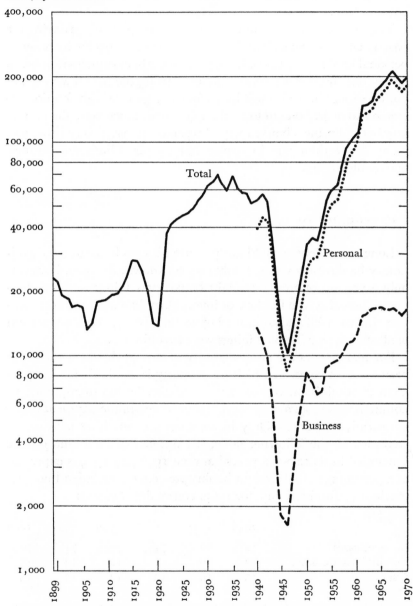

Sources: *Annual Report of the Attorney General of the United States* (through 1939), and Administrative Office of the U.S. Courts, "Tables of Bankruptcy Statistics" (1940–70).
a. Separate figures for personal and business bankruptcies are not available before 1940.

1952, the number declined below the previous year's, and after 1967, filings declined two years in a row, then increased again in 1970.

The dramatic increase in the rate of bankruptcy filings during the past twenty-five years has been caused largely by an increase in personal bankruptcy cases. In 1946 business bankruptcies numbered nearly one in every six bankruptcies. During the next few years, as both personal and business bankruptcy rates rose, this fraction increased to nearly one in four, then declined. Since 1961 the annual number of business bankruptcy filings has increased very little, and today fewer than one in twelve bankruptcy filings are business bankruptcy cases.[1]

CATEGORIES OF CASES

Long ago a debtor could not procure his own bankruptcy; involuntary bankruptcy was the only process known. By 1946, however, only 3 percent of annual straight bankruptcy filings were involuntary. Thereafter the fraction of involuntary bankruptcies rose temporarily, then fell and continued to decline. In 1970 only 0.7 percent of all straight bankruptcy filings were involuntary.

For many years the great majority of straight bankruptcies have been no-asset cases, in which no property is available for the payment of administrative expenses or for distribution to creditors. In nominal-asset cases any property is consumed in the payment of administrative expenses. Only in asset cases is anything paid to the creditors. In the following table, the number of each kind of case concluded in six selected years between 1946 and 1969 is expressed as a percentage of all straight bankruptcy cases concluded that year (excluding dismissed and, for 1969, consolidated cases):

	1946	1950	1955	1960	1965	1969
No-asset cases	72%	72%	74%	75%	74%	70%
Nominal-asset cases	13	10	11	12	13	15
Asset cases	15	18	15	13	13	15

1. These figures are taken from "Tables of Bankruptcy Statistics," issued annually by the Administrative Office of the U.S. Courts, Washington, D.C. Unless otherwise indicated, all bankruptcy statistics appearing in this section come from this source.

These data show no discernible trend. In particular, the number of no-asset cases has not increased faster than the number of cases in the other two classes. But the average *size* of asset bankruptcy cases has declined during the past twenty-five years, probably because of the much larger proportion of personal bankruptcies. In 1946 payments to creditors in asset straight bankruptcy cases totaled $7,490 a case; in 1968 creditors were paid just $3,087 a case. Meanwhile the claims of creditors in the same cases decreased from an average of $44,769 a case to $19,602. During this interval administrative costs declined roughly in proportion to the fall in payments to creditors, consuming in all years about one-fourth of the proceeds in asset cases.

The number of chapter proceedings filed each year has increased since World War II about as fast as the number of straight bankruptcy filings. In 1946 about 15 percent of all bankruptcy filings were of chapter proceedings; in 1970 they were about 16.5 percent of the total. Much the largest number of chapter proceedings are filed under the provisions of Chapter XIII—in the last few years about thirty thousand cases annually, or more than 95 percent of all chapter filings. Cases filed under Chapter XI, dealing with business arrangements, have fluctuated around one thousand a year since 1961. Filings under all other chapters have totaled less than two hundred a year.

WHAT CREDITORS RECEIVE

A few more statistics will show clearly how little creditors get out of bankruptcy proceedings. Let us look first at payments to creditors in straight bankruptcy cases. During the four fiscal years 1965 through 1968, according to the Administrative Office of the United States Courts, the average annual total of the claims of creditors in asset bankruptcy cases was nearly $431 million. Payments to creditors averaged just over $70 million a year—a return of just 16 cents on the dollar. The return varied among different classes of creditors: secured creditors, whose claims during this interval totaled 11 percent of all creditors' claims in asset bankruptcy cases, received an average of 66 cents on the dollar; priority creditors, who held 9 percent of all claims, received 35.5 cents on the dollar; the largest class—the unsecured creditors, whose claims were 80 percent of the total—received an average of just 7 cents on the dollar.

The return in Chapter XIII cases is much better because virtually all the wage plans provide for the full payment of creditors' claims over an extended period of time. From 1965 to 1968 creditors received $19 million out of $20.5 million—about 93 cents on the dollar.

Statistics on the amounts paid to creditors in Chapter XI proceedings are not as reliable as those on payments made in straight bankruptcy cases. A typical arrangement in such a proceeding calls for the immediate payment of part of a creditor's claim plus an extension of the time within which the debtor must pay another part, often after the debtor has left the court's supervision. Creditors typically agree to accept partial payment of their claims under the terms of the arrangement. The fault in the payments data is that they show nothing about the subsequent fulfillment of these agreements; they disclose only the amounts debtors paid to creditors, or agreed to pay to creditors, under the arrangements concluded each year in Chapter XI proceedings. (No comparable data are published for cases completed under the provisions of other chapters.)

If the default experience under these payment plans was good and creditors received nearly all they were promised, the payments made to creditors in chapter proceedings would have been nearly as large as those made in straight bankruptcy cases. Between 1965 and 1968, creditors were either paid or promised payment of an average of more than $45 million in the Chapter XI cases concluded each year. Their total claims averaged nearly $125 million, meaning that they would have received a return of 36.5 cents on the dollar.

There are obstacles in the way of putting these figures together to arrive at an average return to creditors in all bankruptcy cases. We have so far ignored no-asset and nominal-asset straight bankruptcy cases, because in these the creditors of the bankrupt are paid nothing. But their claims cannot be overlooked in computing an average return to creditors. No figures have been published since 1964 on the amount of claims allowed in no-asset bankruptcy cases. The claims of creditors in all bankruptcy cases concluded in that year, including Chapter XI and Chapter XIII proceedings, totaled $1,808 million, while creditors were paid or promised payment of about $99 million. So the average return to all creditors in bankruptcy cases in 1964 was no more than 5.5 cents on the dollar.

We attempted to update these figures to 1968 by estimating the growth of creditors' claims in no-asset cases since 1964 as the annual number of cases increased. We also tried to eliminate the double counting of some creditors' claims that occurs when husband and wife file separate petitions and list the same debts in their schedules. Our procedures are described in Appendix B, section 2. The estimates we prepared suggest that the claims of creditors in cases concluded in 1968 amounted to $2,168 million; that the creditors were paid or were promised payment of $131 million;[2] and that they thus received an average return of just over 6 cents on the dollar.

Personal bankruptcies greatly outnumber business bankruptcies, but the average business bankruptcy case is concerned with very much larger debts and assets than the average personal bankruptcy case. Of the $2,168 million in claims we estimate were allowed in all bankruptcy cases concluded in 1968, about $1,400 million must have been allowed in business bankruptcy cases and the rest in personal bankruptcy cases (see Appendix B, section 2). We are less sure what fraction of the $131 million of payments in all these cases was made to the creditors of business bankrupts, but it almost certainly was greater than the ratio of the claims in business cases to the claims in all cases.

How do the amounts paid to creditors in the bankruptcy courts compare with normal repayments of debt? The relevant statistics are poorly organized to facilitate such comparisons; but no matter what assumptions we make to cover gaps in the data, the amounts distributed to the creditors of bankrupts are negligible beside normal debt repayments. In calendar year 1968, for example, repayments of consumer installment credit totaled $88.1 billion.[3] In fiscal year 1968 the creditors in straight bankruptcy cases received $65.9 *million.* Only a portion of the latter amount is comparable to the repayment of consumer installment credit, since a large part of all such distributions goes to the creditors of business bankrupts, not to those of personal bankrupts. Even the distributions in personal bankruptcies are not made exclusively to installment creditors. On the other hand, $21.3 million must be added for payments made in cases closed that year to creditors under Chapter XIII wage plans. But whatever corrections are made to the statistics, distributions in

2. The estimate of $182 million that appears in Appendix B, section 2, includes $51 million of discharged debts that bankrupts later agreed to repay.

3. *Economic Report of the President, February 1971,* Table C-59, p. 267.

bankruptcy court remain inconsequential beside the total amounts that are repaid normally each year.

FACTORS IN THE GROWTH RATE

Since a person usually seeks the relief of bankruptcy only after he becomes hopelessly burdened with debt, the obvious place to turn first for an explanation of the recent increase in the personal bankruptcy rate is to the statistics of debt formation. These take us much of the way toward understanding the trend in bankruptcies, though they fall short of providing all the answers we seek. On the next several pages we review some of the evidence that can be extracted from credit and unemployment statistics to explain much of the increase in the personal bankruptcy rate. Then we consider an apparent relation between state wage garnishment laws and personal bankruptcy rates.

PERSONAL INDEBTEDNESS

It is plain enough why the bankruptcy rate declined sharply during the last several years of World War II and rose after the war ended. Many goods that were ordinarily bought on credit were scarce during the war (automobiles are a prime example); consumers were encouraged to save a large part of their incomes, and tight credit controls were put into effect. As a result the aggregate indebtedness of consumers declined sharply early in the war and remained low while personal income was rising, causing the bankruptcy rate to fall. Once the war was over and economic conditions returned to normal, consumers began adding to their indebtedness at a rapid rate, and the bankruptcy rate started rising.

The steady increase in aggregate personal indebtedness during the next twenty years probably explains most of the concurrent increase in personal bankruptcies. The relevant numbers are shown in Table 3-1. In constructing the table, we took statistics on outstanding debt between 1945 and 1970, adjusted them to reflect the growth in personal income during this period, and compared them with bankruptcy rates adjusted to reflect the increase in the nation's population during the same years. Because no credit statistics of

TABLE 3-1. *Personal Bankruptcies, Personal Debt, and Debt–Income Ratio, 1945–70*

Year[a]	(1) Personal bankruptcy filings	(2) Personal bankruptcy rate[b]	(3) Increase in personal bankruptcy rate[c] (percent)	(4) Personal debt outstanding[d] (billions of dollars)	(5) Personal debt as a percentage of personal income[e]	(6) Rate of increase in debt–income ratio[f] (percent)
1945	11,051	12.0		24.3	14.2	
1946	8,566	9.1	−23.6	31.4	17.7	24
1947	10,234	10.8	17.9	39.8	20.8	18
1948	13,537	14.1	30.6	47.7	22.7	9
1949	19,144	19.6	39.4	55.0	26.5	17
1950	25,040	25.3	29.0	66.7	29.3	10
1951	27,806	27.6	9.2	74.4	29.1	−1
1952	28,331	27.8	0.7	86.0	31.6	9
1953	33,315	32.4	16.3	97.5	33.8	7
1954	44,248	42.6	31.6	108.2	37.3	10
1955	50,219	47.9	12.4	127.0	40.9	10
1956	52,608	49.7	3.7	141.3	42.4	4
1957	63,617	59.5	19.7	152.6	43.5	3
1958	80,265	74.3	25.0	162.8	45.1	4
1959	88,943	81.6	9.8	182.4	47.6	6
1960	97,750	88.8	8.8	197.4	49.2	3
1961	131,402	118.3	33.2	211.0	50.7	3
1962	132,125	117.7	−0.5	230.3	52.0	3
1963	139,190	122.7	4.2	253.9	54.6	5
1964	155,209	135.0	10.1	277.9	55.9	2
1965	163,413	140.5	4.1	303.2	56.3	1
1966	175,924	149.5	6.4	321.1	54.7	−3
1967	191,729	161.1	7.8	338.2	53.7	−2
1968	181,266	149.4	−7.2	364.4	52.9	−1
1969	169,500	137.4	−8.0	389.3	52.0	−2
1970	178,202	142.2	3.4	401.1	50.1	−2

Sources: Col. 1: "Tables of Bankruptcy Statistics," issued annually by the Administrative Office of the United States Courts. Col. 2: col. 1 plus population estimates by age groups, *Economic Report of the President, February 1971*, Table C-21, p. 221. Col. 4: ibid., Tables C-58 and C-60, pp. 266 and 268. Col. 5: col. 4 plus estimates of personal income from ibid., Table C-14, p. 213.

a. Cols. 1, 2, and 3 are for fiscal years; cols. 4, 5, and 6 are for calendar years.

b. Number of filings of personal bankruptcy cases per 100,000 population aged 20 or over at beginning of fiscal year.

c. Equal in year t to (personal bankruptcy rate in year t minus personal bankruptcy rate in year $t − 1$)/(personal bankruptcy rate in year $t − 1$).

d. Sum of total consumer credit and mortgage debt outstanding on nonfarm one- to four-family properties on December 31 of year.

e. Debt as of December 31 of year. Income is that received during year.

f. Equal in year t to (entry in col. 5 in year t minus entry in col. 5 in year $t − 1$)/(entry in col. 5 in year $t − 1$).

exactly the kind we needed have ever been published, we made do with available substitutes. We selected the Federal Reserve Board's series on total consumer credit[4] and on mortgage debt outstanding on nonfarm one- to four-family houses. According to the 1963 Survey of Financial Characteristics of Consumers, these two credit components account for much the largest part of all the debt incurred by families in the United States, and more than 90 percent of the debt incurred by families in the income classes from which most bankrupts come.[5] The amounts of personal debt shown in column 4 of Table 3-1 are estimates of the amounts outstanding at the end of each year. In column 5 the debt figures are expressed as a percentage of personal income received that year, and it is this figure (hereafter called the "debt–income ratio") rather than the unadjusted debt that we shall pay attention to. The bankruptcy rate is expressed in column 2 as the number of personal bankruptcy cases filed per 100,000 persons in the United States who were twenty years of age or older at the start of the fiscal year. Columns 3 and 6 express the annual growth in the personal bankruptcy rate and debt–income ratio as a fraction of the figure for the preceding year.

There are sound reasons for supposing that changes in the personal bankruptcy rate would roughly parallel changes in the debt–income ratio, and indeed this seems to have happened. In 1946 the personal bankruptcy rate began a rise that was interrupted only once during the next twenty-one years. The rate fell substantially for the first time in fiscal 1968, and it fell again in 1969. The debt–

4. The Board defines consumer credit as "all short- and intermediate-term credit that is extended through regular business channels to finance the purchase of commodities and services for personal consumption, or to refinance debts incurred for such purposes." Board of Governors of the Federal Reserve System, *Supplement to Banking & Monetary Statistics*, Section 16 (new), "Consumer Credit" (Washington, 1965), p. 2. A few types of credit covered by this definition are not included in the series, for reasons explained in the source.

5. Alternatively we might have constructed estimates of the amount of household debt from the flow of funds accounts of the household sector, published periodically in the *Federal Reserve Bulletin*, which contain the most comprehensive tabulations available anywhere of what we call personal indebtedness. Besides true households, however, the household sector includes nonprofit organizations, and their debts would have to be separated from the totals. If we deleted those debts and eliminated other items that are in the nature of fixed charges against assets and impose no recurring burden on income, we would be left with little more than the sum of total consumer credit and household mortgage debt—nearly the same series as the one we used.

income ratio grew steadily between 1945 and 1965, turned down in 1966, and continued to decline in the succeeding years. Why the decline in the bankruptcy rate should have lagged more than a year behind the fall in the debt–income ratio is not clear, though the lag may be simply the time that elapses between a person's contracting more debt than he can afford and his decision to throw off the burden in bankruptcy court.[6] This pattern suggests that the fall in the debt–income ratio in the mid-1960s was closely related to the subsequent fall in the bankruptcy rate. To be sure, the bankruptcy rate has begun climbing again, despite the continuing decline in the debt–income ratio, but this reversal is probably due to the recent rise in unemployment, illustrating the close link between the bankruptcy and unemployment rates.

UNEMPLOYMENT

Although changes in the debt–income ratio appear to explain much of the postwar growth in the bankruptcy rate, the way that growth has fluctuated suggests that other economic forces have also affected it. The most important of these has probably been the state of the economy as reflected in the unemployment rate. This is as we would expect: whatever the amount of debt outstanding, an increase in unemployment is bound to touch a number of debtors who were already hard-pressed to meet their obligations, and will certainly force some of them into bankruptcy.

Thus in fiscal 1961 the personal bankruptcy rate increased sharply over the rate of the year before while the national unemployment rate was rising to its highest level of the postwar period. The unemployment rate fell throughout fiscal 1962, and the bankruptcy rate declined slightly that year. Similarly, as the economy entered recessions in fiscal years 1954 and 1958 and the unemployment rate rose, the personal bankruptcy rate spurted upward. Much the same thing happened in the late 1940s, when the debt–income ratio was growing rapidly; the personal bankruptcy rate showed its sharpest growth of the postwar period in fiscal 1949, when the recession of

6. A similar, though shorter, lag appears in the credit and bankruptcy statistics at the end of World War II, when the personal bankruptcy rate continued to fall for a time after the debt–income ratio had begun to rise. A more detailed comparative analysis appears in Appendix B, section 3.

28   BANKRUPTCY

1949 began. High rates of unemployment persisted until after the
beginning of the Korean war, and the bankruptcy rate reflected
this. The small increase in the bankruptcy rate in fiscal 1952 probably resulted from the slight decline in the debt–income ratio in
1951, along with the low rate of unemployment in fiscal 1952.

WAGE GARNISHMENT

A characteristic of bankruptcy in the United States is that the
rates differ greatly among the states, as is shown in Table 3-2. In

TABLE 3-2. *Number of Personal Bankruptcies per 100,000 Population,
by State, Selected Fiscal Years*[a]

State	1957	1962	1967	1969
Alabama	273	277	288	255
Alaska	2	13	49	62
Arizona	36	145	209	170
Arkansas	10	20	40	43
California	72	144	197	167
Colorado	87	128	223	165
Connecticut	20	33	47	38
Delaware	4	10	11	14
District of Columbia	10	12	8	11
Florida	2	7	19	18
Georgia	59	148	166	131
Hawaii	16	26	53	39
Idaho	38	92	135	136
Illinois	80	135	125	109
Indiana	15	77	136	134
Iowa	12	53	69	76
Kansas	57	124	143	184
Kentucky	48	85	151	151
Louisiana	17	54	77	108
Maine	69	153	183	168
Maryland	2	5	7	8
Massachusetts	13	16	27	23
Michigan	35	77	95	65
Minnesota	42	79	95	78
Mississippi	5	19	44	41
Missouri	28	74	119	101
Montana	23	73	88	115
Nebraska	25	42	79	79
Nevada	28	115	301	282
New Hampshire	13	60	123	98

TABLE 3-2 (*continued*)

State	1957	1962	1967	1969
New Jersey	5	12	18	16
New Mexico	13	53	103	130
New York	14	23	36	29
North Carolina	b	1	5	7
North Dakota	5	19	34	33
Ohio	57	132	178	141
Oklahoma	36	74	155	116
Oregon	113	202	246	208
Pennsylvania	1	4	9	10
Rhode Island	25	28	57	49
South Carolina	b	3	5	5
South Dakota	4	11	25	22
Tennessee	104	183	260	199
Texas	b	2	5	8
Utah	51	66	155	130
Vermont	20	42	78	66
Virginia	53	88	112	89
Washington	75	106	154	129
West Virginia	38	66	90	74
Wisconsin	38	73	94	82
Wyoming	22	77	124	143
All states	38	72	98	85

Source: National Consumer Finance Association, "Report on Nonbusiness Bankruptcies by States," Table 3, relevant annual issues (Washington; processed).
a. Population as of beginning of fiscal year.
b. Less than one personal bankruptcy per 100,000 persons.

1967 the median bankruptcy rate among the five states having the lowest rates was 5 personal bankruptcies per 100,000 residents of those states; among the five states with the highest rates, the median rate was 260 personal bankruptcies per 100,000 residents—more than fifty times greater. No obvious economic or demographic differences among the states explain such striking variations, particularly when marked differences in rates appear among adjoining states that otherwise have much in common. What, then, accounts for this pattern?

Some observers have suggested that bankruptcy rates might be related to the ease with which the laws of the various states allow creditors to attach the wages of debtors in garnishment proceedings.[7] They reason that the filing of a petition in bankruptcy is

7. See, for example, George Brunn, "Wage Garnishment in California: A Study and Recommendations," *California Law Review*, Vol. 53 (December 1965), pp. 1214-53.

commonly precipitated by a creditor's threat to have a part of a debtor's wage withheld at its source for eventual payment to the court and thence to the creditor in satisfaction of his claim. Our own study tends to support this view with evidence collected in interviews with former bankrupts. The garnishment process is controlled by state laws, except that federal law now limits the fraction of earnings that can be taken. Because the state laws vary, it is not equally convenient everywhere to cause a person's wages to be garnisheed. Creditors, the explanation continues, will more often invoke the threat of garnishment, and the threat will be more credible, where garnishment is easy than where it is not; hence, the bankruptcy rate will be higher in one state than in another.

There are obvious difficulties in measuring how easily wages can be garnisheed in any state. Many features of the law ought to be considered, some of which cannot be expressed numerically. But one important variable usually can—the wage exemption each state provides. Every state exempts some part of a debtor's wages from garnishment, and the amount of this exemption could affect a creditor's readiness to institute a garnishment action. For the larger the exemption, the smaller will be the amount the creditor can collect at any time, and the longer it will take to satisfy his claim. Consequently, the size of the exemption should be correlated with the bankruptcy rate.

We tested this idea with the data in Table 3-2 on the number of personal bankruptcies filed in the various states in fiscal 1967. The size of the wage exemption in each state was taken from a commercial handbook published in August 1966.[8] Forty-nine states (all but Arkansas, whose exemption provisions were exceptionally difficult to reduce to figures) and the District of Columbia were ranked both by their bankruptcy rates and by the size of their wage exemptions, and the two rankings were set side by side. Using a statistical technique called rank correlation analysis, we tested the hypothesis that there was *no* relation between wage exemptions and bankruptcy rates. The hypothesis failed the test at a significance level of 99 percent, meaning that there is less than one chance in a hundred that the coincidence between high exemptions and low bankruptcy

8. Commerce Clearing House, *Handbook on Assignment and Garnishment of Wages* (Chicago: CCH, 1966).

rates and low exemptions and high bankruptcy rates found in these statistics could have appeared purely by chance. The result persuades us that wage exemptions and bankruptcy rates are related in the way supposed.

A complete description of this test appears in Appendix B, section 4, and includes a discussion of how we ranked states whose wage exemptions are not expressed as a simple fraction of a person's earnings.

It should not be expected that all states with high (or low) wage exemptions have low (or high) bankruptcy rates. A few examples of the opposite might be cited, such as Kansas, which exempts a generous 90 percent of a person's wages from garnishment yet has a rate of personal bankruptcies notably higher than the national average, or Massachusetts, which provides a relatively small exemption but has a low bankruptcy rate. All that these examples show, however, is that still other factors contribute to variations in the rate. The laws of some states, for instance, encourage both spouses to file in bankruptcy if one plans to do so.

Our understanding of these relations would be improved if we could examine the effects on bankruptcy rates of changes in wage garnishment provisions; but unfortunately few states have recently made important changes in their garnishment laws. Iowa permitted garnishment for the first time in 1957, and thereafter its bankruptcy rate rose more rapidly than the national average. Illinois increased the size of its wage exemption in 1961; by 1967 its bankruptcy rate had declined by 7 percent, while the rate in every other state (though not in the District of Columbia) was increasing.[9] Although these developments are not conclusive in themselves, they reinforce the conclusions we reached on the basis of our statistical test.

If wage garnishment laws do indeed have a pronounced effect on personal bankruptcy rates, the national bankruptcy rate may soon be affected by two recent events. The first was the passage of the Consumer Credit Protection Act of 1968. This law may be ex-

---

9. A large firm in Illinois informed us that it had received only 462 garnishments in 1965, whereas before the exemption was liberalized in 1961 it had received about 110 in a single week. However, in interviews with persons familiar with the Illinois bankruptcy scene, we heard no suggestions that the change in the garnishment law had been so significant. Another explanation of the decline in the bankruptcy rate in Illinois may be the tightening of procedures for cognovit judgments in the state. See below, p. 51.

pected to reduce bankruptcy rates in many states by its establishment of a national minimum wage exemption from garnishment. Beginning July 1, 1970, the law exempted 75 percent of a person's weekly disposable earnings (earnings after the deduction of taxes) or an amount in one week equal to thirty times the national minimum hourly wage, whichever is greater.[10] The act also prohibits an employer from discharging an employee the first time his wages are garnisheed, a provision that may keep some debtors from rushing to file in bankruptcy when garnishment proceedings are begun against them.

A year later, the Uniform Consumer Credit Code was passed by two state legislatures, Oklahoma and Utah; four more states passed it in 1971. The Code, as proposed by the National Conference of Commissioners on Uniform State Laws, abolishes garnishment before judgment;[11] exempts 75 percent of disposable earnings or a weekly amount equal to forty times the national minimum hourly wage, whichever is greater; and forbids discharge of an employee because of garnishment.

WILL THE RATE CONTINUE TO GROW?

We have seen that the growth of the personal bankruptcy rate since the end of World War II has been due primarily to a marked increase in personal indebtedness. In the short run, the bankruptcy rate has also been strongly affected by changes in the state of the economy. These things seem clear but at least one apparent puzzle remains: Why have changes in the personal bankruptcy rate been so much greater throughout this period than the changes in the debt–income ratio that apparently caused them? When the debt–income ratio increased, the bankruptcy rate increased more; when the debt–income ratio declined, the bankruptcy rate declined more.

10. In revising its garnishment provisions in 1969, New Hampshire exempted an amount in one week equal to fifty times the national minimum hourly wage. Other states can be expected to adopt similar standards.

11. This is consistent with the Supreme Court's decision that provisions of the Wisconsin statute allowing prejudgment wage garnishment were unconstitutional. *Sniadach v. Family Finance Corp. of Bay View et al.*, 395 U.S. 337 (1969).

Between 1946 and 1966 the bankruptcy rate grew at an annual rate nearly four times as great as the annual rate of growth in the debt–income ratio.

ROLE OF THE DEBT–INCOME RATIO

We say "apparent" puzzle because this inequality in growth rates may have a rather simple explanation. At any point in time we would expect that the debt–income ratio for the preponderance of families would be at or close to the average ratio for all families, and that very few would have the highest ratios. Suppose, then, that there is a "critical value" of the ratio above which the risk of financial failure and eventual bankruptcy grows appreciably. As families add to their debt faster than their income increases, more and more of them will have the higher debt–income ratios and the number whose ratios are above the critical value will grow—at first slowly, then more rapidly as the large group whose ratios cluster around the average begin to exhibit ratios that approach the critical level. Much would depend on the density of this cluster around the average and on the difference between the average and the critical value, but these might well be such that a uniform increase in the debt–income ratio among all families could generate a larger than proportionate increase in the personal bankruptcy rate.

A highly simplified example may clarify this idea. Suppose the critical value is 0.50 and that half of all families attaining that ratio enter bankruptcy. For simplicity, assume that all families fall into only three groups and that they exhibit only three debt–income ratios: 25 percent have the highest ratio, 25 percent the lowest, and 50 percent have exactly the average in between. At the opening of our example, the ratio increases so as to bring the upper 25 percent across the risky 0.50 line, and thus 12.5 percent of all families enter bankruptcy. The increase is also such that the 50 percent of the families at the average move to the 0.40 line. Now families again add to their debt faster than their incomes rise and the average debt–income ratio rises by 25 percent to 0.50, bringing these 50 percent to the critical value of the ratio and making half of them, or 25 percent of all families, bankrupt. Thus an increase of 25 percent in the debt–income ratio has brought about a doubling of the bankruptcy rate—from 12.5 percent to 25 percent of all families.

The artificiality of some of the assumptions in this explanation hardly needs pointing out. In particular, the idea of a critical value of the debt–income ratio greatly oversimplifies the relation between a family's debt burden and the soundness of its finances. But the explanation is serviceable and, within broad limits, does not depend on the kind of assumptions we have made. It would be consistent with many kinds of distributions of families according to their debt–income ratios—for example, with relatively more or fewer families in the lower ranges, and with relatively smaller concentrations around the mean. Moreover, it could accommodate a change from the simplistic notion of a single critical value to a probability distribution that measured the likelihood of a family's going into bankruptcy, given its debt–income ratio.

Regardless of the assumptions, the explanation finds empirical support in evidence that the difference between the rates of growth of the bankruptcy rate and the debt–income ratio widened as the mean debt–income ratio climbed to higher levels. It is a corollary of the preceding explanation that the entry of families into a region of high debt–income ratios, in which the likelihood of bankruptcy is high, accelerates as the mean ratio in the population comes nearer the critical value. Something akin to the illustration above seems to be shown by the statistics. Early in the 1950s the bankruptcy rate grew at slightly more than twice the rate of the mean debt–income ratio. By the early 1960s, when the mean debt–income ratio was half again as high as it had been ten years before, the rate of increase in the bankruptcy rate was more than three times that of the debt–income ratio. Care must be taken in interpreting this evidence, however, and no more is claimed here than that it is consistent with the mechanism sketched above to explain the difference between the growth rates of the two series.

PROBLEMS OF PREDICTION

So long as the debt–income ratio continues to fall, the personal bankruptcy rate is likely to fall too. The debt–income ratio declined in fiscal 1970, but the bankruptcy rate—far from falling—rose slightly over that of the previous year, probably because of an increase in unemployment. If the unemployment rate were to continue to rise, the bankruptcy rate might also rise, despite a continuing fall in the debt–income ratio.

It would be rash to speculate whether the debt–income ratio will rise or fall during the 1970s. Much will depend on whether the growth of mortgage debt accelerates; for mortgage debt has not grown as fast as personal income since 1964 and has thus accounted for the decline in the debt–income ratio since 1965. The other component of total personal debt, total consumer credit, remained a nearly constant fraction of total personal income between 1964 and 1969.

The decline in the ratio of mortgage debt to personal income must have been caused at first by the decrease in new housing starts between 1963 and 1966. In 1966 fewer new housing units were started than in any year since 1946. By 1968 construction activity had revived, but personal income was showing its most rapid growth since 1951, owing to the general inflation of prices then occurring; and so the ratio of outstanding mortgage debt to income continued to decline.

If inflation abates soon and the rate of growth in personal income slows, and if new housing starts increase as interest rates fall, mortgage debt may again increase more rapidly than personal income. Assuming that total consumer credit continues to grow at least as fast as personal income, the debt–income ratio will once more increase, and if past experience is a reliable guide the personal bankruptcy rate should increase too. How high will it rise? We have no well-tested theory to indicate whether there is some limit the debt–income ratio will eventually approach but never exceed.

Finally, we have noted that recent legislative and judicial actions could make the garnishment of wages more difficult in the future and thus have the effect of lowering the personal bankruptcy rate. If their effect is potent enough, this decline may occur even if the debt–income ratio increases.

EFFECTS OF FUTURE RECESSIONS

We pointed out earlier that the personal bankruptcy rate was much affected by increases in the unemployment rate during the several short recessions that followed World War II. After the recession of 1960–61 the economy entered a period of sustained prosperity that lasted the rest of the decade, and though the bankruptcy rate continued to increase for several years, it showed no

upward surge comparable to the jumps associated with earlier recessions. This record of prosperity prompts the question whether
the nation has so succeeded in smoothing out business fluctuations
that we can hereafter ignore the effect of economic conditions on
the bankruptcy rate.

For an answer we need only look at recent experience. After de-
clining two years in a row, the bankruptcy rate rose in fiscal 1970,
presumably because unemployment began rising early in calendar
1970. Fluctuations in the level of prosperity will no doubt continue
to be reflected in the annual number of bankruptcy filings. And
we must not suppose that, because no major depression is likely to
happen again, future economic fluctuations will be minor in effect
and will have no more than a marginal impact on the personal
bankruptcy rate. The Great Depression of the 1930s had little more
effect on the bankruptcy rate than have some of the moderate recessions since World War II. The number of all bankruptcies in
fiscal years 1933 through 1937 was 34.0 percent greater than the
number for the five years 1923–27. In fiscal 1932, when more bankruptcy cases were filed than in any other year during the depression,
the number of filings was 55.3 percent greater than the average
annual number of filings in fiscal years 1923 through 1927. By
comparison, during the short but sharp recession in fiscal 1961 the
number of bankruptcies filed increased by 33.3 percent over the
number filed the year before.

Even the moderate recessions of the past twenty-five years may
have been more severe than any economic shocks the U.S. economy
is likely to experience in the years ahead. Among the reasons for
thinking so are increased governmental confidence and skill in the
use of fiscal and monetary tools to maintain a high level of national
output, the high degree of stability built into the system through
heavy reliance on a progressive income tax and a high level of welfare expenditures and unemployment benefits, and the consensus
of government leaders, private organizations, and the public at
large in favor of using whatever means are appropriate to maintain
national prosperity. Perhaps the bankruptcy rate will never again
rise as sharply as it did during the postwar recessions. But from time
to time we shall no doubt see moderate increases in unemployment,
whose impact on the bankruptcy rate will be certain and unmis-
takable.

WHO BEARS THE COSTS?

As noted, about $2 billion of debts were discharged in the bank-
ruptcy courts in 1968. Of this amount we estimate that about $1,400
million of debts were discharged in business bankruptcy cases and
the rest in personal bankruptcy cases. Can it be said that this measures the economic "cost" of the bankruptcy process in the United
States, against which its benefits must be set?

The answer, of course, is no, since no real resources are consumed
when debts are discharged. The bankruptcy process operates instead as a kind of redistributive mechanism whereby goods and
services are supplied to one group at the expense of another. In
personal bankruptcies, the first group consists of persons whose
debts are discharged. The losses incurred by the merchants who sell
to them are probably made up in part by sales to cash customers at
higher prices than would prevail if debt losses were lower. Another
part of these losses is borne by responsible users of credit who pay
their debts and who bear their share in the form of higher credit
charges or prices. But the costs of the goods and services consumed
by bankrupts may not be distributed uniformly among all borrowers
if bankrupts regularly come from a class of high-risk borrowers
whose characteristics lenders are quick to recognize and who can obtain credit only by paying a higher charge than other borrowers. In
that case the costs may be borne largely by other members of the
high-risk group who do repay their debts (or pay cash). It is also
conceivable that lenders themselves may bear a part of the costs, at
least in a period when bankruptcies are increasing rapidly, if the increase is so rapid that lenders are unable to raise credit charges fast
enough to earn a normal profit. In this case the costs of the goods
and services consumed by bankrupts would be borne in part by taxpayers, because of the abnormally high bad debt losses that would
be charged against lenders' taxable income. All this is necessarily
speculative. There is little empirical evidence to show how these
costs are actually distributed, and in the following discussion we
simply assume that bankrupts' debts are paid for by borrowers.

With that in mind, let us consider what effects would follow if
discharges of debts were no longer permitted. First we must know
how many discharged debts might have been repaid. If the answer

is none, then discharges do no more than give legal sanction to an accomplished fact. But no doubt some debts that are now discharged would eventually have been repaid. Creditors would harry debtors until many of them bought relief by paying a part or all of their creditors' claims. Some critics of the system assert that a majority of bankrupts could pay their debts if they wanted to; and in this spirit bills have been introduced in Congress that would require wage earners to persuade a referee that their financial problems could not be solved with a Chapter XIII wage plan before they would be put in bankruptcy and discharged from their debts.

This position finds support in several studies of the finances of bankrupts in limited geographical areas, which conclude that many bankrupts could have paid their debts.[12] Some of these conclusions are based on uncommonly bold assumptions. One study assumed that an "adequate" income for a family of four in Flint, Michigan, in 1963 was $2,763 a year and concluded that, if all of the debtor's income above this amount were devoted to debt repayment for three years (the debtor presumably incurring no new debts in the meantime), 49 percent of the bankrupts in the area could have paid their debts.[13] Such studies say nothing of the bankrupts' willingness to pay, and it is unlikely that if relief had been withheld from them in bankruptcy court these debtors would have subjected themselves to the harsh discipline necessary to pay their debts. Probably a substantial part of these debts would have gone unpaid until they were written off by creditors as uncollectible.

If discharges were not permitted and if a large part of the personal debts that are now discharged in bankruptcy court were eventually repaid, the repayment would affect national levels of saving and spending through its effects on the price of credit and on the income of persons who buy on credit. Some of the effects would oppose one another, and it is impossible to know what the net effect on the level of national income would be.

12. See, for example, Robert Dolphin, Jr., *An Analysis of Economic and Personal Factors Leading to Consumer Bankruptcy*, Occasional Paper No. 15 (Michigan State University Graduate School of Business Administration, Bureau of Business and Economic Research, 1965); Edward W. Reed, "Personal Bankruptcies in Oregon" (University of Oregon, Bureau of Business and Economic Research, 1967; processed); Grant L. Misbach, *Personal Bankruptcy in the United States and Utah* (University of Utah Press, 1964).

13. Dolphin, *Analysis*, pp. 98–99.

Consider first the effect on prices. Bad debt losses would fall, and a decline in the price of credit might be expected to follow. As the price of credit fell, people presumably would make more use of it; more goods would be bought on credit, possibly fewer with cash. The increase in the demand for goods bought on credit, if not offset by a decline in the demand for goods bought with cash, would generate a round of increases in national income by the classical multiplier effect.

On the other hand, the persons who would otherwise have been discharged from their debts would now have to devote part of their income to repaying those debts. Think of their repayment as a transfer to other borrowers, who would receive it in the form of lower credit costs. The disposable income of the first group would fall, while that of the second group would rise. It cannot be assumed that this transfer would have no net effect on savings and spending, for one group might be composed largely of "savers" and the other group of "spenders." Since persons who are hard-pressed to pay their debts are probably spenders rather than savers, the transfer might have the effect of increasing savings and diminishing consumption, thus working against the price effect. Which effect would predominate would be impossible to foretell, but the net result would surely be small beside the normal fluctuations in national income that arise from other sources.

Business bankruptcies are quite another matter. Although the amount of debts discharged in business cases each year is about twice the amount discharged in personal cases, the action has far less practical effect in business cases. While individuals might eventually repay their debts by reducing their consumption, few insolvent firms could ever do the same if their debts were not excused by the bankruptcy court. The cost of these losses is presumably borne by other purchasers of business supplies and services and in turn by their customers, and so is widely diffused among the population.

SUMMARY

A willingness to seek and extend credit is essential to the smooth functioning of the U.S. economy, whose institutional structure efficiently accumulates the nation's savings and channels them into the hands of borrowers. In the process, situations inevitably arise in which the borrower is unable or unwilling to repay. Indeed, the absence of credit losses would be an indication of economic inefficiency, since it would suggest that the marketplace was not being allowed to work and that lenders were withholding funds from marginal borrowers as a class, even though such borrowers would be willing and able to pay interest rates sufficient to cover losses on bad debts.

Total private debt has grown rapidly in the last two decades, but there is little empirical evidence that the debt burden is too great for borrowers as a whole. Unless there is a downturn in economic activity considerably worse than anything the United States has experienced in almost thirty years—a possibility that most economists think unlikely—the existing and expected debt level is not alarming.

Some $2 billion of debts were discharged in the bankruptcy courts in 1968—about 0.2 percent of the private debt outstanding. This may be viewed as a cost of the existing credit system—a cost that is widely diffused throughout the economy, being borne partly by borrowers as a whole, through higher interest rates, but principally by customers of business borrowers, through higher prices.

Business bankruptcy rates have been relatively stable for the past decade. Personal bankruptcies, however, have sharply increased in number since World War II, though at a diminishing rate, and actually decreased in 1968 and 1969. The growth apparently resulted primarily from the increase in the amount of indebtedness of the population rather than from deteriorating credit standards or a greater willingness of persons to enter bankruptcy.

Bankruptcy, then, is not so much a problem to the American economy as it is a human problem, and a problem in court procedure and in government administration, as the following chapters demonstrate.

4

The Personal Bankrupts

This chapter looks at personal bankrupts and debtors—their backgrounds, their reasons for being in bankruptcy court, their debts, events after bankruptcy, and their reactions to the whole experience. Most of the information comes from interviews with 400 persons in seven of the eight districts about two years after their cases were closed. They were among some 3,600 names chosen at random from files of bankruptcy cases closed in fiscal year 1964. It proved difficult to locate and interview these former bankrupts, for some represent highly mobile parts of the population and some have become wary of talking to strangers. The 400 who were found and were willing to be interviewed probably were more stable, better satisfied, and in better financial condition than those who had disappeared or who refused to be interviewed. Readers should keep this in mind in interpreting the results of the interviews.[1]

The seven districts in which the interviewing was done are: Northern Ohio, Northern Alabama, Maine, Northern Illinois,

1. There is some overlapping here. The 400 people interviewed by Chilton Research Services in the summer of 1966 include as many personal bankrupts of the 1,675 in the Brookings sample as we could reach. For those we could not get in touch with, we added bankrupts from the same city and in the same time period from adjacent positions in our list.

In this chapter the term "debtors" is used to refer to all interviewees instead of the awkward but precise "former bankrupts and debtors." Except for Northern Alabama, where more than three-quarters of the interviewees had filed under Chapter XIII (the wage earners' repayment plan), the debtors were mostly (80 percent) straight bankruptcy cases.

Oregon, Western Texas, and Southern California. As noted in Chapter 1, after the interviewing was completed, we added Southern New York to our study in order to get more business cases in our sample. See Appendix A, section 3, for more methodological detail on this interview study.

PERSONAL CHARACTERISTICS OF DEBTORS

The typical debtor interviewed in these districts was an industrial worker, earning a little over $100 a week. At the time of the interview he was nearly forty years old. He had finished three years of high school. Married more than twelve years at the time of his bankruptcy, he had four people dependent upon him. Thus he presents a picture of neither poverty nor instability.

Looking at the group more broadly, we find them spread over various age groups: 19 percent in their twenties, 32 percent in their thirties, 30 percent in their forties, and the rest older. Three out of every four debtors were men. As to family status, 76 percent of the total group were married, 6 percent separated, 9 percent divorced, and 2 percent (all women) widowed.[2] Among the women the divorce figure was higher: 17 percent, as against only 6 percent of the men. Of the married debtors all but 19 percent had been married five years or more.

EDUCATION

The debtors who were interviewed did not come from the poorly educated groups in the population. Three-quarters of them had been to high school—well above the 1960 average of the general population, 60 percent.[3] Some 18 percent of those interviewed had

2. All fractions and percentages presented in this chapter are based on replicated totals of the number of persons interviewed or the number of files sampled in each district. Actual numbers are therefore not stated in text or tables. Appendix Table A-3 gives the number of persons interviewed and the sampling rates.

3. Data on education of the general population (twenty-five years old and older) are from the 1960 census. U.S. Bureau of the Census, *Statistical Abstract of the United States, 1966*, p. 113.

been to college, about the same as the general population. Here are the proportions of the debtors at various educational levels:

Highest grade completed	Percent
Grades 1 to 4	5
Grades 5 to 8	20
Grades 9 and 10	17
Grades 11 and 12	39
College, 1–3 years	11
College, 4 years	6
Postgraduate (any)	1
No answer	1

The median number of years of schooling was 11.4, slightly better than the 10.6 years for the general population.[4]

OCCUPATION

Blue-collar workers dominate the statistics in this bankruptcy study, as well as in others (see Appendix A, pages 219–20). Three out of every five of those interviewed were in this category—28 percent of them craftsmen or skilled workers, 32 percent semiskilled or unskilled. Following them were clerical workers, 12 percent; service workers, 7 percent; professionals and semiprofessionals, 7 percent; proprietors and managers, 5 percent; sales employees, 2 percent; farmers or farm workers, 1 percent; and others, 7 percent. The total percentage of blue-collar workers (60 percent) is high compared to the total for the general employed population, which was 36 percent in 1960.[5]

These figures for the interviewees are fairly close to those showing occupations of the bankrupts and debtors in our sample from bankruptcy court files. The main differences are the higher proportion of proprietors (10 percent) and unemployed (10 percent) among the straight bankruptcy cases and of semiskilled or unskilled workers (65 percent) among the debtors in the Chapter XIII (wage earner plan) cases. (See Appendix Table C-1 for details.)

Tabulation of the group interviewed by type of employment

4. Ibid. Medians in this chapter are grouped medians, unless otherwise stated.
5. Ibid., p. 229.

showed that nearly half (49 percent) worked for manufacturing or industrial concerns. Others were engaged in:

	Percent
Business and trade	17
Services (hotels, utilities, transportation, and so forth)	15
Government (federal, state, local)	10
Military	9

Agriculture showed less than 0.5 percent, as did other fields. Again, these results were close to those found in the bankruptcy files. (See Appendix Table c-2 for comparison.)

Some of the debtors, although employed at the time of bankruptcy, had been in business within the previous six years. These "former business" debtors constituted 13 percent of our straight bankruptcy cases and 1 percent of those under Chapter XIII. Most of these businesses were in the retail and service fields. In the first category, restaurants, automotive dealers (including gas stations), and wearing apparel outlets were most frequently mentioned. Automobile repair shops, recreation facilities, and medical supply businesses led the list of bankrupt service enterprises. From the limited data available, these ventures appeared to be "one-shot" efforts of employees who had aspired to having their own businesses.

INCOME

Asked about their earned income in the year 1965 (after their cases were closed), the debtors gave a wide range of replies, but the median was a little over $100 a week. Such incomes were distributed by amount in this way:

Annual income, in dollars	Percent
None	3
Under 3,000	14
3,000–5,999	44
6,000–7,999	23
8,000–9,999	9
10,000–14,999	6
15,000 and more	1

They ranged from medians of $6,421 in Southern California down to $3,590 in Northern Alabama, with a median of $5,237 for the entire group. Their take-home pay was of course less—11 percent less for all these districts. Except in one district, Western Texas, take-home pay rose substantially between the year the debtor filed in bankruptcy (usually 1963) and 1965. This increase for all districts combined was 19 percent. The higher income reflects the generally rising wage level in the nation during this period, but is also large enough to suggest an improvement in the economic situation of these debtors.[6] A few (9 percent) received unearned income—such as interest, pensions, gifts, insurance proceeds, welfare payments—amounting to a median of $1,820. Fewer than 1 percent of the debtors had unearned income but no earned income.

BACKGROUND GROUPINGS

Debtors were also sorted into groups based on ethnic or national-origin backgrounds, according to judgments by their interviewers. The most significant result is the large disproportion of blacks— 38 percent of the debtors. In the districts with substantial black populations the percentage of blacks is high (see Table 4-1). Personal background percentages of debtors interviewed in all seven districts are shown in Table 4-2. Note the large proportions of Spanish-speaking debtors in Western Texas and Southern California and of those with a French-Canadian background in Maine.

MOBILITY

Debtors were asked about recent job changes and home address changes to see if they were more or less mobile than the general population. The results are not conclusive, although the interviewees moved around less than the authors had expected. At the time of the interviews 39 percent were working for the same employer as when they went into bankruptcy court, and 42 percent were living at the same address.

6. In manufacturing industries nationwide, average net spendable weekly earnings for a production worker with three dependents went up from $87.58 in 1963 to $96.78 in 1965 (in current dollars), an increase of 10.5 percent (*Statistical Abstract of the United States, 1966*, p. 238).

TABLE 4-1. *Blacks as a Percentage of Debtors Interviewed in Six Court Districts Compared with Percentage of Black Population of Selected Cities in Those Districts*[a]

District and city	As a percentage of debtors interviewed	As a percentage of population, 1960
Northern Alabama	78	
Birmingham		40
Anniston		34
Northern Illinois	51	
Chicago		23
Northern Ohio	43	
Cleveland		29
Akron		13
Canton		10
Southern California	20	
Los Angeles		14
Santa Ana		2
Oregon	5	
Portland		4
Western Texas	4	
San Antonio		7
El Paso		2

Sources: Col. 1, interviews with 400 debtors in seven federal court districts by Chilton Research Services, Philadelphia; col. 2, U.S. Bureau of the Census, *County and City Data Book, 1967*, Table 4.
a. While these figures are only roughly comparable, a very high proportion of the bankruptcies filed in these six districts came from the cities listed.

TABLE 4-2. *Backgrounds of Debtors Interviewed, by District*[a]
In percent

Ethnic group	Seven districts	Northern Ohio	Northern Alabama	Maine	Northern Illinois	Oregon	Western Texas	Southern California
Anglo-Saxon	45	40	21	64	22	90	50	64
Black	38	43	78	—	51	5	4	20
Oriental	—	—	—	—	—	—	—	—
Spanish-speaking	6	—	—	—	4	2	36	13
Slavic	2	3	—	—	4	—	—	—
Italian	4	5	—	5	11	2	4	—
Jewish	2	2	—	—	2	—	—	4
French-Canadian	1	—	—	26	—	—	—	—
Other	1	—	1	2	2	2	4	—
Uncertain	2	7	—	3	2	—	4	—

Source: Interviews with 400 debtors in seven federal court districts by Chilton Research Services.
a. Because of rounding, percentages may not add to 100.

CAUSES OF PERSONAL BANKRUPTCY

Why did the debtors go to the bankruptcy court? Those who were interviewed were first asked about underlying problems—why they were in financial difficulty.[7] The leading reason, given by 31 percent, was poor debt management—too many debts, unwise refinancing, overspending. Their decisions about borrowing or buying depended only on whether or not they thought their current income could support another monthly payment. All too seldom did they evaluate the total cost involved or their future prospects.

Next as underlying causes were family health reasons (sickness, injuries, babies, death), 28 percent, and job problems like layoffs, strikes, and loss of overtime, 20 percent. Then 13 percent cited threats of legal action or hounding by creditors, followed by 10 percent who mentioned actual legal action—suit, garnishment, repossession. Another 10 percent referred to emotionally based problems such as marital troubles, drunkenness, or excessive gambling. Then came "to avoid paying debts," 7 percent, and calamities not associated with health (house burned, car wrecked), 6 percent. Nine percent of the debtors, who had been in business, gave business reasons like poor sales, poor collections, loss of a big customer, management problems, or insufficient capital. Other scattered reasons were also given.[8]

Then debtors were asked about immediate causes—specifically, why they went into bankruptcy court. Their reasons naturally overlap those above, but the main cause is clear: 43 percent mentioned threats of legal action—of garnishment, attachment, repossession, suit. Typical comments were: "I knew I had to work, and this was the only way I could hold my job. I had lost a job on account of garnishee." "All I was getting was threats every way I turned. Yes, threats. Oh, I mean about garnishing."

Other persons we interviewed—referees in bankruptcy, attorneys (both for debtors and creditors), and welfare authorities—also emphasized fear of garnishment or suit as a leading cause of bankruptcy. Garnishment can be the cause of the debtor's losing his job, because his employer does not want to become a collection agent.

7. The question was "open-ended"—they could give any reasons that occurred to them.

8. Multiple replies were possible.

Nearly 40 percent of the employers we interviewed had policies permitting discharge of employees whose wages were repeatedly garnisheed. Those with union contracts reported that garnishment-inspired discharge was not an employment policy issue to which their unions gave high priority.

Other "immediate causes" were generally like the underlying reasons but with different emphasis. Here is the full list:[9]

	Percent
Threats of legal action	43
Poor debt management	20
Actual legal action	18
To avoid paying debts	15
Poor health; babies; death in family	11
Job problems	9
Lawyer (expert) advised	9
Business problems	6
Marital, other emotional problems	5
Nonhealth calamities	2

Some of these interviewees gave various combinations of reasons.

Other persons interviewed (not debtors) said that defendants in lawsuits—especially negligence cases resulting from automobile accidents—went bankrupt to avoid paying damages. We rarely found debts resulting from such suits in the case files or in debtors' interviews, but we tested this allegation by further research. A representative sample of trial attorneys completed questionnaires describing their experience as plaintiff's counsel from 1964 through 1966. Their replies do *not* support the idea that such suits are an important cause of bankruptcies. Sixty-five percent reported that no defendant had actually obtained a bankruptcy discharge during that three-year period.[10] Another 26 percent of the attorneys said that there had been discharges in from 1 to 5 percent of the cases

9. Causes of bankruptcies were also given in some of the files examined in this study —in 48 percent of the straight bankruptcy cases and 28 percent of the Chapter XIIIs. These causes were not separately identified as either underlying or immediate causes. The leading causes given for straight bankruptcies were: debt overload, 30 percent; health reasons, 13 percent; actual legal action, 10 percent. For Chapter XIII: actual legal action, 15 percent; debt overload, 8 percent; health problems, 6 percent.

10. A related problem mentioned repeatedly in Northern Illinois was the insolvency of insurance carriers.

they handled; 9 percent reported discharges in more than 5 percent of their cases. Asked about settlements resulting from threats of bankruptcy, the attorneys had little more to report. Fifty-one percent of them had not settled any case because of such a threat; 28 percent had settled for this reason in from 1 to 5 percent of their cases, and 21 percent in more than 5 percent of their cases.

STATE LAWS AFFECTING CAUSES OF PERSONAL BANKRUPTCY

The prominence of actual or threatened legal actions among the reasons for debtors going bankrupt naturally draws attention to the state laws under which such actions are taken. The diversity among the states is striking.

Wage garnishments. We showed in the previous chapter how bankruptcy rates in various states appear to be related to their garnishment laws.[11] An employee who can be hard hit by garnishment either has his income reduced drastically or may be fired, or both, so he files in bankruptcy.

How hard he can be hit depends on where he lives.[12] Among the eight states in this study, one extreme at the time of our field research was found in Maine, where only $30 of the debtor's monthly earnings were exempted from garnishment.[13] At the other extreme was Texas, where wages are immune from garnishment. In between were the other six states we studied: Alabama, Oregon, Illinois, Ohio, California, and New York. Their laws let the debtor keep from 50 to 90 percent of his earnings, but there are various minimums, maximums, and exceptions.[14] California and New York give

11. The term wage garnishment is not used in all states; for example, "trustee process" is used in Maine, "income execution" in New York.

12. See discussion in Chapter 3. The processing of exemption claims in general, and property exemptions in particular, is discussed in the next chapter.

13. In 1967 Maine's exemption laws were amended to permit the debtor to keep earnings of up to $40, and in no event less than $10, a week.

14. Alabama—75 percent of wages exempt from garnishment.

Oregon—50 percent exempt, but no less than $25 or more than $250 a month.

Illinois—85 percent exempt, but no less than $50 ($65 for heads of families) or more than $200 a week.

Ohio—80 percent of first $300 a month and 60 percent of the balance exempt, but no less than $150 for heads of families, and $100 for others (the wage earner trusteeship procedure, described later in the chapter, bars garnishment of earnings).

California—50 percent of debtor's earnings exempt, and all such earnings if neces-

their courts considerable discretion to vary the amounts exempted from garnishment to fit the circumstances. Illinois and New York permit only one creditor to garnishee at a time, and the initial garnishment is continued until the claim is satisfied. This rule makes things easier for the debtor and harder for other creditors.

In other states all kinds of factors affect the size of garnishment: the amount of wages; when they were earned; the number of creditors; the nature and size of the debts; the debtor's family status; and the stage of the litigation against him. In recent years there has been a general tendency to liberalize wage exemptions with respect to their size, the manner in which they are defined (the trend is from dollar to percentage amounts), and the flexibility of their application. Such liberalization has been most pronounced in the more populous and urbanized states.[15]

Wage assignments. Even if a debtor's income is not garnisheed he may be persuaded to assign some of it to his creditors—and may sign away too much unless protected from such an error by state laws.[16] Such laws range all the way from categorical prohibition of wage assignments to virtually complete laissez-faire.

In making the present study we found no evidence that wage assignments lead to bankruptcy, largely because in all but one of the states studied (Maine) the laws are very restrictive. In seven states (including Alabama, Ohio, and Texas), wage assignments are for all practical purposes quite unenforceable. In twenty-seven other states (including California, Illinois, New York, and Oregon), wage

---

sary for use of the debtor's family, unless the creditor's claim was incurred in supplying "the common necessaries of life."

New York—90 percent exempt, but in no event less than $30 a week if he resides or works in a city with a population of 250,000 or more—otherwise $25 a week, or as much as the court may find necessary. New York now forbids an employer to fire an employee because his wages have been garnisheed unless this occurs more than once in a twelve-month period.

15. The federal Consumer Credit Protection Act, which became effective in 1970, provides a minimum standard for wage exemptions. See the discussion in Chapter 3. For a general description, discussion, and evaluation of wage garnishment proceedings, see Commerce Clearing House, *Handbook on Assignment and Garnishment of Wages* (Chicago: CCH, 1966), pp. 25–50; see also George Brunn, "Wage Garnishment in California: A Study and Recommendations," *California Law Review*, Vol. 53 (1965), p. 1214; J. M. Boddington, "Garnishment of Wages in Pennsylvania: Its History and Rationale," *Dickinson Law Review*, Vol. 70 (Winter 1966), pp. 199–212.

16. For a general description of state laws governing wage assignments, see CCH, *Handbook on Assignment and Garnishment of Wages*, pp. 11–24.

assignments are permitted, but with many safeguards designed to frustrate creditors' overreaching. Finally, in the remaining seventeen states, restrictions on wage assignments are either nonexistent or give the debtor little protection.[17]

Cognovit clauses ("confessions of judgment"). Another forerunner of bankruptcy may be a promissory note containing a so-called cognovit, or warrant-of-attorney, clause. This lets the creditor "confess judgment," that is, obtain a judgment without notice to the debtor in case of default. The holder of such a note may well garnishee wages, and this sort of threat to the debtor may result in his seeking bankruptcy.[18]

Pressure of this kind clearly existed in two of the states studied. In Cleveland, Ohio, an official of the wage earner trusteeship court[19] estimated that 70 percent of the claims paid through his court resulted from cognovit judgments. In Illinois six of the thirteen debtors' attorneys and seven of the eleven creditors' attorneys interviewed said that such clauses were a major cause of formal insolvency proceedings. Ohio is one of five states where the law puts little or no restriction on the use of cognovit clauses. Illinois is one of thirty-two where such clauses are limited by certain procedures or are excluded from certain transactions. California, Maine, New York, and Oregon are also in this category. The other fourteen, including Alabama and Texas, forbid cognovit clauses entirely.

Repossessions and deficiency judgments. If a man fails to pay for a refrigerator he has bought, the seller (if the debt was secured by the property) may repossess it and resell it. If he does not get enough to pay for the costs of the action and to satisfy the debt he may get a deficiency judgment for the remainder. Then he may use any legal collection methods—wage garnishment, for example.[20]

17. These state law categorizations and others in this book are based on statutes in effect in January 1969.

18. For a more detailed description, discussion, and evaluation of cognovit clauses, see Dan Hopson, Jr., "Cognovit Judgments: An Ignored Problem of Due Process and Full Faith and Credit," *University of Chicago Law Review*, Vol. 29 (Autumn 1961), pp. 111–58; "Confessions of Judgment," *University of Pennsylvania Law Review*, Vol. 102 (February 1954), pp. 524–28; Robert M. Hunter, "The Warrant of Attorney to Confess Judgment," *Ohio State University Law Journal*, Vol. 8 (December 1941), pp. 1–16.

19. This is a state alternative to the federal wage earner (Chapter XIII) proceeding. See the next chapter for further discussion.

20. See the Uniform Commercial Code, art. 9, pt. 5 (1962), for the reciprocal rights and duties of the secured creditor and the debtor in the event of default. The UCC has

Since the property has been repossessed, however, the debtor will probably care little about a deficiency judgment, unless strenuous collection efforts are made. In that event, particularly if the debtor's wages have been garnisheed, the judgment may lead to his filing in bankruptcy.

Deficiency judgments are barred by statute in California when the security is personal property (except automobiles)[21] but are freely obtainable in the other seven states studied. Nevertheless, they were not named as significant causes of bankruptcy by any but three of the six federal district judges interviewed in Northern Illinois.

Imprisonment. The most extreme collection practice related to bankruptcy is the jailing of debtors (called "capias execution") in Maine and, less extensively, in Illinois. A creditor with a judgment in excess of $10 may have the debtor imprisoned if he fails to disclose (at a formal hearing) the extent of his assets. The creditor must pay $1.75 a day for board for jailed debtors, but this sum may be added to the amount of the judgment. In practice, debtors are usually released after short periods of imprisonment even if they have produced no assets, because the creditors grow weary of paying the board bill. Some debtors who are threatened with this measure, however, avoid it by filing in bankruptcy.

Credit controls. In a broad sense, all state laws that affect consumer credit are preliminaries to bankruptcy. If the laws are so lax, or so poorly enforced, that debtors are encouraged to overcommit themselves and pay excessive rates and charges, more debtors "go broke." Some of the creditors' attorneys and the federal judges interviewed in this study made this point. It may be said in rebuttal that an ignorant, imprudent, or unscrupulous debtor will merely be delayed in his journey to the bankruptcy court by stringently worded or enforced credit laws.

This study of bankruptcy processes and institutions cannot be stretched into a study also of the consumer credit industry, despite the large areas common to the two fields.[22] Readers interested in

---

been adopted in forty-nine states and the District of Columbia—Louisiana, alone among the states, still has not enacted it. For an incisive analysis and discussion of these Code provisions, see Grant Gilmore, *Security Interests in Personal Property* (Little, Brown, 1965), pp. 1211–80.

21. Cal. Civ. Code, Sec. 1812.5. See also Sec. 580(b).

22. But see the discussions of garnishment and of credit in Chapter 3.

more intensive analysis of credit problems that precede bankruptcy should consult the literature of both consumer and business credit and the trade associations in those fields.[23] The development of a proposed uniform consumer credit code by the National Conference of Commissioners on Uniform State Laws is particularly relevant.[24]

HELP FOR THE DEBTOR

After the debtors had talked about the causes of their money problems they were asked, "Did you ask anyone for assistance with these problems?" Yes, said 71 percent; no, said 29 percent. "Whom did you ask?" was the next question. The leading answers are given below:[25]

52 percent had asked a lawyer, or a friend who was a lawyer (answer given by 56 percent of those who filed in straight bankruptcy, 36 percent of those in Chapter XIII);

23 percent had asked creditor(s) or a collection agent (32 percent of Chapter XIII cases, 20 percent of straight bankruptcy cases);

10 percent, a relative who was not a lawyer (mostly straight bankruptcy cases);

9 percent, a personal friend (nonlawyer);

8 percent, the boss, foreman, supervisor;

5 percent, a government official (welfare worker, veterans' adviser, Small Business Administration official);

4 percent, a Legal Aid office.

Other replies were scattered and negligible.

How did they find their lawyers? The largest percentage—45—used an attorney suggested by a friend or relative. The next largest

23. Particularly the National Association for Credit Management, the National Association for Consumer Finance, the National Retail Credit Men's Association, and the Associated Credit Bureaus of America.

24. National Conference of Commissioners on Uniform State Laws, "Uniform Consumer Credit Code" (Chicago, 1969; processed). The UCCC has now been challenged by a National Consumer Act, which takes stronger positions on behalf of the consumer. "National Consumer Act," prepared by the National Consumer Law Center, Boston College Law School, Brighton, Mass. (1970; processed).

25. Some respondents gave more than one answer.

group, 13 percent, found their lawyers themselves by consulting telephone books or other directories or by going to a building occupied by law firms. Ten percent used a lawyer who was a friend or relative; another 10 percent used one who had already done other legal work for the debtor; and 8 percent were referred by another lawyer.

Lawyer or otherwise, what did the advisers suggest? "Go into bankruptcy," said 60 percent. "Go into Chapter XIII," said 15 percent. Eight percent of the debtors recalled that the advice received was unhelpful or unsympathetic.

Later the debtors were asked specifically who advised them to file in bankruptcy. The straight bankruptcy debtors were more inclined to mention their lawyers. Chapter XIII debtors were more likely to have filed on the advice of friends or relatives.

CONSUMER CREDIT COUNSELING SERVICES

Some debtors have a chance to get help from nonprofit consumer credit counseling offices, organizations that are largely supported and staffed by the credit industry. Only a few were in existence in our sample districts during research for this study, but more information later became available as a result of a study sponsored by the Family Service Association of America. In the thirty-two offices covered it was found that 75 to 90 percent of the staffs' time was spent on cases involving counseling *and* administration of payment plans. Almost all of the rest was used for "counseling only" cases. A negligible share of staff time went to group educational efforts.[26] This emphasis on payment plans suggests that these offices are more collection agencies than public service organizations.[27] They cannot give legal advice, so debtors must be referred to attorneys if a creditor's claim needs to be challenged or if terms of a repayment plan need to be negotiated. Bankruptcy is ignored:

It appears to be practically universal that the possible use of bankruptcy is not discussed even though the credit counseling service counselor may believe it to be the only possible solution. The absence of any factual dis-

26. Perry B. Hall, *Family Credit Counseling—An Emerging Community Service* (New York: Family Service Association of America, 1968), pp. 20, 22, 25.

27. Recognizing this possibility, Hall recommends broadening the service rendered and the sources of staffing and financial support. Ibid., pp. 34–43.

cussion of bankruptcy is heavily related to the desire to avoid the appearance of promoting bankruptcy with the resultant potential criticism of the service from the creditors. It is also related to the desire to avoid criticism from the legal community.[28]

Offices in the Family Service study reported that between 15 percent and 50 percent of their applicants were in such serious financial difficulty the service could not help them. Among these are some of the persons who ultimately file bankruptcy petitions.

FREE LEGAL SERVICES

Some debtors may be able to get free help from attorneys. When the cases sampled for this study were filed, the burden of making volunteer legal service available to debtors of limited means was borne chiefly by local units of the National Legal Aid and Defender Association. Traditionally, Legal Aid representation for bankruptcy petitioners was very limited. Many of the bankrupts' incomes were too high to allow them to qualify for service under local eligibility standards. Another deterrent was the fact that major creditors and local bar associations were contributors to the community funds that supported the Legal Aid program.[29] Even if the danger of financial repercussions was more imagined than real, clients had a hard time getting Legal Aid help on bankruptcy matters. Only divorce was more restricted as a field for free legal advice.[30] In 1966, policy in the units we visited varied from outright rejection of straight bankruptcy cases to thorough consideration of the necessity for filing. The usual practice was to refer potential Chapter XIII cases to the practicing bar, because counsel fees could be paid as part of the payment plan.

Meanwhile the Office of Economic Opportunity began its program of neighborhood legal services. Funds were made available to community action agencies to provide legal advice for citizens otherwise unable to afford it and to educate them on their legal rights and responsibilities. Widespread opening of Neighborhood

28. Ibid., p. 21.

29. See Jerome E. Carlin and Jan Howard, "Legal Representation and Class Justice," *UCLA Law Review*, Vol. 12 (December 1965), p. 415.

30. See Lee Silverstein, "Eligibility for Free Legal Services" (American Bar Foundation, 1966; processed), pp. 34–37, for a discussion of the social policy considerations underlying such restrictions.

Legal Services offices occurred during the fiscal year beginning July 1, 1966. To capitalize on existing know-how and to blunt opposition from local bar associations, the Office of Economic Opportunity frequently selected the local Legal Aid office as its delegate agency. The OEO contributed 55 percent of the total Legal Aid budget in calendar year 1966, 72 percent in 1967, and 80 percent in 1968. The OEO contribution in 1968 was almost seven times the total Legal Aid budget for civil cases in 1965.[31]

The Neighborhood Legal Services program has done more than expand the existing Legal Aid offices. In some localities Legal Aid and NLS offices operate independently; elsewhere, NLS programs are present where no Legal Aid office had existed. Thus more help is available not only on bankruptcy, but also on the wide range of economic and family problems that Legal Aid had handled.[32] So far, however, the bankruptcy work is negligible, according to early (and fragmentary) figures. Reports filed with OEO by NLS attorneys revealed that they were responsible for less than 1 percent of the nationwide bankruptcy filings.

Other facilities for free legal advice about bankruptcy are the products of local initiative, usually in metropolitan areas. Some religious organizations maintain panels of volunteer attorneys. A union may have a lawyer on retainer for consulting purposes. Sixty-eight percent of the employers we interviewed had facilities for counseling (usually through the personnel office) on financial problems, but only one provided its employees with full legal representation under such circumstances. Occasional county or city departments refer clients to staff attorneys. Coverage under such conditions cannot be uniform, and it is impossible to estimate how many bankruptcies would be averted and how many filed if such assistance were generally available.

31. Legal Aid reports on a calendar year basis, while OEO uses the U.S. government fiscal year. Data taken from National Legal Aid and Defender Association (NLADA), "Statistics of Legal Aid and Defender Work in the United States and Canada" (Chicago, 1966–68; processed).

32. "Consumer and employment problems" constituted 18 percent of the NLS caseload in fiscal 1967. Included in this category (which totaled 52,579 cases) were 6,018 potential bankruptcies. "Family problems" (102,581) were almost twice as numerous. Office of Economic Opportunity, *Community Services Program Progress Report (Legal Services)* for the fiscal year ending June 30, 1967. For calendar year 1966, 23 percent of the new cases handled by Legal Aid involved economic problems and 41 percent family problems. NLADA, "Statistics of Legal Aid."

HOW MUCH THE DEBTORS OWED AND OWNED

When the debtor goes into bankruptcy court, what kind of financial picture does he present? (The information here comes from the sample of bankruptcy files.)

Our typical personal bankruptcy debtor:

If he had formerly been in business, owed about $10,000 to twenty-six creditors, primarily to merchandise suppliers and lending institutions;

If he had not been in business, owed about $5,000 to twelve creditors, primarily to finance companies, retail merchants, and banks;

If he filed under Chapter XIII, owed about $2,500 to seven creditors, also mainly to finance companies, retail merchants, and banks;

Had assets he valued at about $500.

(More detailed figures on amounts and kinds of debts and amounts of assets appear in Appendix Tables c-3 to c-8.)

Two kinds of facts about these debtors and debts should be emphasized if debt figures are to be properly understood. First, we found that 14 percent of the straight bankrupts were persons whose spouses had also filed.[33] This is important, because debts are often joint obligations of a husband and wife. Even though both are liable, the figures obviously overstate the family's debt. In our sample, considerable duplication was possible because 40 percent of debt listed in "former business" cases was of persons whose spouses had also filed. Twenty-two percent of the "nonbusiness" debt was similarly affected. Only 5 percent of the Chapter XIII files represented separate petitions by spouses.

Second, a large portion of the debt for both the nonbusiness and Chapter XIII cases was listed as secured. If much of his debt is secured, a bankrupt will gain little from his discharge, because it does not affect valid liens. After bankruptcy he will either have to

33. This figure is low because no uniform cross-referencing system existed for such cases in the official court records. We pursued any indication of a spouse's filing in petitioners' files and also checked files adjacent to those in our sample. However, 26 percent of the married debtors who were interviewed replied that their spouses had filed at the same time, with an additional 6 percent reporting filings at other times,

pay his secured creditors or possibly have the property repossessed. The situation is most acute in the nonbusiness cases, where only 39 percent of the total indebtedness was unsecured. The chances of significant relief appear to be much better for bankrupts with former business connections, because 70 percent of their total indebtedness is unsecured.

Secured debts also affect confirmed payment plans under Chapter XIII. First, a Chapter XIII plan cannot deal with debts secured by real estate. Then there are two problems with debts secured by liens on personal property: (a) if the referee requires that creditors with such liens receive payments outside the proceeding while unsecured creditors are paid through the court, the debtor may not be able to make a realistic payment proposal; or (b) if the referee requires that secured creditors be paid first under the plan, the unsecured creditors may be unwilling to accept the proposal.[34]

ASSETS

We have said that a typical bankrupt's assets (as scheduled with his petition) amount to about $500. This is only an approximation because of the way information is put into the schedules. Some debtors' attorneys deducted secured liabilities before listing assets; others did not; and for a third group, it was impossible to tell.[35] (See Appendix Table c-8 for details.) Whichever alternative was used, there were more assets in former-business than in nonbusiness cases.

Modest as the asset estimates seem, they are still generous. Attorneys frequently scheduled assets at the maximum value allowable under the state's exemption laws[36] without making a serious effort to determine the potential market for the property.

EARLIER INSOLVENCY PROCEEDINGS

To complete the debtors' financial picture we should know how many were new to bankruptcy (or comparable state proceedings)

34. See Chapter 5 for a fuller discussion of how Chapter XIII plans work.
35. If the reader concludes from this that it is difficult to understand the debtor's financial situation from the official schedules, he is correct. See Chapter 8 for other observations on bankruptcy forms and records.
36. See Chapter 5, pp. 81–84, for explanation of how exemptions work in the bankruptcy process.

and how many were "repeaters." The files showed that at least 3 percent of the bankrupts and 22 percent of the Chapter XIII debtors had had prior experience with federal or state proceedings:[37]

	Straight bankruptcy	Chapter XIII
Prior bankruptcy	2%	13%
Prior Chapter XIII	—	9
Prior state proceeding	1	—

All but one of the state proceedings reported were municipal trusteeships in Northern Ohio. Of the bankrupts, a little over 1 percent had filed a previous petition after 1956. Remember that the sample cases were closed in 1964. A discharge cannot be granted in a second proceeding begun within six years of the filing of an earlier proceeding in which a discharge was granted.[38] This means that a few of the bankrupts were getting a discharge about as soon as it was possible to do so.

A majority of the Chapter XIII repeaters had refiled within three years, and they were concentrated in Northern Alabama. This phenomenon is discussed in more detail in Chapter 5.

PAYING DEBTS AFTER BANKRUPTCY

As the bankruptcy process winds to a close, the debtor almost always receives a discharge. This does not entirely relieve him of concern for the debts he started with, for three reasons. First, he may want to do business with some of his old creditors; second, he probably has some secured debts; and third, creditors may sue anyway, alleging that their claims are excepted from the discharge.

37. These figures are understated for a variety of reasons. The statement of affairs that accompanies the petition requests information about earlier insolvency proceedings for only limited time periods before the current filing. Moreover, some statements may have been incomplete in this respect, as they were in others. No national roster of bankrupts and Chapter XIII petitioners exists, so there were no provisions for disclosing out-of-state proceedings.

38. In 1966, the Supreme Court held that the six-year bar would not apply to subsequent Chapter XIII petitions which sought an extension of time for full payment of debts. *Perry* v. *Commerce Loan Co.*, 383 U.S. 392 (1966).

The first problem is obvious. The debtor wants to buy from a store or borrow from a finance company he has dealt with before. Either one may decide not to extend credit unless the old (presumably discharged) debt is included in a new account. And creditors are more likely to get their money this time because by law the debtor cannot receive another discharge for six years.

A debtor does not get rid of obligations secured by liens, usually on his house, car, or household appliances. He pays such debts outside the bankruptcy process or the security is repossessed or the debt is "revived."

Over one-third of our interviewees who had been through straight bankruptcy had agreed to repay some of the debts they owed when they went into bankruptcy court.[39] They were then asked, "What kinds of debts?" Because of the vagueness of this phrasing, the replies included both the purposes for which the debts were incurred and the kinds of creditors. The answers thus overlap considerably but the patterns are clear:

Purposes	*Percent*
Debts for appliances or furniture	48
Debts for automobiles	30
Home mortgages	9
Loans (unspecified)	8
Medical and hospital bills	6
Debts for clothing	5
Debts for jewelry	3
Debts for business equipment or inventory	2
Debts for tools	2
Utility bills	1
Debts for food	1

Kinds of creditors	
Loan companies	30
Garages, filling stations	2
Loans from employers	2
Credit unions	2
Loans from individuals	1
Creditors—identity not clear	1
Other	8
Don't know	2

39. Over half of the bankrupts in a study by Herbert Jacob (*Debtors in Court* [Rand McNally, 1969], pp. 109–10) agreed to reaffirmations of debts.

They revived on the average almost $1,000 in debts (one-fifth of what the typical nonbusiness bankrupt owed). Why? Forty-five percent answered that they wanted to keep the car, stove, or whatever. Another 32 percent said they wanted to pay the creditors—they had been lenient, fair, considerate, or the creditor was a friend. Other replies were far less numerous: 8 percent said this action was advised, insisted on, or arranged for by their attorneys, and 5 percent said "to save my job"—usually this covered debts to employers. Another 4 percent said they had gone bankrupt to get rid of debts other than those revived.

Frequently, creditors attempt to collect even unsecured debts after debtors have been through bankruptcy. A creditor may wait until a discharge has been granted and then sue in a state court on the original obligation. The typical suit alleges that the debt was fraudulently incurred and should therefore be excluded from the discharge. Unless the bankrupt asserts his discharge as an affirmative defense to the complaint, judgment for the plaintiff will be granted as if bankruptcy had not intervened. The bankrupt, from ignorance (and unwillingness or inability to incur further legal fees), is not likely to put up a defense.

The reaction of the local courts and of the debtors' counsel to such collection efforts affects the creditors' choice of tactics. Some state court judges are not receptive to postdischarge suits. Or debtors' attorneys may have warned creditors "not to try it on my clients."

Forty-one percent of those interviewed (including 44 percent of those in straight bankruptcy and 29 percent of the Chapter XIII debtors) reported postbankruptcy collection efforts. Among creditors who made such efforts, loan companies again led the list, being named by 38 percent. Others most often mentioned were furniture stores (11 percent), department stores (10 percent), doctors, hospitals, nurses, and other health-related services (10 percent), clothing stores (6 percent), banks (6 percent), other retail stores (5 percent), and individual creditors (5 percent).

"What did you do?" was the next question. "Nothing," "Tore it up," or "Ignored it" were replies given by 32 percent of those whose creditors had tried to collect. Nearly as many, 27 percent, turned the collection letter over to their lawyers. Fourteen percent told the creditors that they were bankrupt and therefore would not pay, but another 12 percent *did* pay without consulting anyone. Other answers: 4 percent paid on advice of attorneys; 4 percent let secured property be repossessed; 3 percent told creditors they would pay later; and 7 percent gave various other replies.

To remedy this general (and unwholesome) problem, it was proposed that bankruptcy courts be authorized to decide whether a particular debt was dischargeable. Legislative efforts to create this authority succeeded in 1970 after a fifteen-year struggle.[40] The debtor, if a creditor attempts to collect its claim through a state-court suit, now has the option of asking the bankruptcy court for a ruling on the issue of dischargeability. If the claim is dischargeable, the creditor will be barred from pursuing the debtor further unless the creditor is able to induce the discharged bankrupt to revive the obligation by a new promise to pay.

GETTING CREDIT AFTER BANKRUPTCY

Debtors *can* get credit after going through bankruptcy, but many of them find this more expensive or more difficult than before. Some creditors offer to sell or lend to them *because* they have been in bankruptcy (and cannot receive a discharge for six years). Here is an example of a flyer mailed to all bankrupts on the court records in one of the cities covered in this study:

Dear Future Customer:

I can finance an automobile for you now, regardless of your bankruptcy.

I am prepared to give you a *fair* and *honest* deal. We have many cars of all makes and models to choose from.

Dear customer, do not wait!!! Call me now. See what I can do for you.

Call now———

XYZ, Inc.

P.S. No monthly payments on the car until July.

Bankrupts who succumb to such offers find the relief afforded by bankruptcy to have been very short-lived.

40. P.L. 91-467, 84 Stat. 990 (1970). For the history and implications of this new legislation, see Vern Countryman, "The New Dischargeability Law," *American Bankruptcy Law Journal*, Vol. 1 (1971), p. 1.

One-third of the debtors find it harder to get credit after bankruptcy. Those who were interviewed said:

	All debtors answering	Straight bankruptcy only	Chapter XIII only
Harder	35%	31%	44%
Same	35	36	35
Easier	8	10	2
Depends	9	9	10
Haven't tried	12	13	8
Hopeless, impossible	1	1	1

Chapter XIII debtors feel the pinch more than straight bankrupts, possibly because creditors think a Chapter XIII debtor can still obtain a discharge at any time.

Seventy percent of those interviewed had made major purchases on credit since bankruptcy, and 41 percent had borrowed money. The median amount borrowed was $568. A motor vehicle was the item purchased most frequently (percentages below are based on the number of interviewed debtors who had made major purchases on credit since bankruptcy):

Purchase	Percent
Car, truck, motorcycle	60
Appliance	41
Furniture	34
House	9
Clothing	8
Jewelry	4
Boat	1
Business equipment, supplies	1
Other	7

Source of purchase	
Motor vehicle dealer	58
Furniture store	36
Appliance store	23
Department store	11
Real estate developer	9
Clothing store	7
Retail store	7
Jewelry store	5
Individual	3
Boat dealer	1
Other	6

When the debtors were asked about the terms on which they had bought or borrowed, they usually answered by naming the amounts of their monthly payments—which resulted in a median of $64 for those who had made purchases, $34 for those who had borrowed, and $73 for those who had done both. The amounts of most of the payments were not unreasonable in relation to income (the median debtor made about $400 a month), but it must be remembered that many of the debtors were already making other payments on revived debts.

Local units of the Associated Credit Bureaus of America checked their records to see how many of the debtors in our sample received credit after bankruptcy. Table 4-3 shows the strong variations among the districts. The credit bureaus also attempted to report

TABLE 4-3. *Percentage of Debtors Receiving Credit after Bankruptcy, by District*[a]

District	Straight bankruptcy	Chapter XIII
Northern Ohio	71	45
Oregon	67	79
Northern Alabama	65	74
Western Texas	64	0
Maine	63	62
Northern Illinois	41	67
Southern California	25	30
All districts	43	67

Source: Files of the Associated Credit Bureaus of America.
a. Percentages are those debtors who received credit after bankruptcy—shown as a percentage of those in our sample who are still listed with the credit bureaus in their area. The figures cover bankrupts and debtors from the Brookings file sample and interview sample in the seven districts shown.

the postbankruptcy payment records of the bankrupts and Chapter XIII debtors whose files they examined (see Tables 4-4 and 4-5). Note that a majority of the straight bankrupts for whom such information existed had poor payment records in every district, with the possible exceptions of Southern California and Northern Illinois, for which very little information was available. The payment record for Chapter XIII debtors was even worse, except in Oregon. In all the districts covered by this study it was bad enough to throw doubt on the rehabilitative effect of the proceedings.

TABLE 4-4. *Postbankruptcy Payment Record of Straight Bankrupts, by District*
In percent

| District | Payment record[a] | | |
	Good/satisfactory	Slow/bad	No information
Northern Alabama	23	40	37
Northern Ohio	20	50	30
Oregon	16	37	47
Maine	15	46	38
Western Texas	12	26	62
Southern California	12	9	79
Northern Illinois	5	15	80
All districts	13	22	65

Source: Files of the Associated Credit Bureaus of America.
a. Percentages may not add to 100 because of rounding.

TABLE 4-5. *Postbankruptcy Payment Record of Chapter XIII Debtors, by District*
In percent

| District | Payment record[a] | | |
	Good/satisfactory	Slow/bad	No information
Oregon	26	49	26
Southern California	13	11	76
Northern Ohio	9	36	55
Maine	9	55	36
Northern Illinois	8	39	53
Northern Alabama	2	60	38
All districts	5	52	43

Source: Files of the Associated Credit Bureaus of America. Western Texas is excluded because of the small size of the sample.
a. Percentages may not add to 100 because of rounding.

REACTIONS TO THE EXPERIENCE OF BANKRUPTCY

Looking back at least two years after bankruptcy, the four hundred debtors interviewed expressed both favorable and unfavorable attitudes about the experience. Their attitudes varied not only from person to person and from district to district but also with the wording of the questions and their placement in the interview.

The interviews began with: "How satisfied are you with the way things in general have turned out for you since you went into bankruptcy court?" Replies tended to be favorable:

	Percent
Wonderful; fine; much better off	23
Good; satisfied; all right	34
Had to; couldn't help it; no other way out	5
OK, but it's hard to get credit	14
Dissatisfied; worse off; should not have gone bankrupt	18
Other	6

Differences between the straight bankrupts and the Chapter XIII cases were not significant, but there were some differences in the degree of satisfaction expressed by debtors in the various districts. When answers were grouped as "satisfied," "neutral," or "dissatisfied," Maine and Northern Illinois yielded significantly more "satisfied" answers, and Oregon fewer. Oregon was the only district showing significantly more "dissatisfied" answers than the others as a group.

In all districts, however, responses were more likely to resemble these actual answers:

"Well, I've been satisfied, I ain't got as many debts as I had."

"Fine, everything worked out fine for me . . ."

than these:

"Bankruptcy didn't help me much."

"Displeased about it all; the lawyer charged as much as paying the bills."

In interpreting the favorable answers, the reader should again recall that a relatively stable group of debtors were interviewed, that economic conditions were on the whole favorable, and that the debtors had a natural wish to assure themselves and the interviewer that they were "doing OK."

Later in the interview they were asked to evaluate their financial situation, and again the response was favorable. More Chapter XIII debtors than straight bankrupts felt better about their situation.

"How would you describe your own financial situation now, compared with when you went into bankruptcy court?"

Reply	All debtors	Straight bankruptcy only	Chapter XIII only
Much better	33%	34%	34%
A little better	32	29	41
About the same	26	28	18
Even worse	6	8	4
Much worse	2	2	4

(Percentages do not add to 100 because of rounding.) To this question significantly more favorable answers came from Maine, Oregon, Northern Ohio, and Northern Alabama; less favorable from Southern California, Northern Illinois, and Western Texas. Note that this pattern of district replies does not correlate at all with that for the previous question.

Reactions are clearly different—more negative, more defensive—when the question is put this way: "How do you feel about having been in bankruptcy?" The main reactions can be listed in three categories: favorable, neutral (but with a tinge of defensiveness), and unfavorable, as shown in Table 4-6. There are several clear attitude patterns. The neutral responses are most numerous, unfavorable are second, and favorable are fewest. There is more satisfaction among the Chapter XIII debtors, more dissatisfaction among the bankrupts. A higher proportion of bankrupts gave neutral answers. Again, the straight bankrupts were less likely to complain of difficulty in getting credit. A comparison of answers among districts shows Northern Alabama (predominantly Chapter XIII cases) and Northern Ohio debtors significantly better satisfied than the others. Oregon debtors were clearly most dissatisfied, with Western Texas and Northern Illinois also contributing high proportions of negative answers.

A few sample quotations:

Favorable—"I feel relieved I don't have to pay those bills." "This was a lifesaver and my only solution." "I'm better off now."

Neutral—"OK as far as I can see." "I feel justified in having gone through bankruptcy." "Some days I'm glad. Some days I'm distressed."

Unfavorable—"I feel guilty. I wasn't brought up that way." "It's

TABLE 4-6. *Attitudes about Bankruptcy Experience, as Expressed by Bankrupts and Chapter XIII Debtors*

In percent

Responses[a]	Total group[b]	Straight bankruptcy only	Chapter XIII only
Favorable			
Wonderful; fine; much better off; very satisfied	4	4	5
Good; satisfied; all right	11	9	19
Satisfied because I can still get what I want	4	4	4
I learned not to overextend myself creditwise; won't let it happen again	4	2	6
Good because I got rid of one (or two) troublesome debt(s)	3	4	1
Glad I could pay (Chapter XIII only)	4	—	17
Feel good because I kept my property	1	1	2
Neutral			
Had to; couldn't help it; no other way out	31	33	24
OK, but can't get credit; hard to get credit	12	9	19
It has made no difference; doesn't bother me	8	10	3
Unfavorable			
Feel bad; lost self-respect; stigma; embarrassed; ashamed	24	28	9
Dissatisfied; worse off; should not have gone bankrupt; things are worse	12	12	15

Source: Interviews with 400 debtors in seven federal court districts by Chilton Research Services.
a. The replies of many of the debtors fell into more than one category. Percentages thus total more than 100.
b. Includes a few who had filed in both straight bankruptcy and Chapter XIII and a few "Don't know's."

a crime to any working man. It sets him back five years. He gets taken." "I would not do it again. I would do almost anything to keep from it. It will take many years to overcome the mess I'm in."

To generalize very grossly: the typical debtor interviewed feels fairly satisfied with his overall situation after bankruptcy but feels badly that he went through the experience.

The debtors were also given another chance to second-guess their decision to file in bankruptcy: "If you had it to do over again, would you rather pay off your debts—even though it would mean temporary hardships for you—or would you rather go through bankruptcy?" Half of them answered that they would rather pay off their debts. A quarter (24 percent) of the total group said they would go through bankruptcy. Only a third (34 percent) of the Chapter XIII debtors said they would go bankrupt—indicating that the rest were satisfied with (or at least accepted) the wage earner relief process. Another quarter (26 percent) of the entire group gave inconclusive replies—"Don't know" or "I had no choice."

By and large the personal bankrupts were mature, settled heads of families working as blue collar or service employees. Most of them had incomes well above poverty levels. They had piled up debts to an unmanageable amount and went into bankruptcy court because some sort of legal action had been taken or threatened. They turned to advisers they knew and found their lawyers on the basis of acquaintanceship. Over a third of them revived debts. Some were victims of creditors' attempts to collect "discharged debts." After bankruptcy 70 percent obtained credit, though a third of these found it more difficult than before bankruptcy. They expressed themselves either numbly or unfavorably about having been through bankruptcy but considered their financial situations better than before.

It is well to remember that candid responses to some of the questions would have required the interviewees to confess to bad judgment or gullibility. Some did and some did not. Responses are probably also influenced by a natural desire to assure the interviewer—and oneself—that all is now well.

5

❊

The Personal Bankruptcy
Process

Here we explain and analyze what happens after the troubled
debtor decides to take some formal step to resolve his financial difficulties. The narrative takes him first through some state-authorized
proceedings short of bankruptcy, next through the straight bankruptcy process, then through the alternative "wage earner" plan
(Chapter XIII), under which the debtor pays off all or part of his
debts under court supervision. These descriptions will prepare the
reader for the business bankruptcy process (discussed in Chapter 7),
which goes through variations of the same basic steps.

STATE ALTERNATIVES TO BANKRUPTCY

There are several kinds of state proceedings that serve some of the
same purposes as bankruptcy: collection, liquidation, and distribution to creditors of the debtor's property. Such proceedings are
alternatives to bankruptcy if they are successful, precursors of bankruptcy if they fail. (The ultimate relief of a discharge from debts is
not usually available under state laws.)

Two of these alternatives are concerned with personal bankruptcies: debt pooling and wage earner trusteeships. Two apply to
both personal and business cases: the informal composition and

extension. Two relate mainly to business bankruptcies: assignments for the benefit of creditors (both common law and statutory)[1] and receiverships, and therefore will be discussed in Chapter 7.

DEBT POOLING (PRORATION)

Under this remedy[2] the debtor regularly pays part of his income to an agent who, usually for a fee, turns over shares of this payment to the creditors. The agent may offer counseling as well as repayment services.

Debt pooling has a number of weaknesses. Creditor cooperation cannot be compelled. The debtor may not be aware of this, and indeed may be misled by the debt poolers' advertising. Moreover, the fees charged usually have been uncontrolled and the safeguards against misuse of the collected funds few. Thus the debtor's financial burden frequently has been increased rather than diminished by debt pooling. And creditors, too, have had no assurance that they will be treated fairly.[3]

Disturbed by these and other shortcomings, many state authorities have taken remedial measures. Thus some twenty-eight states (as of 1971) have by statute absolutely prohibited or drastically curtailed debt pooling, except as an adjunct to legal counseling or as a nonprofit community service. At least twelve other states have circumscribed and regulated its practice. Still other states, without specific laws, have judicially imposed restraints that render debt-pooling operations difficult, if not impossible.

The eight states in the present study vary greatly in this as in other respects. Four of them—Maine, New York, Ohio, and Texas

1. Such assignments are also, though infrequently, used by individual insolvents.
2. Firms specializing in this business may also use the terms "debt management," "debt counseling," "budget planning," "debt liquidating," or others.
3. For two accounts of surveys of businessmen's attitudes toward debt pooling, see Joe B. Birkhead, "Debtors Misled and Deceived by Pro-Raters, Kansas City Better Business Bureau Finds," *Personal Finance Law Quarterly Report*, Vol. 16 (Fall 1962), pp. 116-19; and Allan E. Backman, "Debt Adjustment Abuses Cause Many Complaints to Better Business Bureaus," *Personal Finance Law Quarterly Report*, Vol. 9 (Spring 1955), pp. 44-45. For an evaluation of the comparative efficacy of debt-pooling arrangements and Chapter XIII proceedings under the Bankruptcy Act, see George R. Kennedy, "Debt-Pooling Arrangements vs. Chapter XIII Proceedings," *Journal of the National Association of Referees in Bankruptcy*, Vol. 32 (October 1958), pp. 109-10.

—prohibit the practice generally; three—California, Illinois, and Oregon—regulate it; and one—Alabama—has no statutory limitations, though some debt poolers have been attacked on other grounds, such as fraud and "failing to meet community standards."

WAGE EARNER TRUSTEESHIPS

A few states have provided for a formal payoff process for wage earners. Typically, the laws require the debtor to send his wages to a trustee appointed and supervised by a local court for distribution to his creditors. As in Chapter XIII cases, the debtor's property is protected against legal action by creditors. Such trusteeships have a few advantages over Chapter XIII proceedings:[4] they are locally administered and therefore probably more convenient for the debtor; they are less costly than Chapter XIII proceedings;[5] and they do not depend on creditor consent. On the other hand, the trusteeships are less flexible: they are intended to include *all* the debtor's nonexempt earnings. Trusteeships also give less relief: they do not permit the debtor to reject onerous contracts; do not spare him the burden of further defending debt-collection actions; do not stop the running of interest on claims against him; and do not permit the discharge of his unpaid obligations under any circumstances.[6]

Ohio is the only state of those covered in this study that provides for wage earner trusteeships. The Cleveland municipal court,

4. Discussed below, pp. 94–105.

5. If a debtor invokes Chapter XIII proceedings, he must pay an initial filing fee of $15; thereafter, 5 percent of all moneys paid under the plan may be retained by the trustee as his fee, plus a 3–5 percent increment to defray his expenses; and $15 ($10 if his liabilities do not exceed $200) plus 1 percent will be withheld for the Referees' Salary and Expense Fund. The attorney who works out the plan and files the petition for the debtor will usually charge a fee of $75 to $250 for his services. In Ohio, however, if the debtor invokes wage earner trusteeship proceedings, he must pay an initial filing fee of only $2.50; thereafter, only 2 percent of all moneys collected may be retained by the trustee as his fee; and the attorney—and normally none is employed—who refers the debtor to the trusteeship department is limited by the Bar Association's recommended fee schedule to a $5 consultation fee for his services.

6. For a more detailed examination of the relative advantages and disadvantages of Ohio's statutory wage earner trusteeship vis-à-vis Chapter XIII proceedings, see Morris G. Shanker, "Comparison of Chapter XIII Proceedings and State Wage Earner Relief Plans," *Personal Finance Law, Quarterly Report*, Vol. 19 (Fall 1965), pp. 153–55.

visited in our field research, has furnished debt repayment and counseling service to thousands of debtors. In 1967, for example, 1,894 trusteeships were filed, and payments to creditors totaled $825,960.

Although the law required the debtor to send the trustee all of his nonexempt earnings, the Cleveland court required less in cases where all would have meant great hardship for the debtor. Creditors went along with this practice, recognizing that it made the best of a bad situation for all concerned.

Creditors interviewed by the Brookings research staff in Northern Ohio said this trusteeship plan was cheaper, speedier, and more productive than any other formal means of dealing with personal insolvencies. Nevertheless, the plan failed to solve the problem of some debtors, who later went bankrupt. At least 4 percent of the bankrupts in the Northern Ohio sample for this study had previously been in wage earner trusteeship proceedings.[7]

This state proceeding would probably have been less popular if Chapter XIII proceedings had been effectively encouraged by the bar.

INFORMAL COMPOSITIONS AND EXTENSIONS

The oldest, simplest, and perhaps the most satisfactory state-sanctioned technique for resolving the insolvent debtor's difficulties is the informal, out-of-court settlement, which may take the form of either of two common-law devices—the composition or the extension, or both. The former is an agreement between the debtor and at least two of his creditors that a partial payment will be made in full satisfaction of the debts owed these creditors. An extension provides for a lengthening of the time for payment; the creditors who agree are barred from trying to collect in other ways from the debtor until the agreed time has elapsed.

Both remedies are relatively quick and inexpensive. They are most likely to be used when the debtor seems to be in temporary trouble and creditors expect to do satisfactory business with him in

7. The actual percentage was probably higher. Some bankruptcy case files had scanty prefiling data. The 4 percent were cases in which funds were actually transferred from the municipal court trustee to the bankruptcy trustee.

the future. Their main limitation is that they bind only the parties who agree to them and thus have no effect on other creditors.[8]

These common-law insolvency remedies were used in all eight of the states surveyed. Creditors and creditors' attorneys interviewed generally said the remedies were cheaper and speedier than more formal measures. When creditors' attorneys, however, were asked, "In your experience, what is best for creditors of *individual* debtors?" the answers were different. Of the forty-two who had an opinion, twenty-two said "Chapter XIII" and only fifteen said "composition agreement."

CHOICE OF REMEDY UNDER THE FEDERAL BANKRUPTCY SYSTEM

If the debtor or (more likely) his attorney decides that he must file a federal bankruptcy proceeding, he must then choose between straight bankruptcy or Chapter XIII. Four out of five choose the former, but there are great variations among the courts in how frequently Chapter XIII is used. The proportions of *all* bankrupts in the seven districts in our study demonstrate this:[9]

	Chapter XIII	Straight bankruptcy
Northern Alabama	76%	24%
Maine	52	48
Western Texas	28	72
Southern California	11	89
Northern Ohio	7	93
Oregon	5	95
Northern Illinois	4	96
Seven districts	18	82
All districts in U.S.	17	83

8. For a more detailed description, discussion, and evaluation of the common-law composition and extension, see Garrard Glenn, *Law Governing Liquidation* (Baker, Voorhis, 1935), Chap. 9; Charles E. Nadler, *The Law of Debtor Relief* (Harrison, 1954), Chaps. 2 and 3; see also Arthur Linton Corbin, *Contracts: A Comprehensive Treatise on the Working Rules of Contract Law* (West, 1962), Sec. 1283, for a brief, but lucid and authoritative discussion of the legal basis of the common-law composition.

9. Administrative Office of the U.S. Courts, "Tables of Bankruptcy Statistics" (1968; processed), Tables F 2 and F 3, voluntary cases. These figures include businesses, which cannot use Chapter XIII. As noted in Chapter 1, only business cases were studied

These diverse patterns result mainly from the attitudes of debtors' attorneys and of referees in bankruptcy—which may combine to form firm local usages. In Northern Alabama, the use of Chapter XIII has been established for more than thirty years as a means of getting relatively low-income citizens to repay their debts through a government-managed system.[10] Maine referees encourage debtors to file under Chapter XIII also, but elsewhere we found little interest in it from bench and bar.

Ideally a debtor should choose between straight bankruptcy and Chapter XIII after he and his lawyer determine which is more appropriate to his situation. But if attorneys "oppose Chapter XIII on principle because it results from unjustifiable pressure to deprive citizens of their legal rights" or feel that "it is much better for the debtor to get cleared up and out," it is not likely that their clients will file Chapter XIII petitions. On the other hand, the debtor's choice will be biased in favor of Chapter XIII if his attorney either believes that "Chapter XIII is morally correct" or if he tries "to avoid straight bankruptcy because if the debtors would go bankrupt, then the creditors would lose confidence in the courts of bankruptcy as a means of solving their problems."[11]

A substantial majority (70 percent) of the debtors' counsel whom we interviewed said that the debtor's ability to pay was the chief consideration in their recommendation for or against Chapter XIII (that is, if he seemed able to pay, Chapter XIII would be used). It must be remembered, however, that we interviewed these attorneys because they were experts in bankruptcy. Whether or not a debtor finds such an expert to represent him is a matter of chance.

The attorney's choice is also influenced by knowledge of a referee's basic attitude toward Chapter XIII.[12] If the referee

---

in New York. Since California has been redistricted, the figures for "Southern California" are a total of filings in the districts of Southern and Central California plus one-half of filings in Eastern California, and are thus not strictly comparable with the Southern California District as it existed when our field research was done. See Chapter 1, note 1.

10. For a discussion of the Alabama history, see Harry H. Haden, "Chapter XIII Wage Earner Plans—Forgotten Man Bankruptcy," *Kentucky Law Journal*, Vol. 55 (1966–67), pp. 581–84.

11. Quotations are from the interviews conducted by the Brookings research staff.

12. The impact of the referees' attitudes toward Chapter XIII in four Wisconsin cities is discussed by Herbert Jacob, *Debtors in Court* (Rand McNally, 1969), pp. 66–68.

strongly opposes it, he can cause or permit various obstacles to arise. Some lawyers told us of being handicapped by clerical red tape, inordinate delays, and excessive compensation to the Chapter XIII trustee. Others said that they did not file Chapter XIII cases because referees would allow such brief time periods for repayment that there would be little improvement in their clients' situations. At the opposite extreme are referees so partial to Chapter XIII that they encourage this choice even when a debtor is in such straits that an attempted repayment plan is unlikely to succeed.

HOW A STRAIGHT BANKRUPTCY CASE PROCEEDS

The straight bankruptcy process really begins when the debtor files his petition. If he does so voluntarily (and all but a fraction of 1 percent of our sample from the bankruptcy files did so) he is automatically declared (adjudicated) a bankrupt.[13] Then the process of liquidating his assets—if any—can begin.

THE FIRST MEETING

The referee then calls the first meeting (it usually is the last one too) of the creditors named by the debtor in his petition. Here they have an opportunity to examine the bankrupt and to select the trustee who will administer the estate—that is, collect and liquidate nonexempt assets. Such opportunities are presumed to assure "creditor control" of bankruptcy proceedings.

Creditor interest. We could not find out in cases drawn from the files how many creditors actually participated in the first meetings because the records were haphazard and often nonexistent. Where information did appear it often showed attorneys' (or law firms') names without indicating which claims they represented. In cases where creditors were identified, usually no more than one or two creditors (or their representatives) appeared. Secured creditors who

13. In involuntary bankruptcy cases, which are extremely rare, creditors file the petition, and the referee decides whether to adjudicate the debtor a bankrupt. Some straight bankruptcies start as Chapter XIII cases (3 percent of our sample did) and are then adjudicated when the repayment plan seems headed for failure; sometimes even before the plan is confirmed.

showed up were likely to use the first meeting for the purpose of locating their collateral and for negotiating with the bankrupt about future payments. With this limited objective in mind, they were unlikely to be interested in the administration of the estate.

Interviews with creditors confirmed that most of them did not participate actively once a bankruptcy was filed. They said they attended first meetings (multiple replies were possible):

	Percent
Never	32
Seldom	22
Always	17
When debt is large	11
Usually	6
Frequently	2
Other	14
Don't know	3

Forty-six percent reported that they always turned the entire file over to their attorneys, who sometimes attended the meetings. They said that their time was better spent in creating new business than in participating in formalities that usually yielded little or no return.

Use of receivers and trustees. The referee may appoint a receiver if he thinks this is necessary to protect the creditors' interest in the bankrupt's property until the trustee can start work. This was done in only 6 percent of our former-business cases and less than 1 percent of the nonbusiness cases.

Selection of a trustee is not always necessary. It can be dispensed with if the debtor's petition "discloses no assets *and if no creditor appears.*"[14] Trustees were *not* used in only 25 percent of our personal bankruptcy cases, although 64 percent of our sample had no assets. These no-trustee cases were concentrated in four districts—Northern Illinois, Northern Alabama, Western Texas, and Oregon.

One of the dilemmas of bankruptcy administration is whether trustees should be used in apparent no-asset cases. If used, they may uncover some truly significant assets or their presence may deter debtors from concealing assets. Yet in many cases where there

14. General Order 15. "No assets" has been construed to mean no assets beyond those allowed as exempt. *Smalley* v. *Laugenor*, 30 Wash. 307, 70 Pac. 786 (1902), *writ of error dismissed*, 196 U.S. 98 (1905). Emphasis in text supplied.

78 BANKRUPTCY

are no assets at all, the use of a trustee merely wastes time and money. One solution, discussed in Chapter 10, is to have a salaried official available to serve in effect as standing trustee.

Choice of trustees. The law says that if creditors (or their representatives) fail to elect a trustee, the referee can make the appointment. Among our districts, methods of selection varied, with creditors electing as few as 1 percent of the trustees in Northern Illinois but as many as 53 percent in Northern Ohio (see Table 5-1). In a handful of cases, the person already serving as receiver was elected or appointed trustee.

TABLE 5-1. *Percentage of Personal Bankruptcy Cases in Which Trustees Were Used, by Method of Selection and District*

District	Trustee appointed	Trustee elected	Total
Maine	97	3	100
Northern Ohio	47	53	100
Southern California	90	9	99
Oregon	53	15	68
Western Texas	39	14	52
Northern Alabama	24	7	32
Northern Illinois	20	1	22
Seven districts	57	17	75

Source: File sample of personal bankruptcy cases. Percentages may not add to totals because of rounding.

The trustee's pay comes from assets found in the estate (except for $10 of the filing fee), so there is little incentive to compete for the job in small personal bankruptcies. In any event it is not difficult for creditors' attorneys to arrange elections among themselves. In one district, we observed attorneys who regularly appeared in bankruptcy proceedings comparing claims before the court session was called to order. Whoever represented the creditor with the largest claim voted for himself,[15] and no one else voted. The following trustees were "elected" in a succession of seven cases on one day: X, Y, Y, X, Z, Z, Z; X and Z are law partners. This situation existed despite the judges' and referees' attempts to maximize competition for the trustees' jobs by limiting each attorney to one vote without regard to the number of claims he represented.

15. An attorney appearing on behalf of a creditor obtains a proxy (or signed authorization) that enables him to vote for the trustee at the first meeting.

In a majority of the sample cases, the referee had to decide whom to appoint. The most typical solution reported by the referees interviewed was to select trustees from a small group of persons who could handle complicated as well as simple cases. The referees said this approach gave them confidence in the expertise of the trustees. It also solved the practical problem of finding persons who were willing to handle no-asset cases for the $10 fee provided by law. They could expect their compensation to average out in the long run if they were assured of receiving enough of the more complex and better-paying cases.

Yet a trustee who relies on such income has no economic incentive to challenge either the inefficiency of the system or the rulings of his particular sponsor, whether referee or judge. Similarly, referees who are comfortable with the performance of a small group have little reason to increase their own workload by encouraging new candidates to apply for such positions. In combination, these considerations produce a dedicated allegiance to the status quo.

Examination of the bankrupt. At the first meeting the bankrupt is examined, either by the trustee or by the referee if no trustee is appointed. Creditors can also participate. Those who do are usually secured creditors who are interested in locating their collateral or, much less frequently, those who wish to object to the bankrupt's discharge.

The amount of time spent with each debtor and the decorum of the proceedings depend on the volume of cases to be heard. To save time, bankrupts in two of our sample districts took their oaths en masse before being examined individually.

The practice and tone of the examination varied with the referees. Many simply made perfunctory requests for information supposedly contained in the petitions. Some probed selectively into suspicious circumstances involving the disposition of property. A few took the opportunity to discuss the future with the bankrupt, and gave limited advice on budgeting. Least decorous was the long-standing Cleveland practice of having several trustees conducting simultaneous examinations, often in the same room. The referees drifted around to some of them and listened in on parts of the questioning.

This examination also gives referees a little-used chance to suggest some other course if they think the debtor should not go through straight bankruptcy. In interviewing referees we asked, "Have you experienced cases in which you felt that the debtor should not have been in bankruptcy even though he was statutorily entitled to a discharge?" Every referee who answered said yes. Despite this, 64 percent felt that there was nothing they could do about it.

Referees who did intervene gave various kinds of advice. Some encouraged the use of Chapter XIII, while others advised an out-of-court settlement. A third group adjudicated the debtor a bankrupt, but discussed the wisdom of the choice with the attorney. (The adjudication would not prevent a petitioner from converting the proceeding to Chapter XIII at a later date.) Both referees in Maine said that they suggest Chapter XIII to straight bankruptcy petitioners when they feel that straight bankruptcy is unnecessary.

The bankrupt's attorney. In the courts we visited the bankrupt was sometimes not represented at all in the first meeting. If his attorney is not present the bankrupt is at a serious disadvantage, both during the examination and in negotiations with creditors trying to get him to revive debts.[16] Some referees and trustees did try to advise the unrepresented bankrupt, but they were inadequate substitutes for effective debtor's counsel.

The reader should not conclude that all counsel who appeared were effective. Occasional instances of conscientious representation were in sharp contrast to the typical performance. Frequently, attorneys could identify their clients only by calling their names and waiting to see who answered. The fact that counsel was looking at a given file for the first time *during* an examination was usually painfully obvious to the referee and trustee, not to mention the debtor (and us). A common excuse for the low level of performance was that the appearance was the attorney's first as counsel for a bankrupt. Whatever the reason, the apathetic bungling often displayed by individual bankrupts' attorneys is one of the most appalling aspects of the present system.

The general performance of bankrupts' counsel looked worse to us than it did to their clients (who were not accustomed to effective

16. In Southern California referees formerly adjourned first meetings if the bankrupt's counsel did not appear. This added delay to the bankrupt's other problems. To avoid such adjournments the "in pro per petition" was developed, whereby the petitioner appears on his own behalf after paying a slightly reduced fee to someone who prepares the bankruptcy schedules and then sends him off to court alone.

representation). Of the interviewees who had been through straight bankruptcy, 69 percent were "very satisfied"; 15 percent were "fairly satisfied"; 6 percent were "a little satisfied"; and 10 percent were "not satisfied." Those in the last two categories were asked to specify their complaints. They mentioned inadequate explanation of bankruptcy's advantages and disadvantages, laziness and inexperience, poor advice about debts secured by personal property, and high costs.

EXEMPTIONS

When the bankrupt files his petition, he lists the property he claims as exempt under his state law (that is, his property which cannot be taken from him and liquidated in the bankruptcy proceeding). This property is supposed to be valued by the trustee, then "set aside" so that the creditors will not get it. The procedure has a worthy purpose: to ensure that the bankrupt has enough to earn his living and maintain his family before other assets are apportioned to his creditors. Nevertheless the treatment of exemptions is characterized by both inequities and waste motion.

Unrealistic state laws. The inequities are largely due to the often obsolete and extremely diverse provisions of state exemption laws. This became a problem only with the Bankruptcy Act of 1898, which made each bankrupt subject to the exemption laws of his home state.[17] (The earlier federal bankruptcy acts had uniform exemption provisions, although the 1867 act also allowed property to be exempted under state *or* federal laws.) The state laws now in effect tend to reflect the values of rural life in the nineteenth century and vary greatly in specificity and generosity.[18]

17. He is also subject to certain exemptions in federal laws, for example, civil service pensions and social security benefits.

18. To complicate this already difficult situation, there are many exceptions to state exemption laws. In some states a debtor may waive his exemption rights by agreement with a particular creditor or by failure to claim exemptions soon enough. Moreover, an exemption may not be good against certain classes of favored creditors—typically an unpaid merchant with a valid purchase money security interest, a government holding tax liens, and a wife and children armed with an alimony or support order. Finally, in transactions with multistate contacts, conflict-of-laws rules may effectively nullify exemption laws.

Laws of the eight states covered in this study show the wide variety we have already emphasized. Some of them are rigidly explicit in their definitions. Thus, Texas law exempts five cows and their calves, two mules, and other specified livestock (not much help to a city apartment dweller). A similar specificity runs through the laws of California, Maine, New York, and Oregon.

The exemption laws of the remaining states, however, are couched in more general terms. Alabama, in lieu of a detailed list of assets, exempts personal property to be selected by the debtor up to a specified maximum value; Illinois law does the same. Ohio law permits the debtor to choose between a homestead exemption and an exemption for other real or personal property of a specified maximum value. These latter laws meet debtors' needs better, but they become obsolete because the specified maximum values are stated in dollar amounts that do not fluctuate with the cost of living or any other economic index.

Exemption laws also differ in generosity, as we pointed out in the Chapter 3 discussion of wage exemptions. There are further differences in how much the debtor may keep in real estate, furniture, life insurance, tools, and all sorts of personal possessions.

Impact on the bankruptcy process. All these differences put a difficult burden on those who administer the bankruptcy process, primarily the trustees and referees. The debtor suffers if the law is unrealistically severe, and the creditor suffers if it is unduly lax. Variations in exemptions also appear to affect bankruptcy filing rates. We have already shown the relation of garnishment, wage exemptions, and bankruptcy. At the other extreme, liberal state exemption laws, as in Texas, tend to discourage bankruptcies. Our judgment on this is confirmed by five of the eight creditors' attorneys interviewed in Western Texas.

Unquestionably, it is appropriate for a state to determine the extent to which property and income of debtors should be shielded from creditors who are trying to collect debts under its laws, even if its lawmakers retain archaic and unjust statutes on the books. It is clearly undesirable, however, for such laws to be, in practical and legal effect, part of the federal Bankruptcy Act. If bankruptcy proceedings are to be fair to all parties, humane, and efficient, there must be uniform and realistic exemption provisions. This requires a change in federal law.

THE PERSONAL BANKRUPTCY PROCESS

Handling exemptions in court. The bankrupt may claim as exempt, at the first meeting, property that he neglected to list previously. Such omissions had been encountered by 65 percent of the referees we interviewed. Thirty-five percent attributed this to the ineptitude of the bankrupts' attorneys, but only 20 percent had intervened to see that the exemptions were properly claimed and not waived. Here again the debtors' interests are not fully protected either by their lawyers or by the referees.

Then, if the exemption law imposes value limits, the property claimed as exempt is valued. This is done by the trustee if there is one; otherwise the referee decides what is to be allowed. In a large majority (71 percent) of the sample cases exemptions were allowed as claimed. This occurred in 82 percent of the no-asset cases, but in only 58 percent of the nominal-asset cases and 54 percent of the asset cases.[19] Both bankrupts and creditors can object to exemption allowances, but they did so in only 0.5 percent of the cases.

Trustees usually do not take a careful look at property claimed as exempt. Those who were interviewed mentioned these methods of valuing such assets (some mentioned more than one):

	Percent
Take a look; it's a matter of feel	43
Rely on debtor's schedule, testimony	34
Use "Blue Book" for cars	31
Not important; no problem	24
Use appraisers for real estate	22
Everything covered by liens anyway	7
Value real estate by address	4
Attorney for trustee handles this (Northern Illinois only)	4

Only one trustee claimed that an appraiser was used in every case. Several said that it was not practical to hire appraisers unless assets were large enough to pay them.

Most of the trustees were convinced that the value of the typical bankrupt's property was less than the maximum value allowed as exempt. The practical effect of this conclusion was that, unless suspicious circumstances appeared, the bankrupt was allowed to keep whatever he had as long as the *category* of property (clothing,

19. These figures are based on *all* bankruptcy cases in the file sample, business as well as personal.

car, and so forth) was exempt. The exemptions allowed by referees generally differed very little from those claimed by the bankrupt (see Appendix Table c-9).

In fact, most of the paperwork involved in claiming and allowing exemptions was waste motion. Very few creditors were interested enough to insist on a careful valuation of the bankrupt's assets. Trustees usually did not spend time inspecting property that was not likely to be included in the estate (and that consequently would yield no compensation for their efforts). There is little, therefore, to deter a bankrupt who is tempted to understate values. A realistically higher, and nationally uniform, set of exemption provisions in the law would save trouble and increase fairness to both debtors and creditors.

RESTRAINTS ON CREDITOR INTERFERENCE

The trustee can ask the referee for a restraining order to keep creditors from interfering with the bankrupt's property while decisions about which assets belong in the estate are being made. Such orders were rarely entered in the cases studied, except in Northern Illinois, where some attorneys routinely requested them in every case. Only once was a restraining order denied—in that case the creditor proved that his claim was a secured debt.

LIQUIDATION

All the above steps are preliminaries to the main activity of a straight bankruptcy—obtaining and liquidating the assets that remain after exemptions.

Sales. In 12 percent of the file sample of personal bankruptcy cases some of the bankrupt's property was sold.[20] Most of these sales (including 89 percent of those in Northern Ohio) yielded less than $200:

Yield (in dollars)	Percent
Under 200	8.0
200–499	2.0
500–999	1.0
1,000–2,499	0.5
2,500 and over	0.5

20. Similarly, 13 percent of the debtors interviewed by Chilton Research Services reported sales.

These small sales reflect the practice prevailing in Northern Ohio, though to a lesser extent elsewhere, of locating and selling enough nonexempt property to pay the trustee's fee.

We could not compare sale prices with the value of the property sold because it had so seldom been appraised. One exception: accounts receivable in former-business cases were sold for only 2 percent of their face amount.

What was sold? In the former-business cases, 45 percent of the total money received from sales came from inventory and equipment. Next were licenses, accounting for 19 percent, and real estate, for 18 percent. Leading categories for the nonbusiness cases were real estate (70 percent), motor vehicles (15 percent), and household appliances (5 percent). Most (83 percent) of the sales (in cases where this information was available) were held privately by solicited bids instead of by public auction.

Who bought the property? The bankrupt or a relative did so in a majority of cases in which we had information about the purchaser. The usual purchasers of household goods and cars were the bankrupts themselves.[21] Their interests in real estate were most often bought by relatives. Creditor purchasers concentrated on appliances, real estate, and cars, in that order.

Collections. There are two other common assets in personal bankruptcies: income tax refunds and wages (above exemptions) earned but not yet paid at the time of filing. Both produced small amounts, usually used to pay the trustees.

Debtors who are carefully advised and who can wait do not file in bankruptcy until tax refunds have been cashed and spent—frequently for attorneys' fees and costs. Twelve percent of the personal bankrupts in our sample did have to turn over refunds to the trustees. None of the refunds yielded as much as $1,000, and two-thirds of them amounted to less than $200.

Local attitudes affected the practice concerning the collection of tax refunds. None of the cases in Northern Alabama showed this type of asset. Some (though not all) referees in Southern California read a statutory provision giving them discretion to pay trustees up

21. Because bankruptcy does not affect income earned after the petition is filed, a bankrupt can accumulate enough money from that source to buy back his used personal property. Alternatively, he can use cash or bank deposits that have been allowed as exempt, or can even borrow money to make such purchases.

to $150 from the available assets of the estate as permitting them *not* to collect tax refunds under that amount.[22] (This policy is humane to debtors but a questionable use of referees' authority.) Elsewhere, the tax refund was often the only source of compensation for the trustee.

Wages payable, which were collected in 13 percent of the sample, produced even smaller sums—only 1 percent of the cases reporting amounts over $200. Referees and trustees in seven districts followed widely differing policies: wages payable were collected in 57 percent of the cases in Oregon, 23 percent in Northern Ohio, 3 percent in Maine, 2 in Northern Illinois, 1 in Southern California, and none in Northern Alabama or Western Texas.[23]

Tax refunds and nonexempt wages payable were very rarely scheduled as assets by the bankrupts, so the referee or trustee had to exert some effort to discover their existence. Seventy percent of the tax refunds were recovered from the bankrupts only after formal turnover orders were issued by the courts. An even larger percentage of the nonexempt wages required the same procedure. Frequently the bankrupt had received and spent the refund or wages *after* the petition was filed but *before* the first meeting, when the subject was explored. If his case came before a referee who required that he reimburse the estate out of his future earnings, the bankrupt's family would experience hardship to provide pay for the trustee.

There are some other sources of funds that are infrequently collected: accounts receivable, bank deposits, and deposits with utilities—each of which appeared in less than 1 percent of our personal bankruptcy cases. The amount recovered rarely was more than $100.

All these collections of small amounts to pay the trustee are cruel to the bankrupt and productive of costly paperwork. Higher exemption allowances and a better method of paying costs would eliminate the problem.[24]

Abandoned items. Not all nonexempt assets are picked up and

22. If other administrative expenses have been paid, the referee can pay the trustee as much as $150 without regard to the statutory formula for calculating compensation as a percentage of amounts disbursed.

23. Northern Alabama referees apparently ignored this item as they did tax refunds. In Texas all wages are exempt.

24. See Chapter 10.

liquidated. The trustee may decide to abandon an asset if the debt it secures exceeds its present value or if the liquidation process would be uneconomic.[25] Following are the percentages of our personal bankruptcy cases in which assets (by type) were officially abandoned, according to the case files:[26]

	Percent
Automobiles	14
Real estate	6
Household goods and appliances	4
Accounts receivable	2
Bank deposits	2
Nonexempt wages	1
Equipment	1

THE ESTATES

The liquidation process we have described produces funds for the estate in bankruptcy. The money is used first for administrative expenses, and then distributed to creditors if there is any left. None was left for them in 84 percent of the cases analyzed, which explains the creditors' lack of interest mentioned above.[27] There were sharp variations among the seven districts in the percentage of cases in which creditors did receive something (Table 5-2). The leaders in this respect were Oregon and Northern Ohio (where nonexempt wages and tax refunds were rigorously administered), Maine (where the sale of automobiles and household goods supplemented collection of tax refunds), and Western Texas (where estates came from the liquidation of other assets).

Cases in which there was something for administrative expenses and nothing for creditors (nominal-asset cases) amounted to 20

25. For example, proceeds from the pursuit of very old accounts receivable are often insufficient to pay the administrative expenses incurred in the chase.

26. The files do not really tell the whole story. In Northern Alabama, for example, the referees consistently ignored income tax refunds and nonexempt wages payable without so noting in the files. Real estate interests in Maine were neither allowed as exempt nor formally abandoned. Closed files usually failed to record the disposition of the scheduled assets, whether or not they were claimed as exempt.

27. This percentage of no-asset and nominal-asset cases is low. According to the "Tables of Bankruptcy Statistics," 89 percent of the straight bankruptcy cases concluded in fiscal 1964 (excluding dismissed cases) yielded nothing for creditors—13 percent of them being nominal asset and 76 percent no asset. Our sample was drawn in such a way that the frequency of asset cases is somewhat overstated (see p. 7).

TABLE 5-2. *Percentage of Personal Bankruptcy Cases in Which Creditors Received Money, by District*

District	All cases	Former business	Non- business
Oregon	36	48	34
Maine	33	30	33
Western Texas	23	46	7
Northern Ohio	22	24	22
Northern Alabama	15	62	9
Southern California	11	32	8
Northern Illinois	6	30	4
Seven districts	16	33	14

Source: File sample of personal bankruptcy cases.

percent of the personal bankruptcy sample. Maine, Oregon, and Northern Ohio were again the high states.

Creditors who participate are playing for small stakes indeed. The median total estate in an asset case was only $311; in a nominal-asset case, $93.[28] Sixty-nine percent of the asset cases were under $500; 86 percent, under $1,000 (Table 5-3). Nominal-asset cases were of course even smaller.

TABLE 5-3. *Personal Bankruptcy Cases, by Size of Estate*
In percent

Size of estate (in dollars)	Type of case	
	Asset	Nominal asset
Under 100	17	54
100–199	22	32
200–499	30	12
500–999	17	2
1,000–2,499	9	—
2,500–4,999	3	—
5,000 and over	2	—

Source: File sample of personal bankruptcy cases.

CREDITORS' CLAIMS

While the liquidation process is going on the creditors may file proof of their claims with the bankruptcy court—they are allowed six months from the date of the first meeting to do this. Once a proof

28. Medians are based on grouped data.

of claim is filed it can be changed. Sometimes the creditors submit amendments. A claim can also be objected to by the trustee, the bankrupt, or by other creditors, and the referee decides whether the claim will be allowed, and for how much. This provides one means of seeing to it that the bankrupt and all creditors are treated fairly under the law. The trustee is the most frequent source of objections. He usually takes this action near the end of a case, when he can see how much there will be in the estate. (There is no point in challenging claims if the creditors are not going to be paid anyway.)

Few objections; few changes. Despite the importance of this safeguard, it was little used. Objections were filed in only 3 percent of the cases in the personal bankruptcy sample. In those cases where objections were filed, only one claim was involved in each. The trustee was the *only* one to act in the former-business cases. Other creditors and the bankrupts each objected in less than 1 percent of the nonbusiness cases.

Of the claims attacked, 19 percent were reduced and 34 percent were disallowed. Twenty percent were allowed as originally filed, while 27 percent were allowed in a different status from that which had been claimed, such as unsecured rather than secured. Apparently there was merit in many of the objections that were made.

Few referees in the seven districts issued orders allowing claims. Most of them merely showed what claims were allowed by approving distributions to creditors.[29]

Few claims proved and allowed. Many creditors told us that they did not bother to file proofs of claims because they were likely to be paid so little (if anything). Yet we did encounter a few creditors who had filed routinely and were pleasantly surprised to be paid in full since so many others had given up. Table 5-4 shows that the claims actually proved are only a small percentage of those scheduled at the start of these bankruptcy cases.

The percentages of secured creditors shown in Table 5-4 are so small for four types of reasons. First, bankrupts' lawyers often list debts as secured even if there is doubt about the validity of the security. Some may therefore become unsecured claims later. Second, the creditor may attempt to reclaim the property from the

29. If there were neither objections nor distribution and if there was no formal order allowing claims, our data on proved claims are drawn from docket sheets, where court clerks enter the claims proved.

TABLE 5-4. *Claims Proved in Personal Bankruptcy Cases as a Percentage of Claims Scheduled, by Class of Debt*[a]

Class of debt	All cases	Former business	Non-business
Secured	5	9	5
Priority	32	35	31
Unsecured	11	17	10

Source: File sample of personal bankruptcy cases.
a. Some creditors who were not scheduled filed proofs; thus the table overstates the extent of activity by scheduled creditors.

bankrupt, so his proof will be incidental to a reclamation petition, not a proof of claim. Third, the creditor may collect outside the bankruptcy case by having the bankrupt revive the debt, or in other ways. Fourth, the property may be abandoned, formally or informally, if the secured claim exceeds its value.[30] On the average only one secured creditor proved a claim in each case.

Although priority creditors (usually tax collectors) are first in line for any distribution to creditors, only about a third of the claims listed with the petitions were proved. Proved priority claims also averaged one a case.

OBJECTIONS TO DISCHARGE

Even after controversies over claims have been settled, other forms of objection or appeal must be resolved before payments are made and the case wound up.

The trustee and creditors have a chance to object to the bankrupt's discharge if they think he has been dishonest or uncooperative or has failed to meet certain requirements. They must file objections within a time limit set by the referee. Theoretically, action by creditors at this stage would screen the "good" from the "bad"

30. Also, if the referee determines that the amount the trustee can realize on the property exceeds the creditor's secured claim, he may authorize the trustee either to pay off the debt and dispose of the property later or to sell the item. The referee can order the property sold either free of or subject to the creditor's lien. If the sale is "free and clear," the amount of the claim will be deducted from the sale proceeds and paid directly to the creditor. If the property is sold subject to the creditor's lien, the claim will remain valid against the property in the hands of the purchaser. In either event, the creditor need not file a formal proof of claim in the bankruptcy proceeding to realize on his security.

bankrupts and would prevent the latter from obtaining a discharge. Yet creditors objected to discharges in only 1 percent of the cases in the personal bankruptcy sample. The trustees were slightly more active, filing objections in 3 percent of the cases. Fewer than 1 percent of the personal bankrupts ultimately had their discharges denied in whole or in part.

PETITIONS FOR REVIEW

The right of appeal is another little-used safeguard. Only two cases in the entire personal bankruptcy sample involved petitions for review of a referee's order.[31] Each was an asset case. The only one to reach the formal hearing stage was a petition filed by the bankrupt because the referee had disallowed a tax refund claimed as exempt. The district judge reversed the referee's decision and allowed the exemption. The other case involved a disallowed lien and was settled before being heard.

PAYMENT OF ADMINISTRATIVE EXPENSES

After the assets have been liquidated and contested matters disposed of, the case can be prepared for closing—payments made, bankrupt discharged,[32] and records sent to be filed. As we said above, the administrative expenses come ahead of other payments (except those to secured creditors out of the proceeds of their collateral). *These expenses amounted to 41 percent of the amounts paid out in personal bankruptcy cases.*[33]

Although trustees served in three-quarters of the cases, they were paid from the estate in only one-third. Even so, they got the lion's share of the administrative expense money,[34] followed by attorneys for bankrupts (who may also be paid directly by their clients), and then by attorneys for trustees (see Table 5-5). This miscellany of

31. See Chapter 8, pp. 155–58, for a fuller discussion of petitions for review, including results of all petitions filed in the eight sample districts in fiscal years 1964 and 1965.

32. Unless he was discharged earlier, as is the practice in some districts.

33. This figure combines costs in asset and nominal-asset cases. Administrative expenses constitute a smaller proportion in business cases, where estates are larger. See Chapter 9 for a fuller treatment of this topic.

34. This discussion refers to compensation from the estate and does not take into account the trustee's $10 share of the filing fee.

TABLE 5-5. *Administrative Expenses Paid from Estates in Personal Bankruptcy Cases, by Category*

Category of expense	Percentage of cases in which compensated	Percentage of total administrative expense[a]
Trustee	34.0	44.0
Attorney for bankrupt	10.0	15.0
Attorney for trustee	5.0	11.0
Shorthand reporter	12.0	3.0
Appraiser	8.0	2.0
Receiver	1.0	2.0
Attorney for receiver	0.4	1.0
Auctioneer	0.7	1.0
Administrative rent[b]	0.1	0.3
Attorney for petitioning creditors[b]	—[c]	0.1
Clerical and bookkeeping	0.5	0.1

Source: File sample of personal bankruptcy cases.
a. Miscellaneous "other" expenses totaled 6 percent of administrative costs.
b. Former-business cases only. Attorneys for petitioning creditors were compensated only in Western Texas. Claims for rent incurred by the receiver or trustee are considered administrative expenses.
c. Less than 0.05 percent.

small, infrequent payments to various persons, all of whose appointments and payments are documented, helps show how complex the present bankruptcy system is when it is used in personal cases.

PAYING THE CREDITORS AND CLOSING THE CASE

Creditors were rarely and meagerly paid. Recall that few of them troubled to prove their claims. From our tabulation of the file sample of personal bankruptcy cases we find that of those who proved few were paid:

Secured creditors who proved claims were paid in only one out of five cases and received 8 percent of the amounts proved and allowed. In one-third of the cases less than $100 went to such creditors.

Priority creditors who proved claims received 13 percent of the amounts proved and allowed.[35] More than half of the cases distributed less than $100 each.

Unsecured creditors who proved claims were paid in one out of four

35. Because of an error in the technical tabulating process, the proportion of cases in which priority creditors with proved claims received dividends was not determined.

cases and received only 7 percent of the amounts proved and allowed. Again, in more than half of the cases distributions amounted to less than $100.

Bankrupts actually got some money back in a few cases in which no creditors had proved claims, or after those who did prove had been paid in full. This occurred in a little under 2 percent of the sample cases.

Once all payments have been made, the referee approves the final accounts, discharges the trustee, certifies the records and transmits them to the clerk of the court, and the case is closed.

PERIODS OF TIME REQUIRED

How long does a personal bankruptcy case take? The mean time from filing to closing was 9.7 months for nonbusiness cases and 12.5 months for former-business cases. The mean time from filing to discharge was 6.1 months for nonbusiness and 7.7 months for former-business cases. Former-business bankrupts in Northern Alabama,

TABLE 5-6. *Length of Time between Filing and Closing of Personal Bankruptcy Cases, by Type of Case*
In percent

Length of time (in months)	Type of case			All cases
	No asset[a]	Nominal asset[b]	Asset[c]	
Under 12	85	56	42	72
12–18	12	18	19	15
19–24	1	13	20	6
25–30	1	10	12	5
Over 30	1	3	5	2

Source: File sample of personal bankruptcy cases.
a. 64 percent of sample.
b. 20 percent of sample.
c. 16 percent of sample.

Maine, and Western Texas had to wait substantially longer than their nonbusiness counterparts for a discharge. Nonbusiness petitioners in Western Texas were discharged with great dispatch.[36] Table 5-6 presents the time factor in another way, demonstrating the obvious fact that the more complex cases take longer.

36. See Appendix Table c-10 for breakdown by type of case and by district.

Bankruptcy cases take too long. It is difficult to understand why no-asset cases should stay open more than two months, even allowing for a few that may need investigation. The same is true for nominal-asset cases, which were so often limited to the collection of a tax refund or nonexempt wages, or to the private sale of the bankrupt's property. The reforms proposed in Chapter 10 include provisions for speeding up the process.

HOW A CHAPTER XIII CASE PROCEEDS

A debtor who chooses Chapter XIII, which provides for payments under court supervision, does so voluntarily, but he may be pressed into such a choice. The procedure is well institutionalized in Northern Alabama, particularly in Birmingham, where two referees and a trustee ("supervisor") run the system in a building separate from the regular bankruptcy court. Elsewhere, referees hear Chapter XIII cases along with the regular bankruptcy cases, although all Chapter XIII cases may be assigned to one referee in a single locality.

THE FIRST MEETING AND THE REPAYMENT PLAN

The purpose of the first meeting is to examine the debtor and to permit him to propose a plan for repaying his creditors. Such a plan has to be agreed to by creditors[37] and confirmed by the referee before it can go into effect. The debtor can propose either an "extension"—a plan to pay off all his debts over an extended period, say, thirty months—or a "composition"—a plan to pay off only a portion of his debts, or a combination of the two. Compositions were proposed in only 1 percent of the cases in the Chapter XIII sample.

Examination of the debtor is used to determine whether his proposed plan is feasible. Even though the examination is required by law, the referees in Birmingham did not require the debtor to attend the first meeting if the proposed plan seemed in order. If a problem arose, the first meeting was adjourned and the debtor was asked to appear. Without the examination, first meetings there were

37. A plan must be approved by a majority of the unsecured creditors and by each secured creditor whose claim is dealt with by the plan.

conducted very quickly,[38] and the debtors were saved what was considered to be an unnecessary loss of working time. Frequently, the debtor's counsel did not appear either.

Examinations were conducted in the other districts and helped in evaluating the proposed plans. Creditors generally showed little interest, according to referees interviewed about their attendance (multiple answers were possible):

	Percent
Creditors almost never attend	57
Only secured creditors attend	18
Creditors attend only to get secured debts revived	8
Most creditors attend	2
No experience with Chapter XIII	18
Other answers	16

When they did attend, their participation consisted mostly of raising objections to the proposed payment plans. However, most creditors did not oppose the plans. When Chapter XIII debtors were interviewed about this, only 14 percent said that their creditors had failed to cooperate.

Decisions to confirm payment plans were reached fairly soon. The median time between filing and confirmation was less than two months, except in Northern Illinois, where the interval was slightly longer.

Treatment of secured claims. Often the entire success of a Chapter XIII plan depends on how secured claims are treated. The debtor is in trouble either if he has to pay his secured creditors in full outside the plan or if he has to pay them in full inside the plan before any unsecured creditors are paid. In either event he may not have enough to pay the secured creditors, *or* the unsecured creditors may anticipate having to wait so long for their money that they reject the proposed plan. There were great differences among the districts in how this problem was handled (Table 5-7). These differences result from variations in local customs—diverse mixtures of how attorneys want to handle the cases, what the creditors will take, and what the referees will permit.

38. Our staff observed the following rates of speed: twenty-five cases in forty-five minutes; thirty-three cases in forty minutes; forty-three cases in seventy-five minutes. (The referees had previously reviewed the case files.)

Even among referees in the same district there were differences. At the time of our field research in Southern California, Los Angeles plans called for prorated payments to secured and unsecured creditors, but San Diego debtors had to pay secured creditors first.

In Northern Alabama, the district with the largest volume of Chapter XIII cases, secured creditors were usually paid first (given "preference") in the plans. One referee said he could set lower payments on a secured debt in the plan than the creditor was getting

TABLE 5-7. *Treatment of Secured Claims in Chapter XIII Cases, by District*[a]
In percent

District	Excluded from plan	Paid in full before unsecured claims	Prorated with unsecured claims	Security revalued
Northern Ohio	53	4	44	—
Western Texas	50	50	—	—
Oregon	29	64	7	—
Southern California	3	97	—	—
Northern Illinois	2	58	40	—
Maine	1	4	—	95
Northern Alabama	—	81	19	—

Source: File sample of Chapter XIII cases.
a. Based on cases in which the information was available. Because of rounding, percentages may not add to 100.

under his contract because "it is so much easier for the creditor to collect through this court than to have to hire someone to track the debtor down on the outside." Yet Alabama creditors were usually not required to prove that their claims were secured or to document the amount due unless too many creditors asserted liens on a single piece of property. In that event, the referee would order their claims prorated with the unsecured rather than bother to decide the existence or relative priority of the alleged liens.

The referees in Maine had a system that was much fairer to the debtor and to the unsecured creditors. An appraiser valued all collateral but cars[39] and reported his determination to the referee at the first meeting. Secured creditors were required to prove that their liens had been perfected (properly filed in accordance with law) at that time. If they did so, the referee fixed the amount of the

39. Automobiles were valued by referees, using the Blue Book.

secured claim (limited to the value of the collateral). He then offered to pay the secured portion of the claim before paying anything to unsecured creditors, with the balance of the claim treated as unsecured.[40] Secured creditors who failed to prove that their claims were secured, refused to accept the referee's valuation of their security, or refused to accept the plan were treated as if the plan did not apply to them.[41] Debtors had to deal with these creditors outside the plan.

Treatment of priority claims. These were included in 10 percent of the file sample. Usually they were to be paid first, but a few plans provided either for priority claimants to be prorated with other creditors or for payments outside the plan.

Proof of claims. Since creditors are likely to be paid in Chapter XIII cases, they are much more diligent about proving their claims than they are in straight bankruptcies.[42] The number proved actually was more than the number scheduled in some instances.

TABLE 5-8. *Claims Proved in Chapter XIII Cases as a Percentage of Claims Scheduled, by Class of Debt*

Class of debt	All cases	Northern Alabama[a]	Other districts
Secured	104	135	63
Priority	125	141	105
Unsecured	83	93	62

Source: File sample of Chapter XIII cases.
a. The Northern Alabama statistics are significantly inflated by the customary practice of paying claims incurred after filing. Such claims were also added occasionally in the other districts.

Some claims were proved by creditors who had not been scheduled at all or whose classification had been scheduled erroneously (such as unsecured instead of secured; see Table 5-8).

Objections to claims. Faced with paying these claims, debtors had

40. Both referees allowed 6 percent postpetition interest on the secured portion of the claim. One added the interest to the secured debt; the other paid it along with unsecured claims.

41. This interpretation was essential because a secured creditor whose claim *is* dealt with can effectively block confirmation of a proposed plan by failing to consent to its provisions. This practice has been approved, as long as the plan does not limit the amount of the creditor's claim or restrict the creditor's security interest. *Cheetham* v. *Universal C.I.T. Credit Corp., et al.,* 390 F.2d 234 (1st Cir. 1968).

42. Nonetheless, some referees approved payments on the basis of amounts listed in the petitioner's schedules unless a dispute arose.

a much greater incentive to question the amounts (or classification) than they did in straight bankruptcy. Even so, they objected in only 9 percent of the cases in this sample. Creditors, who also had more to gain from policing these proceedings, raised objections in 4 percent of the Chapter XIII cases. Trustees raised objections in only 1 percent of the cases. Of the claims attacked, 38 percent were allowed as filed. Twenty-nine percent were disallowed completely; 30 percent were reduced; only 3 percent had their classification changed.

EXEMPTIONS IN CHAPTER XIII CASES

Because debts are paid out of income and not out of sale of property, there is no point in finding out how much of the debtor's property is exempt. Though required to do so by the statute, debtors did not even bother to claim exemptions in 63 percent of our cases, and no action was taken on allowances in most of the cases in which requests *were* filed. When referees confirm plans they base their decisions on the needs of the debtor's family, not on the wage-exemption laws of the state. Under these circumstances, the process of claiming and allowing exemptions was simply waste motion.

RESTRAINTS AGAINST CREDITOR INTERFERENCE

A total of 31 percent of the debtors studied, including almost all of them in Northern Illinois and Southern California, sought protection against creditors' collection efforts before confirmation of their proposed plans. As in straight bankruptcy, requests in Northern Illinois were frequently filed routinely with the petition against all creditors, unlike the Southern California requests, most of which focused on specific creditors. Grounds supporting the requests for restraints included: attempted wage garnishment (all of the Northern Ohio and most of the Northern Alabama requests), 42 percent; creditors attempting to collect despite proceedings (most of the Northern Illinois requests), 36 percent; "irreparable harm" (all in Southern California), 13 percent; miscellaneous, 9 percent. Only one request for a restraining order was denied in the cases covered by this study.

COLLECTING FROM THE DEBTOR (OR HIS EMPLOYER)

The referee gets information about the debtor's income[43] from statements filed with the petition and decides, before confirming the plan, how much of this will be taken for the creditors. Since some (12 percent) of the petitioners reported net income, while most (88 percent) reported gross income, it is impossible to give precise data on the variations among districts. However, the proportions varied greatly from one district to another, from a high of 40 percent on a monthly salary of $250 in Western Texas down to 8 percent on a monthly salary of $399 in Northern Ohio.

Money is collected from the debtor and paid to creditors by a trustee appointed by the referee. Usually one trustee handles all of the Chapter XIII cases for a particular referee, in accordance with a general policy of the judicial branch. The trustee is obviously more likely to receive the payments required by the plan if he gets them from the debtor's employer than from the debtor himself. Most employers cooperated (four out of five in the cases in our sample), but collections were made from the debtor if the employer would not agree or was likely to discharge the employee. (Trustees were familiar with the attitudes of various employers.) Employers made the payments in 79 percent of the cases, with percentages varying in the districts from 85 percent in Northern Alabama down to 25 percent in Northern Ohio. Some employers made the required deduction from the debtor's wages and forwarded it directly to the trustee. Others sent the debtor's entire paycheck to the trustee, who deducted the required payment and turned over the balance to the debtor.

The trustee then continues to collect the debtor's money and pay it to the creditors at appropriate intervals in accordance with the plan. This is a relatively routine process which lends itself well to automatic data processing. At the time our data were gathered, such a system was working in Birmingham, and a more simplified version was being used in Tuscaloosa. Other trustees were investigating leased-time arrangements. Some Chapter XIII trustees scattered around the country use data processing facilities in Kansas

43. Income was virtually the only asset administered in Chapter XIII cases. In less than 1 percent of the sample other assets were involved: child support payments (when debtors voluntarily committed them to the plan), or cash collections resulting from a tax refund or previously garnisheed wages.

City, Kansas. The San Diego trustee was the only one from our sample in this group at the time interviews were conducted. More recently, the referees in Bangor, Maine, Chicago, Illinois, and Santa Ana and San Bernardino, California, decided to use the Kansas City facilities. Further comment on the potential for data processing is presented in Chapters 8 and 10.

Modifications of required payments. As the debtor pays his debts under the plan, changes become necessary. Some debtors asked for reductions because of reduced income (loss of overtime, layoffs) or increased expenses (medical bills). Unless such changes had been approved, the plans would have failed.

Other debtors had to increase their payments because of purchases after the plan was confirmed. In Maine the debtors had to get court approval if they wished to add payments for a necessary purchase (such as a car). In Northern Alabama it was common practice for the debtors to be allowed to run up more bills without advance approval from the court. Some creditors allegedly encouraged this practice. One interviewee said, "Certain creditors will sell to these people *only if they are in debtors' court*, and I guess they will be quite open about it."

No creditor *was* that candid, although the Birmingham "red flag" practice supports the assertion. When the referee decided that increased payments required by additional debts had reached the maximum that the debtor could support, he issued a "red flag" order to the effect that no further claims would be honored. Notice of this order became part of the debtor's file at the local credit bureau and was distributed to creditors.

Because of this practice of adding claims, a majority of the modifications in Northern Alabama provided for increased payments. In the other districts, nearly all of the modifications were for decreased or suspended payments. The referee must decide whether to notify creditors so that they have a chance to object.[44]

Dismissals. If the debtor fails to keep up his payments under the plan, the Chapter XIII trustee can seek to have the proceeding dismissed. Such a motion was filed at least once in a majority of the cases involving confirmed plans:

44. The referees in Maine reduced this burden by providing in the confirmation order that temporary modifications lasting not more than ten weeks might be granted without further notice to creditors.

District	Percent
Northern Ohio	82
Maine	72
Northern Illinois	66
Southern California	63
Oregon	59
Western Texas	50
Northern Alabama	49
All seven	53

The hearing on this motion can result in a modification, but most (73 percent) of these cases (including 99 percent in Southern California) were dismissed outright. Seventeen percent were resumed, but ultimately failed; 10 percent were successfully completed.

Year after year, half or more of all the Chapter XIII cases concluded are dismissed, leaving debtors unrehabilitated and creditors dissatisfied. The figures for two years for the whole country as well as for our sample districts are given in Table 5-9.

TABLE 5-9. *Cases Dismissed as a Percentage of Cases Concluded under Chapter XIII, by District, Fiscal Years 1964 and 1968*

District	1964	1968
Northern Ohio	86	62
Northern Illinois	78	70
Maine	69	60
Western Texas	67	37
Southern California	63	63ᵃ
Oregon	60	55
Northern Alabama	45	46
All districts in U.S.	56	57

Source: Computed from Administrative Office of the U.S. Courts, "Tables of Bankruptcy Statistics" (1964 and 1968; processed), Table F 4b. Adjudicated cases are excluded from Chapter XIII statistics and are treated as straight bankruptcies.

a. The 1968 figure for Southern California is based on filings in the districts of Southern and Central California plus one-half of the filings in Eastern California, and thus is not strictly comparable with the Southern California district as it existed when our field research was done or with figures in the 1964 column. See Chapter 1, note 1.

THE ESTATES

There *were* estates (that is, assets to pay expenses or creditors) in 90 percent of the cases. The remaining 10 percent had been dismissed for various reasons before the debtor had paid in anything.

All of the debtors' payments were used for administrative expenses in 7 percent of the cases, and creditors received something in 84 percent.

How large were the estates? About $600 in the average (median) case—about twice as much as in the straight bankruptcy asset cases. The median successful ("arranged") case,[45] however, amounted to about $1,000; the median dismissed case, to $253. There were great variations among the districts, the details of which are shown in Appendix Table c-11. If the Northern Alabama cases (which are lower-debt cases) are excluded from the total, the median arranged case jumps to over $2,100.

Administrative expenses. Out of every dollar in these estates, 17 cents went for administrative expenses—22 cents if Northern Alabama is not included in the arithmetic. Trustees were paid in all but the cases dismissed before the debtors had paid in anything under the plans. Debtors' attorneys were paid from estates nearly as often—in 84 percent of the total cases in the sample. Even shorthand reporters received something in 11 percent of the cases.

What creditors received. Almost all distributions to creditors in the successfully completed cases came to *more than 90 percent of the amounts of the claims proved.* Even in the dismissed cases secured creditors got 39 percent, priority creditors 27 percent, and unsecured creditors 19 percent of proved claims. (Recall that comparable figures for the straight bankruptcy cases were 8, 13, and 7 percent.)

DISCHARGE

The debtor may be discharged after the repayment plan is successfully completed. He may also receive a discharge after three years without completing his plan if the referee decides that his failure to complete it was due to circumstances beyond his control. None of the Chapter XIII files showed any objections to discharge by creditors, although referees in Maine, Northern Illinois, and Southern California reported that they occasionally heard objections in court. The practice in granting discharges varied among the referees. Some did not bother with a discharge if the creditors had

45. "Arranged" is a statistical category used by the Administrative Office of the United States Courts. It covers cases in which an arrangement was confirmed and which were not dismissed, consolidated with other cases, or adjudicated bankrupt.

been paid in full. Others used case closing forms, which granted a discharge simultaneously with closing. The referees in Maine were the only ones who systematically granted discharges to debtors who had failed to complete their payments in three years because of circumstances beyond their control.

LENGTH OF TIME

The typical Chapter XIII case we studied took a year if it was dismissed, two years if it was successful (Table 5-10). The longer

TABLE 5-10. *Median Time Elapsed in Chapter XIII Cases, by District and Outcome of Case*[a]
In months

| | Outcome of case | | |
District	Dismissed[b]	Arranged[c]	All cases[d]
Western Texas[e]	18	29	24
Maine	19	34	21
Northern Alabama	10	22	19
Southern California	11	25	19
Northern Illinois	10	32	16
Oregon	11	23	16
Northern Ohio	12	24	10
Seven districts	11	23	19

Source: File sample of Chapter XIII cases.
a. Medians are based on grouped data.
b. Time between confirmation and dismissal.
c. Time between confirmation and closing. The figures include cases in which discharges were granted after three years despite failure to complete plan.
d. Time between filing and closing.
e. Actual time in first two columns because there was only one case in each category.

times in Maine may have resulted from the referees' practice of authorizing temporary suspensions of payments. The differences among the districts in the last column (time between filing and closing for all cases) are influenced by the different frequencies of dismissed cases.[46]

46. Dismissals occurred in 88 percent of the sample cases in Northern Ohio, 78 percent in Northern Illinois, 70 percent in Maine, 67 percent in Western Texas, 64 percent in Southern California, 60 percent in Oregon, and 45 percent in Northern Alabama. The base of these percentages is number arranged plus number dismissed. Adjudicated cases are not included.

THE "REPEATERS"

At least 23 percent of the Chapter XIII debtors had had previous experience with either straight bankruptcy or Chapter XIII itself. Almost all of the latter group were from Northern Alabama, which supported the allegation made by some of our interviewees that "Chapter XIII is a way of life" for some debtors in that district.

An analysis of a special 0.5 percent sample of the Chapter XIII records in Birmingham in the spring of 1966 showed that about two-thirds of the debtors were repeaters:[47]

Times filed	Percentage of debtors
1	33
2	17
3	20
4	13
5	6
6	4
7	3
8	2
9 or more	2

Half of the debtors had filed three or more times. It is clear that earlier experience with Chapter XIII had not taught them to handle their finances. However, the percentage of debtors successfully completing plans was much greater for repeaters than it was for those who had filed only once:

Times filed	Percentage of debtors
1	38
2	65
3	70
4	81
5	78
6	81
7	91
8	94

47. The special sample was drawn for this limited purpose and is unrelated to the Northern Alabama file sample upon which other figures in this chapter are based.

The percentage total for the repeaters is almost identical with that reported by Harry H. Haden from a sample of petitions filed in Birmingham in 1965 (see "Chapter XIII Wage Earner Plans—Forgotten Man Bankruptcy," p. 600).

Debtors who had filed nine and fourteen times had successfully completed their payments eight and thirteen times, respectively. Some debtors (and their creditors) had apparently become accustomed to using the Chapter XIII court as a collection agency or bill-paying service.

CONCLUSION

By any rational standard, the present system for handling personal straight bankruptcies is seriously deficient. Each time a petition is filed, complex quasi-judicial machinery is cranked up as if adversary issues and substantial assets were involved. Both factors are usually missing. Instead, the referees handle a mass of cases involving uncontested matters and sums of money that are inconsequential from the creditors' point of view.

The petitioner files, undergoes a first-meeting examination of varying quality and tone, and is unlikely to have further contact with the bankruptcy court except for receiving notice of his discharge. While this process may temporarily relieve pressure from creditors, it does not contribute to the bankrupt's financial rehabilitation in any real sense, and it wastes a lot of time.

The present system makes absolutely no provision either for uniform scrutiny of the bankrupt's activities before filing the petition or for advice concerning future money management. If trustees are not used, it is likely that some assets will be withheld from the estate by the bankrupt. If they are used, there is a considerable amount of waste motion in their activities.

Most debtors who file a petition in bankruptcy court go through straight bankruptcy. They use Chapter XIII only if this is favored by local usage or if it is the preference of their lawyers. In either event they go through a slow, unhelpful process. Their creditors are neither interested in nor aided by a straight bankruptcy proceeding and have only a small chance of being paid anything at all.

Compared to straight bankruptcy, the Chapter XIII process is simple and effective—at least in getting creditors paid in the successful cases. The method is *not* effective in rehabilitating debtors, as indicated by the high proportion of both dismissals and "repeater" cases. The chances of getting something for creditors and of helping the debtors would be increased if more use were made of compositions (paying less than the total amount owed). The process would also be more humane and realistic if creditors' claims were closely reviewed and the security valued.

6

The Business Bankrupts

A business bankrupt may be a one-man quick-lunch operation, a hundred-million-dollar manufacturing corporation, or any kind or size of business in between. When a business fails it does not necessarily show up in the federal bankruptcy courts. It may simply shut down with or without the informal agreement of its creditors, or it may be liquidated under state laws.[1]

Earlier in this book we pointed out that business bankruptcies are numerically and economically unimpressive.[2] They represent only about 8 percent of the total number of bankruptcies filed, and the number has not increased in recent years.[3] Nevertheless, business cases take up a disproportionate amount of the bankruptcy courts' time because there are usually more assets and therefore more work to do in acquiring and disposing of property and in settling disagreements.

Businesses, like individuals, may use various types of bankruptcy proceedings, but anything except straight bankruptcy is unusual. Of the business cases filed in 1969:

93.4 percent were straight bankruptcies;

0.6 percent were Chapter X cases (reorganizations of corporations);

---

1. See Chapter 7, pp. 118–20.

2. See Chapter 3, p. 39, for observations on how business bankruptcies affect the economy.

3. 16,302 business bankruptcies were filed in 1963, 16,510 in 1964, 16,910 in 1965, 16,430 in 1966, 16,600 in 1967, 16,545 in 1968, 15,430 in 1969, and 16,197 in 1970. Administrative Office of the U.S. Courts, "Tables of Bankruptcy Statistics," relevant years.

5.6 percent were Chapter XI cases (arrangements to extend or reduce unsecured debts);

0.4 percent were Chapter XII cases (extensions or reductions by unincorporated debtors of debts secured by real estate).[4]

A debtor can start a proceeding under one of the chapters but be adjudicated a bankrupt if it does not work out. The reverse is unlikely, however. When a business is ready for bankruptcy, it usually cannot be saved. If it could be, the creditors would probably have rescued it.

The Brookings file sample of 398 business cases (all closed in fiscal year 1964) was broken down differently, in order to have more chapter proceedings to analyze. Three-quarters were straight bankruptcies, most of the rest Chapter XIs, plus a handful of Xs and XIIs. A little over one-eighth of the straight bankruptcies had begun as chapter proceedings, most of them as Chapter XIs.

KINDS OF BUSINESSES

The businesses in the sample were a mixture of corporations, proprietorships, and partnerships. Straight bankruptcy is attractive to the unincorporated businessman because it is the only federal procedure that discharges him from personal liability for the obligations of the business. Corporations can simply close their doors, unless they wish to continue doing business in the same corporate form.[5] Thus it is not surprising that the typical business bankrupt in our file sample was unincorporated, while corporations were predominant among the Chapter XI cases:[6]

	Straight bankruptcy	Chapter XI
Corporations	38%	79%
Sole proprietorships	48	15
Partnerships	14	6

4. Computed from Administrative Office of the U.S. Courts, "Annual Report of the Director" (1969; processed), pp. V-5, V-6.

5. Piercing corporate veils is not a commonplace activity in U.S. courts. By contrast, the French bankruptcy law passed in 1967 allows the court to decide whether the responsibility for a company's financial failure should be placed directly on its managers; if it so decides, the managers may become personally liable for business obligations.

6. Chapter X is limited to corporations; Chapter XII to unincorporated debtors.

The fields of business of the straight bankrupts and Chapter XI debtors also differed, as shown in Table 6-1. More than half the bankrupts were retail merchants, with restaurants and grocery stores most numerous. Manufacturing was the most common industry among the Chapter XI cases. Clothing makers led this list, followed by textile mills, printers and publishers, and manufacturers of furniture and electrical machinery.

TABLE 6-1. *Business Debtors Classified by Type of Industry*[a]

	Percentage of sample	
Type of industry	Straight bankruptcy	Chapter XI
Retail trade	53	19
Services	13	20
Manufacturing	10	40
Construction	10	2
Agriculture	6	5
Wholesale trade	4	10
Real estate	2	2
Transportation	1	1
Finance	0	1
Unclassifiable	1	0
Total	100	100

Source: File sample of business bankrupts and Chapter XI cases.
a. Using U.S. Department of Labor Standard Industrial Classification.

Only one Chapter X case in our sample succeeded to the point of a confirmed payment plan. The debtor was the General Stores Corporation, which started in the retail tobacco business, branched out by acquiring two drug chains, and later dropped the tobacco line. The case started as a Chapter XI but was converted to Chapter X. The other Chapter Xs, all unsuccessful, included an apartment house construction business, an operator of two diners and one tourist home, a printing firm, a steel fabricator, a bowling alley, and a motel.

Chapter XII (real estate) cases are rare, and only seven of them were successfully completed in fiscal 1964 in the entire country. Five of these were in our sample, and each debtor was in some kind of business—such as a doctor who owned a ranch, or a building contractor.

CAUSES OF BUSINESS BANKRUPTCY

Success or failure in business is compounded of so many dynamic personal and economic factors that it is impossible to say simply why businesses fail. One landmark study of 570 commercial bankrupts in metropolitan Boston in 1932 showed that most of these bankruptcies were caused by inefficient management. Both unwise credit extensions and adverse personal factors were considered important. Other explanations, such as the then-current business depression, insufficiency of capital, and pressures of competition, were viewed primarily as rationalizations. Most of the failures were found to be "a consequence of an unjustifiable entrance into business" aided, in many cases, by "indiscriminate and careless granting of credit to the bankrupts by incurious creditors."[7]

Similarly, Dun and Bradstreet's current annual studies, on the basis of "opinions of informed creditors and information in Dun & Bradstreet credit reports," identify "lack of experience" and "incompetence" as the causes of failure in over 90 percent of the cases.

Our own assessment, presented in Table 6-2 and based on study of case files and on interviews with fifty business bankrupts, is fairly consistent with these other findings. (Note that there is little effort to present causes in the files.) As with personal bankruptcies (Chapter 4), it seemed helpful to present underlying causes separately from immediate causes. We did not find lack of business experience to be a major factor. Only 12 percent of those who were interviewed lacked earlier business experience, and 38 percent had been in business more than ten years at the time of bankruptcy.

The "internal management problems" category covers a multitude of contributing causes. Not necessarily typical but interesting was the corporation president who used company money to buy a luxury car for himself, another car for his daughter, and used a company credit card for personal entertainment—all this according to an embittered associate we interviewed.

The bankrupts could not be expected, of course, to attribute bankruptcy to their own dishonesty, nor did the files in our sample contain indications that dishonesty had contributed to the bank-

TABLE 6-2. *Underlying and Immediate Causes of Business Bankruptcy, from Bankrupts Interviewed and Bankrupts Whose Files Were Abstracted*
In percent

Cause	Interviewees[a]	File cases
Underlying		
Business below expectations	64	5
Internal management problems	46	4
Insufficient capital	26	3
Overexpansion	18	—
Factoring accounts receivable	8	—
General business failure	—	26
Other	4	2
Immediate		
Threatened suit	32	2
Actual suit	30	11
Involuntary bankruptcy petition	22	—
Execution levy	16	—
Tax levy	10	—
Set-off by bank[b]	2	—
No answer	22	52[c]

Source: File sample of business bankruptcies in eight federal court districts and interviews with fifty debtors in six districts by the staff for this study. Percentages add to more than 100 because of multiple responses.

a. Northern Alabama and Southern New York not included.

b. A bank has the right to set off moneys in its possession against another of its claims which is overdue. For example, Company A may have its operating account in a bank that has also lent Company A money for equipment purchases. If Company A fails to pay one of its loan installments, the bank can take ("set off") money from the operating account to cover the missed payment. Usually, the bank will not set off unless it feels that Company A's financial position is very precarious. Thus a set-off may become the precipitating cause of bankruptcy.

c. No information was available in many of the case files, and there was little evidence that creditors sought to examine the bankrupts later about the causes of their financial difficulty.

ruptcies. Nevertheless, there are doubtless some such cases. The Fraud Section of the Department of Justice Criminal Division investigates between two and three hundred bankruptcy cases each year and obtains criminal convictions in fewer than one-sixth of them.[8] Some of these cases involve dishonesty in the bankruptcy proceeding or other wrongdoing that cannot be demonstrated to have caused the bankruptcy. Others result from a particular type of fraudulent activity—the "scam" operation, in which criminal elements set up a business (or preferably take over one with an established credit rating), purchase large quantities of inventory on

8. See Chapter 8, p. 154.

credit, sell it, and disappear with the proceeds.[9] Justice Department officials refer to such operations as "fraudulent" or "planned" bankruptcies, but such terms are misnomers in implying that resort to bankruptcy is part of the fraudulent scheme. Bankruptcy usually occurs after creditors have filed an involuntary petition, not because the culprits want to invoke the jurisdiction of the bankruptcy courts and the Department of Justice.

We conclude that a very small proportion of business bankruptcies—probably from 5 to 10 percent—are attributable to dishonesty, uninsured catastrophe, or personal problems. Many of the rest are doubtless due to incompetence or inefficiency. But inefficiency does not necessarily mean culpability. The small corner grocer cannot compete "efficiently" when a chain store opens across the street. Finally, where culpability exists, it may not always be on the debtor's side. As one attorney put it, "Commercial credit is a very cheap commodity." Here, as with consumer credit, the creditors' emphasis frequently is on volume rather than on careful credit checks and the policing of accounts. And their experience is such that this emphasis is likely to continue. Most of the creditors who were interviewed said that fewer than 1 percent of their accounts receivable were involved in insolvency proceedings; even in these instances, many were frequently able to recoup something on the accounts through informal settlements.

HOW MUCH THE DEBTORS OWED AND OWNED

The financial picture of the debtors in our file sample can be simply sketched from their records:[10]

The median business bankrupt scheduled about $12,000 in assets

9. Sheldon Davidson, "Schemes and Methods used in Perpetrating Bankruptcy Frauds," *Commercial Law Journal*, Vol. 71 (December 1966), pp. 383–87; Nathaniel E. Kossack and Sheldon Davidson, "Bankruptcy Fraud, Alliance for Enforcement," *Journal of the National Conference of Referees in Bankruptcy*, Vol. 40 (January 1966), pp. 12–19, 30–31.

10. Debt schedules filed with business bankruptcy petitions are even less accurate than those in personal bankruptcies. In some instances, the debtor may intentionally fail to schedule the claim of a favored creditor in the hope that he will be able to pay the creditor more outside the bankruptcy proceeding. Moreover, even honest debtors are frequently mistaken about the amount, or even the existence, of claims. Failure to schedule creditors will be of little concern to principals of a corporate bankrupt, except

and owed about $40,000—eight times the debt of the nonbusiness bankrupt, but not a large amount as commercial debts go. He listed 44 creditors when he filed his petition, primarily merchandise suppliers, lending institutions, and landlords.

The median Chapter XI debtor scheduled $167,500 in assets and owed some $245,000 to 105 creditors; the most numerous creditors again were merchandise suppliers and lending institutions, but not landlords.

The bankrupts presumably let landlords go unpaid because they did not plan to continue in business. The Chapter XI debtors apparently planned to continue—or at least to give that impression.

The difference in size of the two types of proceedings can be emphasized in another way. Half of the bankruptcy cases had liabilities between $10,000 and $50,000; another quarter between $50,000 and $100,000. Half of the Chapter XI debtors owed between $100,000 and $500,000. (More detailed figures on debts and assets appear in Appendix Tables c-12 to c-15.) About one-third of the debt in both kinds of business cases was secured, somewhat more of it by personal property than by real property; from 5 to 7 percent was scheduled as priority, mainly to tax collectors; and the rest (about 60 percent) was unsecured.

Nine out of ten creditors in our sample were unsecured. The median numbers, by class of debt, for business bankruptcy and Chapter XI cases were:

	Bankruptcy	Chapter XI
Priority	2	4
Secured	3	5
Unsecured	39	96

Relying on the recorded information about business debtors' assets is risky for the reason already mentioned for personal cases: one cannot tell whether secured liabilities are deducted from the asset amounts reported. The asset figures above ($12,000 for bankrupts and $167,500 for Chapter XI debtors) assume that secured liabilities were not deducted. (See Appendix Table c-15 for more detail.)

in the rare instances in which they plan to continue doing business in the same corporate form. Nonetheless, the schedules provide the best available information on the petitioners' financial situation.

In only a few scattered cases did the files show that the debtor had been in bankruptcy before—less than 1 percent of the bankrupts and only one Chapter XI debtor. There probably were others not reported. In any event, the files would not show cases where the managers of a business were in bankruptcy earlier under a different corporate name.

There were also earlier state cases, notably in Southern New York, where 13 percent of our business bankrupts had been through a formal state insolvency proceeding within a year preceding bankruptcy. This reflects the rather common practice in that district of using the statutory assignment for the benefit of creditors as an alternative to bankruptcy liquidation in business cases (frequently with the New York Credit Men's Adjustment Bureau as assignee).[11] Bankruptcy nonetheless usually follows shortly thereafter, either because a dissatisfied creditor treats the assignment as an act of bankruptcy and files a petition for involuntary bankruptcy or because it becomes desirable to use a bankruptcy trustee's power to set aside transactions. The records also showed earlier formal state proceedings involving a few of the business bankrupts in California and Ohio.

The successful Chapter X debtor, General Stores Corporation, listed nearly $4 million in debts with its petition and nearly $5 million in assets. The seven unsuccessful Chapter Xs are so miscellaneous as to defy text summarization. Details appear in Appendix Table c-16.

The Chapter XII debtors showed very high percentages of secured debt, amounting to as much as 98 percent of the total debt load. Priority claims typically involved taxes. Such a debt profile is consistent with the usual Chapter XII purpose of restraining mortgage foreclosures.

AFTER THE BANKRUPTCY PROCEEDING

Again we skip over the details of the bankruptcy process, which are covered in Chapter 7, and come to the results of the cases studied. With the aid of Dun and Bradstreet, we tried to find out

11. See Chapter 7, p. 119.

the later financial history of both the bankrupts and the Chapter XI debtors. The Dun and Bradstreet reporting staff tested the feasibility of tracing the principals of the liquidated businesses in straight bankruptcy. It was concluded that the results of a search for the bankrupts would not justify the costs required to get the information. Often only a corporate shell remained with no leads on the whereabouts of the persons involved.

The check on the Chapter XI debtors was more revealing—the results appear in Table 6-3. The most striking finding was that *only one-third of the debtors were still operating their own businesses two years after their Chapter XI proceedings were closed.* Another 6 percent of the businesses were continued either under new management or by merger into a parent company. Thirty-eight percent had either discontinued the business in the succeeding two years or used more formal liquidation procedures. This group included half of the cases in Southern New York. An additional 14 percent had had to sell all of the business's assets in order to finance the plan.

The fact that so few businesses remained in operation does not mean that a Chapter XI plan should not have been attempted. As one New York lawyer said, "The only way to find out whether Chapter XI will work is to try it." It does mean that the referees concern themselves very little with the future prospects of the businesses when they approve payment plans. The statutory requirement that a plan be "feasible" has been interpreted in practice to mean that the creditors seem likely to receive what is being promised them, rather than that the debtor seems likely to survive. Such an interpretation may produce more money for creditors than they would receive in straight bankruptcy, but it does not assure rehabilitation of the debtor.

CHAPTERS X AND XII

File information on the aftermath of Chapter XIIs in which plans had been confirmed was sketchy. In two consolidated cases, the business (a motel) was sold in order to finance the plan. In others, a building contractor was unable to meet the payments on his refinanced mortgage, and a doctor's case was closed with no indication of whether he had been able to pay his refinanced debts. Although it is difficult to generalize from so few cases, the proceedings

TABLE 6-3. *Results of Confirmed Chapter XI Plans Two Years after Proceeding Closed, by District*
In percent

Result	Six districts^a	Northern Alabama	Northern Ohio	Maine	Northern Illinois	Southern New York	Southern California
Still in business	33	—	33	—	32	39	18
Business discontinued	30	—	—	—	—	50	—
Assets sold to finance plan	14	—	17	—	28	6	29
Liquidated after plan confirmed	8	—	17	50	20	6	—
Default under plan	5	100	—	—	8	—	11
Business under new control	5	—	—	50	—	—	25
Merged into parent company	1	—	—	—	4	—	—
No data	6	—	33	—	8	—	18

Source: Dun and Bradstreet records, 1967. Percentages may not add to 100 because of rounding.
a. There were no Chapter XI cases in Oregon or Western Texas.

seemed to be more effective in forestalling the immediate problem (mortgage foreclosure) than in producing long-term rehabilitation.

General Stores, reorganized under Chapter X in 1959, with the case formally closed in 1964, did succeed. Except for 1962–64, the company showed a profit in every year after the 1959 reorganization, and its stock never fell below the $1 at which it was issued under the reorganization plan. The company has now been merged into a larger, more diversified corporation.[12]

ATTITUDES OF THE DEBTORS

Business debtors, like our personal bankruptcy debtors, expressed a variety of reactions to their experience: relief, indifference, anger, shame. About two out of five of the fifty debtors interviewed said they felt some degree of shame. One told of building a house in a good neighborhood, and of neighbors remarking, "There's the bankruptcy money." Another lost his "so-called friends," not his "real friends." A third was genuinely distressed and spoke of his bankruptcy as "a terrible thing." Those with opposite reactions included one bankrupt who was quite happy because he was able "to beat all of his debts," and another who said his credit was now "better than ever."

The business bankrupts tended to be small businesses that were inefficient under prevailing market conditions and probably poorly managed. Chapter XI was used by larger businesses either to reduce the amount of their debts or to allow a longer time to pay them off, and resulted in only one-third of the debtors being in business two years after their cases were closed. Chapters X and XII are rarely used, and their results depend entirely on the special circumstances of each case.

12. *Moody's Industrial Manual*, p. 1932 (1960), p. 1443 (1961), p. 1368 (1962), p. 2648 (1963), p. 1659 (1964), p. 347 (1965), p. 383 (1966), p. 262 (1967), p. 114 (1968), pp. 811–12 (July 1969).

7

The Business Bankruptcy Process

Business bankruptcies have much in common with personal bankruptcies but are more time-consuming, complex, and expensive because the game is played for higher stakes. Another important difference is that the discharge, so crucial to an individual debtor, is of no interest to a corporation unless it wants to stay in business. Still, the same basic procedures are followed as in personal bankruptcies.

CHOICE OF STATE OR FEDERAL REMEDIES

Like the personal debtor, the business debtor may find under state law some kind of relief short of formal bankruptcy proceedings. First, he may work out an informal composition or extension, as explained in Chapter 5.

A second possibility is to propose an assignment for the benefit of creditors.[1] By this remedy, long recognized under common law, all of the debtor's nonexempt assets are transferred to an assignee, liquidated, and the proceeds distributed among his creditors. This may hinder particular creditors in the collection of their claims, but it tends to benefit creditors in general. The common law gave the debtor an unqualified right to make such an assignment as long as

1. Such assignments may also be made in personal insolvencies, but they are far more frequent in business cases.

he transferred all of his nonexempt property to the assignee and did not seek to have the assignee delay liquidation longer than was necessary for an orderly conversion of his assets to cash, but the common law of most states did not permit the debtor to obtain a discharge of unpaid balances of his debts. Once the transfer was made to the assignee as trustee for all creditors, individual creditors were not permitted to interfere with the assignee's administration of the estate. In some states the common-law assignment is now regulated by statutes, some of which are almost as detailed as the Bankruptcy Act—but the state statutes cannot give the debtor a release of unpaid balances of his debts.

The main advantage of both common-law and statutory assignments is protection of the debtor's assets against action by individual creditors that might dissipate them or distribute them unfairly. The principal shortcoming of both is that usually the debtor does not receive a discharge from the unpaid balance of his debts—unless his creditors agree.

In three of the eight states studied—Illinois, Maine, and Oregon —the common-law assignment is substantially unchanged. In Alabama only minimal restraints involving routine formal matters have been added. California has enacted a comprehensive statute governing assignments, but little use is made of it because the common-law assignment can be and generally is used instead. In Ohio the statutory assignment has displaced its common-law ancestor. Texas also uses assignments under common law. And finally, in the remaining state, New York, the assignment has assumed its most sophisticated form: regulated extensively and intensively by statute and under close judicial surveillance, the assignment has become in practice—if not strictly in law—a state bankruptcy proceeding except that no discharges are granted.[2]

For a corporation in trouble, there is a third choice: state court receiverships may be used either to liquidate the debtor's assets or to work out an arrangement for paying the creditors. All eight of the states we studied have laws authorizing the judicial appointment and supervision of a receiver for an expiring corporation. Neverthe-

2. For a comparison of New York's general assignment law and the federal Bankruptcy Act, see Sydney Krause, "Insolvent Debtor Adjustments under Relevant State Court Statutes as against Proceedings under the Bankruptcy Act," *The Business Lawyer*, Vol. 12 (January 1957), pp. 186–89.

less, the receivership does not appear to be well regarded as a liquidation method. It was mentioned infrequently by creditors' attorneys who were asked in interviews to list the devices their clients used in collecting claims against business debtors. Only in Maine was the receivership viewed with anything like general favor: seven of the ten creditors' attorneys interviewed there said their clients used the state court receivership. Four of the nine who answered a later question said it was the best remedy against delinquent business debtors.

Which of these state remedies is used—if any are chosen in preference to bankruptcy proceedings—depends on many factors. The debtor and his attorney will normally prefer an informal arrangement, but his creditors may conclude that the time has come for an assignment or liquidation. The choices of creditors and their attorneys depend on the condition of the debtor's business, the history of their relations with it, their judgments about the speed, cost, and productivity of the various remedies, the attitudes of state court judges and referees in bankruptcy, and the usual working habits of the commercial bar in that area. In general, the creditors' attorneys we interviewed, when asked "What is best for creditors of business debtors?" were most favorable to composition agreements, Chapter XI proceedings, and assignments for the benefit of creditors, in that order.

If the debtor decides to go into federal rather than state courts there is another choice to be made: between straight bankruptcy—taken by nine out of ten business debtors—and the rehabilitative proceedings provided by various chapters of the Bankruptcy Act. Chapter X may be used to reorganize corporations. Chapter XI offers a chance of continuing a business with agreement by unsecured creditors that the debtor may pay less or take longer. Chapter XII is available (and almost never used) to ease real estate debt problems. There is room for differences in judgment on the choice—usually between straight bankruptcy and Chapter XI, sometimes between Chapters X and XI. In Southern New York, for example, about 20 percent of the voluntary business cases are Chapter XIs.[3] Attorneys there reported that they advised resort to Chapter XI unless the debtor's situation was obviously hopeless.

3. Computed from the Administrative Office of the U.S. Courts, "Tables of Bankruptcy Statistics" (1968; processed), Tables F 2 and F 3.

HOW A STRAIGHT BANKRUPTCY CASE PROCEEDS

The straight bankruptcy procedure is exactly the same for business as it is for personal bankrupts, starting with the petition, normally filed by the debtor. Involuntary bankruptcies were filed by creditors in 9 percent of our sample of business straight bankruptcy cases; 13 percent started as Chapter XIs, which were then adjudicated; and the remaining 78 percent were voluntary straight bankruptcies.

EARLY PROTECTION OF THE ESTATE

The referees naturally had to do more to protect the estate in business bankruptcies than in personal bankruptcy cases. They appointed receivers in about half (52 percent) of our business cases to look after the assets or to operate the businesses. Referees normally took the initiative in choosing custodial receivers. Half of them served for less than a month; very few served as long as six months. Operating receivers, appointed in only 15 percent of the business cases, were also used for brief periods. Unlike custodial receivers, operating receivers were more likely to be appointed at the request of creditors, who presumably wanted to keep the business running but out of the hands of the previous management.

Restraining orders, almost never needed in personal bankruptcies, were requested in 24 percent of the business cases to prevent creditors from trying to collect before the proceeding was finished. Nine out of ten requests were granted.

THE FIRST MEETING

Deficiencies in the records again kept us from finding out exactly how many creditors showed up at this meeting and how active they were in examining the debtor. However, in the 22 percent of the business cases where the information did appear, the median number of creditors in attendance was four and the median amount of claims represented was $4,050. This is faint interest indeed, considering that the typical business bankrupt had a dozen creditors and $40,000 in debts.

Unless a verbatim record was taken of the first meeting, which
very rarely occurred, there was no information as to how thoroughly
the debtor was examined, or by whom. Additional examinations
later on[4] were shown to have been held in only 11 percent of the
sample cases.

Creditors' committees. Creditors have the opportunity to elect committees that will protect their interests by giving appropriate advice
to the trustee and recommendations to the referee. Here creditor
indifference was again demonstrated. Committees were virtually
nonexistent in our no-asset and nominal-asset cases and were
elected in less than 7 percent of the business asset cases—nearly all
of which were adjudications from unsuccessful Chapter XI proceedings. There were no committees at all in business bankruptcies
in Maine, Northern Ohio, and Oregon.

Selection of trustees. In spite of the higher potential returns to
creditors in business bankruptcies, they did not trouble to elect
trustees with any greater frequency—doing so in 18 percent of the
business cases and 17 percent of the personal cases. In the other 82
percent of the business cases, the referee appointed the trustees,
and half the referees' appointments were of persons they had previously appointed as receivers. In fact, receivers were nearly always
continued as trustees: a receiver was appointed in 52 percent of all
business bankruptcies studied and became the trustee in 48 percent.

The wide variation in how trustees are chosen in the eight districts is shown in Table 7-1. Note that creditor interest (as shown
by elections) is stronger in Southern New York, where cases tend
to be larger. In Northern Illinois each referee "had his own trustee,"
who was used on most cases at the time of our field research. In the
other three districts with high percentages of appointments (Maine,
Oregon, and Southern California), the referees used panels of individuals who were regularly selected as trustees. Creditors in those
districts rarely proposed anyone else.

Proxy solicitation. When trustees are being elected someone must
vote on behalf of a creditor, since corporate creditors cannot appear
in person and most other creditors do not bother to attend. Thus
one attorney could solicit proxies from several creditors, perhaps
enough to control the election of the trustee. Referees we asked

4. These are called "Section 21a examinations" as they are authorized by that part
of the Bankruptcy Act.

TABLE 7-1. *Methods of Selection of Trustees in Business Straight Bankruptcy Cases, by District*[a]
In percent

	Elected		Appointed	
District	Total	Former receivers	Total	Former receivers
Southern New York	77	6	23	—
Northern Alabama	50	30	50	29
Western Texas	48	33	52	30
Northern Ohio	44	18	56	7
Oregon	16	3	84	17
Maine	6	3	94	18
Southern California	6	5	94	51
Northern Illinois	—	—	100	76
Eight districts	18	7	82	41

Source: File sample of business bankruptcy cases.
a. Base for percentages is number of cases in which information was available (91 percent of the straight bankruptcy business cases in the file sample).

about this potential problem tended to minimize it. Some correctly pointed out that in their districts trustees were seldom elected. Others explained that solicitation was done by credit agencies or trade associations. A few assured us that attorneys would not solicit since it would be unethical for them to do so. And there were those who professed ignorance about how proxies were solicited, although such an assertion was hardly believable.

In two districts, voting on behalf of more than one claim was restricted by local rules, to be enforced by the referees. In both districts the referees were satisfied that their rules eliminated any problem. In one, however, we observed that usually only the largest claim was voted—by the proxy-holding attorney, who elected himself trustee.

COLLECTION AND LIQUIDATION OF THE ESTATE

Once the trustee is on the job, he proceeds to convert the assets into cash—or to recommend that they be abandoned. He naturally has more to work with in business cases than in personal cases.[5]

5. Noncorporate business bankrupts may qualify for exemptions, but they do so as individuals. Exemptions are discussed in Chapter 5. The present discussion deals with nonexempt property.

Sales. There was property to be sold in over half (56 percent) of these straight bankruptcy cases. The property usually consisted of equipment and inventory; these accounted for 75 percent of the proceeds of the sales.

It is up to the referee to decide whether a public or a private sale will produce the best results for the kind of property to be sold, and referees' decisions varied from district to district. Overall, 32 percent of the items were sold at public auctions and 45 percent at private sales; information on the other items was unavailable.

In most cases, the public auctions were conducted by private auctioneers retained for the purpose. A few referees conducted their own auctions in open court to dispose of such items as real estate and automobiles. Other referees considered this practice undignified. In some districts the judges had issued an official list of the auctioneers to be used and required them to post bond. In Southern New York, a local rule designates a single company as the official auctioneer for bankruptcy sales.

To show how much local policies vary, our files revealed that private sales (either by negotiation or by receipt of sealed bids) were used more than ten times as often as public sales in Maine and Western Texas, five times as often in Northern Ohio, and about twice as often in Northern Alabama, Southern California, Oregon, and Southern New York.[6] Public auctions slightly outnumbered private sales in Northern Illinois, where six of the referees were convinced that auctions brought better results (some of them reporting that usually the only returns to mailed solicitations of bids were from auctioneers). Another referee in that district said that private sales were better because the auctioneer's fee was eliminated and because he suspected auctioneers of conspiring to "chill the bidding" so that their own men could buy the property.

Except for this referee and one other in Northern Illinois who had recently called on the United States Attorney to investigate a suspected buyers' ring, referees did not believe that such groups were controlling many sales. Some said that appraisals were a protection against such a result, that they occasionally asked an FBI agent to attend an auction, or that they combated the rings by

6. No separate breakdown by district was made for business bankruptcies. Remember, however, that sales took place in only 12 percent of the personal cases and generally yielded small amounts.

"scaring hell out of the auctioneer." Even in Los Angeles, where bidders who regularly attend auctions are colloquially referred to as "the forty thieves," the referees were satisfied that there were enough outside bidders in attendance to prevent the regulars from chilling the bidding. Other referees reported that they would combat suspected chilled bidding by resorting to private sales—a dubious protection.

Although the law requires appraisal of all assets, there frequently was no appraisal of automobiles (to which Blue Book or Red Book values were assigned); and the files often contained no information on the appraised value of other items.

In one-fifth of the cases in which sales were made, the files indicated sales of some assets to the debtor (with the cost presumably being met from borrowings, postbankruptcy income, or exempt property) or to a relative or business associate of the debtor. The property most frequently involved in such sales consisted of automobiles and other equipment, real estate, and household appliances.[7] There were also a few instances of sales to creditors, usually of personal property such as household appliances but occasionally involving realty and, in one case, accounts receivable.

In general our research suggests that controls over bankruptcy sales are loose enough to invite ethical slippages. The findings show a varied collection of familiar procedures casually administered— not a businesslike operation zealously carried on to produce the greatest possible yield for the creditors.

Amounts realized from sales. For the median estate in business bankruptcies, sales of property brought in $1,539. Medians among the districts ranged from lows of $500 in Oregon and $900 in Maine to highs of $4,500 in Western Texas and $5,714 in Southern New York. In a few cases in Northern Illinois, Western Texas, Southern New York, and Southern California sales yielded more than $100,000, and in one instance in Southern New York more than $500,000 was realized.

Collections and recoveries. The trustee also brings money into the estate from other kinds of assets. He may pick up bank accounts, wages due the bankrupt, other money owed the bankrupt, or perhaps inheritances. If necessary, the trustee can get a turnover order

7. This would occur if the bankrupt was a proprietor or partner whose personal assets were brought into the estate.

from the referee to compel the bankrupt to surrender money or property. The kinds of items most frequently obtained for the estate by the trustee, the percentage of cases in which each category was collected, and the median amounts collected were:

Category	Percentage of cases	Median amount (dollars)
Accounts receivable	*31*	373
Bank accounts	*14*	169
Tax refunds	*10*	178
Utilities deposits	*8*	Under 100

Abandonment of assets. The trustee may abandon "burdensome" property that is worthless to the estate. It may be worn out or have liens on it greater than its worth. The most common type of property abandoned in our sample cases was accounts receivable. Such accounts are notoriously hard to collect. "In his anxiety to increase his cash flow" before bankruptcy, "the worried debtor may be more ready to ship defective or substandard merchandise, to ignore the credit ratings of his buyers, or to ship to poor credit risks."[8] Moreover, customers who no longer expect to do business with the bankrupt may say that goods were defective or that payments were not properly credited. Trustees have little incentive to work hard on collections because they cannot earn more than 10 percent for doing so.[9] Lawyers in private practice would charge a great deal more.[10]

8. William E. Hogan, "Games Lawyers Play with the Bankruptcy Preference Challenge to Accounts and Inventory Financing," *Cornell Law Review*, Vol. 53 (April 1968), p. 571, n. 73.

9. Bankruptcy Act, Sec. 48c(1). The 10 percent is on the first $500 disbursed by the trustee from all sources. Thereafter, it is 6 percent on the next $1,000, 3 percent on the next $8,500, 2 percent on the next $15,000, and 1 percent on the balance.

10. Most lawyers in private practice would charge one-third on accounts of $54 or less, 15 percent on the first $1,000, and 10 percent on the rest (with additional fees if a lawsuit is required) for commercial accounts forwarded to them by collection agencies or other attorneys, with the forwarder also charging 5 percent or more. (These are the recommended rates of the Commercial Law League. See *Handbook of Commercial Law League of America* [1967], p. 45.) For nonforwarded commercial accounts they probably, and for consumer accounts they certainly, would charge more. For example, the recommended minimum fee in Massachusetts for consumer accounts is 50 percent on accounts of $100 or less, one-third on the first $750, and 25 percent on the balance, with an additional lawsuit fee. (Massachusetts Bar Association, *Minimum Fee Schedule* [1967], p. 10.)

In any event, accounts were abandoned in 24 percent of the business cases, and the incomplete records in the files indicate a face amount averaging almost $7,000 a case. Other abandonments in business cases included automobiles (17 percent of the cases), other equipment (11 percent), and real estate (10 percent).

SIZE OF ESTATES

All this selling and collecting brought in very little—a median of $3,190 for business straight bankruptcy *asset* cases. (Remember that median debts were $40,000 and median scheduled assets $12,000 for all our business straight bankruptcy cases.) Thirty-one percent of the business bankruptcies studied yielded nothing at all, and 13 percent yielded nothing above administrative expenses.

A majority of the asset cases were below $5,000, but 20 percent did run between $10,000 and $50,000 (see Table 7-2). The median nominal-asset case was only $317.

TABLE 7-2. *Size of Estates in Business Straight Bankruptcy Asset Cases*

Size of estate (in dollars)	Percentage of cases[a]
Under 1,000	23
1,000–2,499	22
2,500–4,999	13
5,000–9,999	12
10,000–19,999	10
20,000–49,999	10
50,000–99,999	3
100,000–249,999	2
250,000–499,999	—
500,000 and over	1
Data incomplete	2

Source: File sample of business bankruptcy cases.
a. Because of rounding, percentages do not add to 100.

CREDITORS' CLAIMS

While creditors are more inclined to prove claims in business than in personal bankruptcies, many still do not trouble to do so. The number of claims proved and allowed in our sample of business cases was only 35 percent of the number scheduled with the petitions.

Claims submitted by creditors were objected to in 31 percent of the sample cases. Almost 90 percent of such objections were filed by the trustee, 2 percent by debtors, 1 percent by creditors, and the rest unknown. The objections apparently had merit, for many of the claims were reduced or disallowed by referees. Of the claims challenged, only 23 percent survived completely. Thirty-seven percent were disallowed, 20 percent reduced in amount, and another 20 percent denied a claimed secured or priority status.

Table 7-3 gives the percentages of the various classes of claims finally allowed, along with the median amounts of claims of each class. Some of the unsecured creditors who did not prove claims could have received money from the estate if they had done so. Referees told of cases they delayed closing while trying to get creditors to prove claims so that they could share in available dividends. If all creditors proved, of course, each would get very little. The successful creditor either systematically or luckily proves his claim in cases where other creditors think this is not worthwhile.

TABLE 7-3. *Scheduled Claims Proved and Allowed, and Median Total Amounts of Claims, by Class of Debt*

| | Percentage proved and allowed | | Median | |
Class of debt	By amount	By number	Scheduled	Proved and allowed
Secured	14	9	$14,922	$ 6,081
Priority	84	60	2,632	1,984
Unsecured	33	34	19,316	15,196

Source: File sample of business bankruptcy cases.

DISCHARGES

If the debtor is not a corporation, his adjudication as a bankrupt operates as an application for discharge. A corporation that wants a discharge must apply for it within six months of adjudication. Only 2.5 percent of our corporate bankrupts did so, and in all cases the discharges were granted without opposition. Why would a bankrupt corporation need a discharge? Normally it has no future; no one wants to preserve its name or continue its operation. We wrote to these bankrupts' attorneys to find out their reasons. None of the replies gave any compelling reason for seeking a discharge—or even indicated that the attorneys knew what they were doing. They said they could not find out from their records or were not experienced in bankruptcy or thought the referee required such an application. One even thought that Mr. John Doe of the bankrupt company John Doe, Inc., "was obligated in some manner, on one or more of the bankrupt's debts, and felt that if the bankrupt received its discharge the end result would likewise relieve him." (If Doe had been obligated, the corporation's discharge would *not* have relieved him.)

Objections to discharge were filed in only 4 percent of the cases involving noncorporate business debtors—by creditors in 3 percent and by the trustee in 1 percent. A discharge was actually denied in only one case; in another, one claim was excepted by mutual consent.

ADMINISTRATIVE EXPENSES

Once the assets of the estate have been liquidated, the referee can make decisions about distributing the proceeds. After secured creditors have been paid, administrative expenses take priority. The largest shares go to trustees and their attorneys (see Table 7-4).[11]

PAYING THE CREDITORS

At the payoff point we find that secured creditors and priority creditors received larger portions of their claims in business cases than in personal cases. Unsecured creditors (the most numerous category) were more often paid than in personal cases but still received a very small part of their claims.

Secured creditors who proved claims were paid in four out of five cases and received 31 percent of the amounts proved and allowed.[12]

Priority creditors who proved claims received 36 percent of the amounts proved and allowed.[13]

11. See Chapter 9 for more extensive discussion of costs and finances.

12. Secured claims were scheduled in 79 percent of the sample business cases but proved and allowed in only 18 percent. The scheduling of such claims is subject to the same conditions in business bankruptcies as in personal bankruptcies and the resulting drop in proved claims is similar. (See Chapter 5, pp. 89–90.)

13. Because of an error in the technical tabulating process, the proportion of priority creditors with proved claims who received dividends was not determined.

TABLE 7-4. *Administrative Expenses Paid from Estates in Business Bankruptcy Cases, by Category*

Category of expense	Percentage of cases in which compensated	Percentage of total administrative expense[a]
Referees' Salary and Expense Fund	69	7
Trustee	67	12[b]
Attorney for trustee	42	20
Appraiser	42	1
Reporter	36	1
Receiver	33	7[b]
Attorney for bankrupt	27	4
Auctioneer	18	8
Attorney for receiver	15	4
Administrative rent	12	3
Accountant	10	4
Attorney for petitioning creditors	8	1
Adjuster[c]	5	—[d]
Clerical and bookkeeping	5	—[d]
Attorney for creditors' committee	1	—[d]

Source: File sample of business bankruptcy cases.
a. Does not total 100 percent, because other irregular allowances are not included. "Other" payments, which totaled 27 percent of administrative costs, included operating expenses in adjudicated Chapter XI cases.
b. Compensation of receivers and trustees is subject to statutory maximums.
c. The trustee is occasionally authorized in Southern California, Northern Illinois, and Western Texas to hire an "adjuster" to perform custodial or other menial tasks for him.
d. Less than 0.5 percent.

Unsecured creditors who proved claims were paid in 44 percent of the cases but received only 8 percent of the amounts proved and allowed. (The comparable figure for personal cases was 7 percent.)

Another way to look at distribution to creditors is to see how the entire amount available was divided among the various classes:

Class of claim		Percentage of total amount distributed to creditors
Secured		25
Priority		35
Wages	6	
Taxes	29	
Federal	13	
State	7	
Jurisdiction not indicated	9	
Unsecured		40

Obviously, the largest bite from what unsecured creditors would otherwise receive is taken by the priority claims (35 percent) and the largest portion of this bite (at least 13 percent of total distribution) is taken by the Internal Revenue Service.[14] Yet the Internal Revenue Service does not compile figures that would indicate the importance to the federal fisc of the priority for tax claims in bankruptcy—not even for use in its largely successful 1957–66 battle against proposals to reduce the number of tax claims that would receive priority and survive a bankruptcy discharge.

In the absence of official statistics, a brief analysis will clarify the major effects of federal tax priorities. Tax claimants received $8,985 thousand in bankruptcy cases closed in fiscal 1964.[15] Our sample of cases closed the same year revealed that such payments were divided, 65 percent going to federal taxes and 35 percent to state and local taxes. If the same division is assumed for all asset cases closed in 1964, the federal share of the $8,985 thousand paid on tax claims would be $5,840 thousand. This sum amounts to slightly more than 0.005 percent of the total gross revenues of $112.3 billion for 1964.[16] But it also amounts to 11 percent of all the $51.2 million distributed to creditors in straight bankruptcy asset cases in 1964 and is almost one-third of the amount paid to unsecured creditors in those cases.[17] Such analyses could be refined in more detail, but the point is clear: the federal tax priority has a minuscule effect on federal revenues but a major effect on dividends paid to unsecured creditors in bankruptcy cases. Repeal of such priority is recommended in Chapter 10.

PERIODS OF TIME REQUIRED

After payments have been made, the case can be closed. For business cases in our sample, the average (mean) time from the filing of the petition until closing was more than twenty-three months— about twice as long as the ten months for nonbusiness cases and the twelve months for former-business cases. The average times in each district were:

14. Our data underestimate the size of the federal share—the government is often a secured creditor because of a tax lien on the debtor's property.
15. "Tables of Bankruptcy Statistics" (1964), Table F 5.
16. *1964 Annual Report, Commissioner of Internal Revenue* (1964), p. 7.
17. "Tables of Bankruptcy Statistics" (1964), Tables F 5 and F 6.

District	Months
Southern New York	48.8
Northern Alabama	27.8
Northern Illinois	22.7
Southern California	22.1
Northern Ohio	20.6
Oregon	18.4
Maine	17.3
Western Texas	13.6
Eight districts	23.4

The length of time required varied with the complexity of the cases (see Table 7-5). Nearly all no-asset cases were closed within

TABLE 7-5. *Length of Time between Filing and Closing of Business Bankruptcy Cases, by Type of Case*
In percent

Length of time (in months)	Type of case			
	Asset	Nominal asset	No asset	All cases
Under 12	13	16	28	18
12–18	21	19	18	20
19–24	20	21	52	29
25–30	16	23	0	13
31–35	5	7	0	4
36–41	8	15	3	8
42–48	5	0	0	3
Over 48	10	0	0	6

Source: File sample of business bankruptcy cases. Percentages do not add to 100 because of rounding.

two years, though a few remained on the dockets for more than three. Fifty-six percent of the nominal-asset cases were closed within two years and the slowest 15 percent exceeded three years. Almost as many (54 percent) asset cases were closed within two years, but the balance took substantially longer and 10 percent took more than four years. We point out again that the simpler cases (no-asset, nominal-asset, low-asset) should be completed in a few months. Only if corporate matters are complex or litigation is prolonged can years of elapsed time be justified.

HOW A CHAPTER XI CASE PROCEEDS

Turning from liquidation to rehabilitation of business, we come to the process followed for Chapter XI cases in six of the districts studied.[18]

The basic steps are simple. The debtor proposes a plan under which he will pay off his unsecured creditors either by an extension of time or a composition (reduction in indebtedness), or a combination of the two. If the creditors accept the plan and if it meets the requirements of the Bankruptcy Act, it is confirmed by the court. After expenses are paid and any payment required by the plan is made to creditors, the case is closed (unless the plan provides that the court retain jurisdiction).

Many Chapter XI proceedings fail, either because proposed payment plans are not accepted or because debtors are not able to make the payments required by confirmed plans.[19] Under those circumstances, the proceeding can be dismissed or the debtor can consent to adjudication. Three out of five Chapter XIs ended in either dismissal or adjudication in fiscal years 1964 to 1968.[20]

PRELIMINARY DECISIONS

In Chapter XI proceedings there is normally no trustee. The court may appoint a receiver to run the business or may continue the debtor in possession. After acceptance of a plan by creditors, the receiver or some other person is designated by the referee as disbursing agent to make distribution under the plan.

Virtually every referee we interviewed except those in Southern

18. There were none in Oregon or in Western Texas and only six cases in Northern Ohio, three in Northern Alabama, and two in Maine. Fifty-four percent of the total were from Southern New York, 24 percent from Southern California, and 16 percent from Northern Illinois. Ninety-one percent of the cases were filed as Chapter XIs; the rest were filed as straight bankruptcies and later converted to Chapter XIs.

19. The outcomes of confirmed Chapter XI cases in our sample are given in Table 6-3.

20. "Tables of Bankruptcy Statistics" (1964–68), Table F 4b in all volumes. Remember that adjudicated Chapter XIs were included in our analysis of business straight bankruptcies. The official statistics understate the frequency of Chapter XI failures. Unless the court has retained jurisdiction, there is no record of the debtor's default under the plan.

California preferred to leave the debtor in possession if he seemed trustworthy, both to avoid a receiver's fee and, as one referee put it, to "encourage the creditors to stick with the debtor."[21] Receivers were actually appointed in only 17 percent of the cases studied. None were used in Southern New York, and practices varied in the other districts.[22]

Restraining orders to prevent suits against the debtor were issued in 78 percent of our cases, all at the request of the debtor except for one case in Northern Ohio and six in Southern California in which receivers obtained the orders. Usually they were blanket orders restraining all suits, although about one-quarter of them were directed against attachments of property or foreclosure of liens.[23]

THE FIRST MEETING

At the first meeting creditors react to the debtor's proposed plan and examine him. (If the plan has not been filed soon enough for creditors to evaluate it before the meeting date, the meeting is adjourned in order to give them this opportunity.)

Only fragmentary information about creditor participation appeared in the files, and the examples found were unimpressive. In Southern New York the median number of creditors represented was seven, and the median amount of claims represented was $35,-000, even though the median debtor owed $305,550. A few cases in Northern Illinois each revealed fewer than ten creditors with claims aggregating less than $50,000, although median scheduled liabilities there were $206,245. In one of the cases in Northern Ohio, which had scheduled liabilities of $28,700, five creditors with claims

21. In Southern California a local rule requires the debtor to bear the burden of persuading the court that it should neither (1) appoint a receiver nor (2) require the debtor to post a bond to indemnify creditors against loss in the event of later bankruptcy adjudication. Referees told us that the latter provision was almost never invoked, because the debtors simply could not get such bonds.

22. Receivers were appointed in 43 percent of the cases in Southern California, in all six cases in Northern Ohio, in both cases in Maine, in two of the three cases in Northern Alabama, and in fewer than 10 percent of the cases in Northern Illinois.

23. Even though Chapter XI cases cannot deal with secured claims, a secured creditor could sabotage a plan through foreclosure or through attachments of property. The court therefore has power to prohibit suits against the debtor, including foreclosures.

totaling $2,500 showed up. Two of the three cases in Alabama revealed better creditor representation—six creditors with claims totaling $12,700 in a case where $13,800 in liabilities was scheduled, and twelve creditors with claims of $18,400 against $20,700 scheduled.

There was no record of the extent to which debtors were examined by creditors at the first meeting. Requests for later examination were made in only 17 percent of the cases and held in 10 percent—less activity than in straight bankruptcy even though the stakes were higher in the Chapter XI cases.

Creditors' committees may be elected at the first meeting to work with the receiver or with the debtor in possession.[24] Such committees were used in most of our Chapter XI cases with assets above $7,500 (see Table 7-6).

TABLE 7-6. *Chapter XI Cases in Which Creditors' Committees Were Used, by Size of Estate*[a]
In percent

Size of estate (in dollars)	Committee	No committee	No data
Under 2,500	33	57	10
2,500–4,999	—	100	—
5,000–7,499	20	80	—
7,500–9,999	79	21	—
10,000–19,999	71	29	—
20,000–49,999	76	24	—
50,000–99,999	88	8	4
100,000–249,999	100	—	—
250,000–499,999	60	7	33
500,000 and over	—	100	—

Source: File sample of Chapter XI cases.
a. Limited to cases with confirmed payment plans.

The referees we interviewed agreed that the creditors' committees used were usually organized by credit associations such as the Chicago-Midwest Credit Management Association, the Southern California Credit Managers Association, and specialized credit associations for particular trades in Southern New York. Most

24. An informal committee may have been set up before the meeting or even before the debtor filed his petition. In such cases the committee may be made official at the first meeting.

referees said also that after being organized the committees tended to be dominated by their attorneys. But referees did not agree about the committees' usefulness. A majority considered them useful in Chapter XI cases because creditors tend to accept plans approved by committees and because committees are a good means of distributing information to creditors. A substantial minority of the referees, however, considered them useless or at least not worth the fees allowed the committee attorneys—"a lawyer's skin game" was the term used by one referee.

A survey of the Food Manufacturers Credit Division of the National Association of Credit Management tends to corroborate the picture of creditors' committees that emerged from our interviews with the referees: general creditor satisfaction with the committees but more activity by lawyers than by the businessmen creditors themselves.[25] Some of the findings: 79 percent were satisfied with the performance of creditors' committees, but only 64 percent usually accepted the recommendations of the committees; 72 percent believed that it was to the advantage of their principals in the business to participate in the selection of the committees, but they did so in only 11 percent of the cases in which they were involved; and 62 percent believed that a ring of bankruptcy lawyers in each district controlled the cases despite creditors' committees.

CREDITORS' CLAIMS

The proof and allowance of claims is a very different (and more important) topic for Chapter XI cases than for straight bankruptcy. The repayment plan must obviously be related to the amounts of the valid claims, and creditors must now prove claims in order to vote on the plan and participate in distributions. At the time most of the cases in the sample were filed, creditors were not required to prove their claims in order to participate in a Chapter XI distribution. Payments were made on the basis of the debtor's schedules unless (1) the receiver or a creditor challenged a claim as scheduled; (2) a scheduled creditor proved for an amount larger than or a status superior to that scheduled; or (3) a creditor who was not scheduled proved a claim.

25. James J. Kelly, "Toward Increasing the Effectiveness of Creditors' Committees" (Dartmouth College, Amos Tuck School of Business Administration, 1966). This survey covers both official committees under Chapter XI and unofficial committees. It is based on replies from forty-three out of the eighty-three members of the division.

Secured claims do not have to be proved and cannot be included in the plan without the secured creditors' consent. Yet secured debts are important to the debtor's financial future and therefore to his plan. So he may, as he develops his plan, make separate agreements with secured creditors to reduce or extend their claims. Where this is done, the secured claims are sometimes proved and allowed in the Chapter XI proceeding. This occurred in 14 percent of our cases, some in each of the six districts having Chapter XI cases except Maine and New York.

Claims were objected to much more frequently in Chapter XI cases (74 percent of the cases) than in straight bankruptcy (31 percent). The reason for the difference is clear. Under Chapter XI, the amount of money a debtor must raise is directly related to the total amount of valid claims, so debtors have a strong incentive to try to get claims reduced or disallowed. Nine out of ten of the petitions objecting to claims were filed by debtors.[26] Those who challenged claims were rewarded for their diligence, because only 7 percent of the claims challenged survived completely. Forty-nine percent were disallowed, 43 percent were reduced in amount, and 1 percent were denied a claimed status as secured or priority debts.

If one compares the median numbers and amounts of claims scheduled with the median numbers and amounts proved and allowed in the cases studied, the figures look like this:

	Median number	Median amount
Priority claims		
Scheduled	4	$ 7,558
Proved and allowed	4	6,964
Unsecured claims		
Scheduled	96	137,500
Proved and allowed	89	94,590

PROVISIONS OF PLANS

The detailed payment provisions of the Chapter XI plans studied were extremely varied and complex. In many cases they were dictated by the amounts and kinds of financing available, as well as by creditors' circumstances and attitudes. It is therefore impossible to summarize such provisions without oversimplification.

26. Receivers (plus one trustee) filed 4 percent, and the rest are unknown. Creditors challenged no claims, according to the files reviewed.

Chapter XI plans are generally of three types: (1) a composition plan, under which unsecured creditors agree to accept less than 100 percent payment; (2) an extension plan, under which unsecured claims are paid in full but over longer periods of time; and (3) a combination of both. Before any type of plan can become effective, the priority creditors must be paid in full unless they waive their right to such payment.

A pure composition plan provides for a single distribution to unsecured creditors (a one-payment plan) to be made promptly after the plan is confirmed. Thirty-eight percent of the confirmed plans were of this type. The remaining 62 percent of confirmed plans provided for deferred payments to at least some creditors. Some of these were pure extensions, and others reduced the amount to be paid. One-payment plans were found in every district except Northern Alabama; deferred payment plans, in all but Maine.

The Bankruptcy Act permits Chapter XI plans to treat unsecured debts alike *or* to divide them into classes and treat different classes in different ways. In our sample cases there was no classification of debts in the one-payment plans. Some of the deferred payment plans classified the creditors, but the basis for classification was often not apparent from the file.[27] "Small" claims, which were likely to be numerous, were sometimes put in a separate class. However, the boundary of small claims was variously set at $25, $50, $250, and $500, and there was no apparent consistency in the manner in which they were to be paid. In some cases, the creditors classified themselves by choosing among options proposed by the debtor. One Northern Ohio plan, for example, gave creditors an option to take 26 percent in cash upon confirmation or 17 percent in cash and an additional 23 percent in installments over a three-year period.

FINANCING THE PLANS

Confirmation of a Chapter XI plan requires a cash deposit to pay administrative expenses and to make the cash payments provided

27. Example of an elaborate plan in Northern Ohio: Class A creditors were to receive 35 percent in cash on confirmation, another 10 percent within twenty months, and a share of all profits earned within twenty-two months, but not to exceed an additional 5 percent. Class B creditors were to receive 55 percent within twenty-two months and up to another 5 percent from profits earned within twenty months. Class C creditors were to receive 6 percent within twenty-three months of confirmation.

for. Debtors with deferred payment plans must also make arrangements for financing to cover the later payments. In our sample the median cash payment was 19 percent of claims in a one-payment plan and 10 percent in a deferred payment plan. Future payments to be made in deferred payment plans ranged from 10 to 100 percent of claims with a median of 25 percent.

Occasionally, money to finance a Chapter XI plan can be raised by the sale of assets not needed for continuation of the business. In some of our cases real estate, vehicles, and stores were sold. The debtor may also bring in cash, bank accounts, accounts receivable, rights to tax refunds, and other collectible items; and these may be augmented or depleted by the operation of his business during the proceeding. In 44 percent of our cases where plans were confirmed there were some funds from the operation of the business which could be used to make a part of the cash deposit required.

In most cases, however, new sources of funds must be located. The files in 43 percent of our confirmed-plan cases indicated that some or all of the necessary funds came from new sources. Another 13 percent of the files contained no indication of the source of funds, though in most of them it was apparent that a new source had to be found. Even where a new source was indicated, it was frequently not possible to determine whether the new contribution took the form of capital investment or of new debt. And even where that much could be ascertained, information was lacking as to the extent of the equity represented by the new capital investment or the terms of the new debt. These points are of course very important in judging the effect of the Chapter XI plan on the debtor's financial future.

THE FEASIBILITY REQUIREMENT

All this important information is not needed by the courts, however, mainly because of the interpretation usually given the statutory requirement that the court be satisfied that the Chapter XI plan "is for the best interests of the creditors and is feasible" before confirming it.[28] The courts determine only that "the creditors must be assured of receiving what is promised them under the arrangement . . . not . . . an assurance of [the debtor's] future business suc-

28. *Bankruptcy Act,* Sec. 366.

cess."[29] In a single-payment plan this interpretation simply means
that the debtor must make the necessary cash deposit before the
plan can be confirmed—never mind what commitments he may
have made to get the cash.[30] But even under deferred payment plans,
where the feasibility requirement has been interpreted to require a
determination that the debtor has "a reasonable chance of success"
at least for the duration of the plan,[31] the files rarely contain adequate information about future commitments to new investors. No
district in our sample required the debtor to make written disclosure
of such commitments in his application for confirmation, and while
the matter may have been explored in the hearings on confirmation,
those hearings were not reported and transcribed.

This whole pattern of interpretations and administration demon-
strates the ineffectiveness of Chapter XI proceedings as a means of
rehabilitation.

CONFIRMATION OF PLANS

A plan can be confirmed when it has been accepted by a majority
of creditors[32] and when the debtor has made the deposit required to
pay administrative expenses, priority debts, and the distribution to
creditors called for by the plan. The confirmation (unlike a Chapter
XIII confirmation) operates as a discharge of the unpaid balances
of claims provided for by the plan.

Fourteen percent of the cases analyzed were dismissed without
confirmation of a plan. Most of these failed because the debtor
could not obtain creditors' consent, could not raise the money to
make the payments, or could not persuade the court to confirm the
plan. The others were dismissed on a happier note for the creditors
—by the sale of assets or by assistance from relatives or associates,

29. *In re American Trailer Rentals Co.*, 325 F.2d 47, 53 (10th Cir. 1963), reversed on
other grounds, 379 U.S. 594 (1965).
30. *In re American Trailer Rentals Co.; In re Admiral Container Corp.*, 95 F. Supp. 723
(D.N.J. 1951), affirmed 193 F.2d 330 (3d Cir. 1952); *In re Slumberland Bedding Co.*,
115 F. Supp. 39 (D.Md. 1953).
31. *United Properties, Inc.* v. *Emporium Department Stores*, 379 F.2d 55, 65 (8th Cir.
1967). See also *In re Transvision, Inc.*, 217 F.2d 243 (2d Cir. 1954), *cert. den.* 348 U.S. 952
(1955).
32. That is, by a majority in number and amount of all creditors affected or, if
creditors are divided into classes, by a majority in number and amount of each class
affected.

the debtor raised enough to pay creditors in full or to make an informal settlement with them. All the dismissals were either at the request of the debtor or on the referee's motion.

All the remaining cases (including all cases converted from straight bankruptcy) were confirmed, although in about one-quarter of them creditors made objections, a few of which resulted in modifications in the plans.

SIZE OF ESTATES

The estate in a Chapter XI proceeding is the cash deposit the debtor must make before a plan can be confirmed. If the plan provides for distribution of the debtor's capital stock to creditors or for deferred cash payments, the deposit may also include stock certificates or notes, but here we do not include such noncash deposits in computing the size of estates.

The median estate for all confirmed plans in the six districts studied was $43,400. Almost one-fifth of the estates were less than $10,000, almost one-fourth exceeded $100,000, and 13 percent exceeded $250,000. The medians by district were:

Maine	$150,000
Northern Ohio	67,000
Southern California	62,500
Northern Illinois	46,400
Southern New York	35,000
Northern Alabama	1,875

ADMINISTRATIVE EXPENSES

Money was available for administrative expenses in all of the confirmed cases in the sample and in one-third of those dismissed before confirmation. Table 7-7 shows the frequency and size of various types of expenses.[33]

The amounts paid to debtors' attorneys and to attorneys for creditors' committees are understated because some of them waive payment throughout the Chapter XI case and are later paid directly by their clients. This is done to reduce the size of the required deposit and thus facilitate confirmation of the plan.

33. See Chapter 9 for further discussion of expenses of administration.

TABLE 7-7. *Administrative Expenses Paid from Estates in Chapter XI Cases, by Category*

Category of expense	Percentage of cases in which compensated	Percentage of total administrative expense[a]
Referees' Salary and Expense Fund	96	15
Disbursing agent[b]	62	5
Reporter	43	1
Attorney for bankrupt	31	41
Attorney for creditors' committee	21	12
Appraiser	14	—[c]
Receiver	13	2
Creditors' committee	12	1
Accountant	12	8
Attorney for receiver	8	2
Clerical and bookkeeping[d]	4	—[c]
Auctioneer	4	1
Attorney for petitioning creditors[e]	3	1
Administrative rent[f]	3	1
Adjuster[d]	2	—[c]
Other	18	11[a]

Source: File sample of Chapter XI cases.

a. An effort was made to exclude from this tabulation all business operating expenses except administrative rent. "Other" payments included an unknown amount of operating expenses. Column does not add to 100 because of rounding.

b. Disbursing agents waived their fees in a few cases and received no separate compensation in a few others in which they also served as receivers.

c. Less than 0.5 percent.

d. Southern California only.

e. Allowances made in Northern Ohio, Northern Illinois, and Southern California to attorneys for creditors who petitioned for appointment of receiver.

f. Southern New York only.

DISTRIBUTION TO CREDITORS

Priority creditors, as we have said, must be paid in full in cash unless they waive their claims or agree to different treatment under the plan. In all but a few exceptional cases in the sample, priority creditors were paid in full.[34]

Unsecured creditors under one-payment plans received a median of 19 percent of their claims.

Unsecured creditors under deferred payment plans present a more complex picture. Cash payments were made upon confirma-

34. The exceptions included some waivers of first-priority administrative expenses and eight cases in which the federal or state governments, or both, agreed to deferred payments; in two of these the federal government accepted partial cash payments.

tion in 60 percent of the deferred payment plans confirmed (this excludes all "small" claims under $1,000, which were treated separately under their respective plans). The median payment was 10 percent of claims. Future payments ranged from 10 to 100 percent of claims, with a median of 25 percent. They were to be paid over periods ranging from ten months to six years. There was no way to tell whether such payments were actually made—except in the few cases (5 percent) in which the court retained jurisdiction.

PERIODS OF TIME REQUIRED

A typical Chapter XI case takes about a year and a half from filing to closing (see Table 7-8)—nearly as long as a straight bankruptcy, which averaged twenty-three months—even though the intent of the law is to get cases closed soon after confirmation (unless a deferred payment plan provides for the court's retaining jurisdiction). In a case with a single-payment plan there is nothing left to do after confirmation but resolve any remaining questions on the allowance of claims and make the distribution before closing the case. Nonetheless, for reasons that do not appear in the files, the time between confirmation and closing ranged from seven to forty-three months. The median time was one year.

Deferred payment plans should take no longer because there is nothing additional to do after confirmation—*unless* the court retains

TABLE 7-8. *Median Number of Months Elapsed between Filing, Confirmation, and Closing of Chapter XI Cases, by District*

District	Filing to confirmation		Confirmation to closing	
	Single-payment plans	Deferred payment plans	Single-payment plans	Deferred payment plans
Northern Ohio	Under 3	3	18	37
Northern Alabama	—a	2	—a	28
Maine	Under 4	—b	10	—b
Northern Illinois	Under 4	5	16	28
Southern New York	8	11	12	8
Southern California	3	7	32	11
Median, six districts	6	9	12	10

Source: File sample of Chapter XI cases.
a. No single-payment plans.
b. No deferred payment plans.

jurisdiction until the payments are completed. The referees, debtors, and creditors we interviewed do not favor the courts' keeping jurisdiction. Many of them explained that it is easier for the debtor to do business unrestricted by a receiver or by his accountability as debtor in possession. Some referees added that they were under pressure from the Administrative Office of the United States Courts to expedite the closing of their cases. Thus there are cases in which payments are made after the case is formally closed. In any event, the median time between confirmation and closing was ten months—less than that for the one-payment plans.

OTHER CHAPTER PROCEEDINGS

Of the various chapters of the Bankruptcy Act that provide for rehabilitative proceedings, only two more are considered here—Chapter X, for the reorganization of corporations, and Chapter XII, covering real estate indebtedness of noncorporate debtors.

CHAPTER XII

The failure rate for Chapter XII proceedings is even worse than that for Chapter XIs. Only 12 percent of the proceedings in fiscal years 1964–68 were successfully completed.[35] There are two apparent reasons. First, it is more difficult to get a plan confirmed, because the consent of creditors holding *two-thirds* of the amount in each class of debts is required; second, it is likely that some Chapter XII petitions are filed not in the expectation of working out a plan, but to obtain delays in mortgage foreclosure proceedings. If an informal settlement can be achieved, the case can be dismissed.

Otherwise, the proceeding is similar to a Chapter XI. A plan must be devised and financed, creditor acceptances must be obtained, and the required funds must be distributed.

CHAPTER X

Chapter X cases are more complex (and usually involve larger businesses) than Chapter XI or XII proceedings. The equity interest of the business can be affected as well as its debt, both secured

35. Fifty percent were dismissed and 38 percent were adjudicated bankrupt. "Tables of Bankruptcy Statistics," Table F 4b, for the respective years.

and unsecured. Another difference is that a district judge presides over the proceedings (although he may refer the matter to a referee in bankruptcy, serving as a master). A final difference involves another participant: the Securities and Exchange Commission (SEC), which plays an influential advisory role as a protection to the stockholding public.

If the debts listed with the petition are less than $250,000, the debtor may be left in possession and may present the reorganization plan. If they are larger, the court must appoint a trustee, who is responsible for developing the plan. The proposed reorganization *must* be referred to the SEC if the debt exceeds $3 million and *may* be referred if the debt is less. The commission's advice, along with other factors in the case, is considered by the judge, who may then approve the plan. This approval is preliminary, for creditors and stockholders are then asked to accept or reject the plan.[36]

If sufficient acceptances are obtained, the judge must decide whether to confirm the plan. He must decide that the plan is "feasible." This standard has been construed to require a determination that a Chapter X plan give the debtor "a reasonable prospect for survival" for the indefinite future.[37] The company's future is very important to creditors, because in Chapter X cases they usually receive stock or long-term debt securities rather than cash.

After confirmation, distribution can begin. This is a slow process, because creditors and stockholders are often widely scattered and getting proper proof of their interests is difficult. The only successful Chapter X in our sample, the General Stores case (see pages 109 and 117), was not closed until more than five years after the reorganization plan was confirmed. Much of the delay resulted from the failure of stockholders in the old corporation to submit their stock for exchange.

All such complexities and delays make it difficult for debtors to survive the Chapter X process. Only one case out of four in fiscal years 1964 through 1968 resulted in a successful reorganization.[38]

36. Acceptance requires a favorable vote by two-thirds (by amount of debt) of each class of creditors and, if the debtor has been found not insolvent, by holders of a majority of the stock in each class.

37. *Group of Institutional Investors* v. *Chicago, Milwaukee & St. Paul Railroad Co.*, 318 U.S. 523, 540 (1943). See also *Consolidated Rock Products Co.* v. *DuBoise*, 312 U.S. 510 (1941).

38. "Tables of Bankruptcy Statistics," Table F 4b, for the respective years.

CONCLUSION

The business bankruptcy process, like the personal bankruptcy process, is characterized by creditor indifference, slowness, and scanty results. The typical asset case (only half of the sample) yields about $3,000, some 30 percent of which goes to costs of administration and 29 percent to tax collectors. Unsecured creditors are paid, but they receive only 8 percent of their proved claims. No wonder they are not interested enough to vote for trustees, establish creditors' committees, or do a good job of examining debtors.

The only perceptible benefits of the process are that the debtors have some unpaid debts discharged, the creditors get an unsatisfactory business situation finally resolved, and those who operate the system (referees, trustees, attorneys, and others) make a living.

Chapter XI proceedings are also slow and time-consuming. They tend to be larger cases, involving more claims and assets of greater value. Creditors' interest appears greater than in straight bankruptcies, and they did better—most priority creditors were paid in full, though unsecured creditors did well if they received 25 percent of their claims.

The courts equate the feasibility of the plans with the likelihood of payments being made to creditors and concern themselves very little with the future prospects of the businesses. The emphasis is on deferred payment plans, and the cases are usually closed after a first payment. Analysis of our sample suggests that only one-third of the debtors whose plans were confirmed continued in business. Thus the Chapter XI proceeding cannot be considered an effective mechanism for business rehabilitation.

8

---◦───◈───◦---

The Administration of
Bankruptcy

Looking at bankruptcy as a governmental administrative system, we concentrate in turn on organization, personnel, and paperwork. In all three respects bankruptcy administration falls below reasonable standards of performance.

ORGANIZATION, SUPERVISION, AND REVIEW

The "organization" for bankruptcy is a multimillion-dollar, loosely connected structure operating in every part of the United States. At the central core of this organization are the offices of the referees in bankruptcy in 155 different locations in 90 districts. As of June 30, 1969, there were 218 referees—183 full-time and 35 part-time—assisted by 855 clerks. Their salaries and expenses in fiscal year 1969 were $13.3 million,[1] all paid from the Referees' Salary and Expense Fund, which will be discussed in Chapter 9.

The most realistic way to look at the organization of the bankruptcy system is to start with the day-to-day administration of the bankruptcy cases. Here the burden of paperwork and detailed discussions falls on the debtors' attorneys, the creditors' attorneys, the trustees, and the trustees' attorneys, with help as needed from ac-

---

1. Administrative Office of the U.S. Courts, "Annual Report of the Director" (1969; processed), p. V-12.

147

countants, appraisers, auctioneers, and other specialists. The referee is, of course, the key adjudicatory official—granting discharges, approving arrangements, ruling on petitions, approving expenses, and exercising all his other powers under the Bankruptcy Act. These powers are extensive; millions of dollars and the entire future of large enterprises may be involved. The referee is also an administrative official. He selects and supervises clerical personnel and outlines detailed work methods, which may vary considerably from court to court. He must answer many questions and make minor decisions on procedural difficulties.

The referee's administrative activities may tend to prejudice the way his adjudicatory functions are carried on. In his more routine work he acquires information that is not properly admissible in an adjudicatory proceeding. He also has numerous informal contacts that would be considered improper in a regular civil court.[2] Our proposal in Chapter 10 attempts to solve this problem by separating administrative from judicial functions.

How is the referee supervised, checked, audited, and reviewed?

ADMINISTRATIVE SUPERVISION WITHIN THE JUDICIAL BRANCH

Referees are supervised by district court judges in several ways. The judges appoint the referees, may promulgate the local rules of court under which the referees work, hear petitions for review, approve fees in some courts, and decide a variety of legal matters under the Bankruptcy Act. In all eight districts studied the general effect of this supervision was superficial. Judges generally stated in interviews that they left the operation of the bankruptcy courts to the referees, taking action only on complex legal problems or on critical problems of ethics or administration.

When the judges were asked, "How do you judge how good a job a referee is doing?" over half of them said that they made judgments when they received appeals (known as "petitions for review") of the referees' rulings. (Such petitions are rarely filed.) Forty-two percent spoke of informal comments or complaints from the bar; 30 percent "read reports"; 18 percent referred to their informal contacts with referees; and 15 percent said, "By general reputation." These

2. For a fuller discussion, see George M. Treister, "Bankruptcy Jurisdiction: Is It Too Summary?" *Southern California Law Review*, Vol. 39 (1966), pp. 78–90.

answers were similar to other statements made by the judges when asked to describe their role in the administration of bankruptcy matters. More candor than modesty is suggested by the second most frequent description (after "handle petitions for review"), which was "almost none."

More general oversight is provided by the Judicial Conference of the United States, the general governing body of the judicial branch. This group is headed by the chief justice and is made up of the chief judge of each circuit and of two special federal courts and of a district judge elected from each circuit. It meets twice a year. The conference oversees bankruptcy matters in several ways: (1) recommending rules of procedure for issuance by the Supreme Court; (2) determining policy on management of the bankruptcy courts; (3) authorizing additional personnel for the courts; (4) endorsing or opposing legislation proposed to Congress; and (5) fixing the amounts of charges to the estates. The conference is kept informed by reports from the Bankruptcy Division of the Administrative Office of the United States Courts. All policy and administrative decisions of the conference are based on recommendations by a committee on bankruptcy administration. Rules are based on recommendations by an advisory committee on bankruptcy rules.

We observed that some Judicial Conference policies were faithfully followed in the districts studied (such as limiting Chapter XIII trustees' commissions to the same amount as the maximum compensation paid to full-time referees). Others were not (for example, a policy that "all first meetings of creditors and continuations thereof should be conducted in the presence of the referee" was flagrantly violated in Cleveland). The conference has little effective power to enforce its will. It could deny staff to recalcitrant referees, but this would punish debtors and creditors as well. It could recommend that a referee not be reappointed, but such a step, even if appreciated and followed by district judges, would come too late and might be unduly severe.

The Administrative Office of the United States Courts provides central administrative services and some coordination of the courts, concentrating mainly on financial, statistical, and office management functions. It offers help and advice, not direction.

This restraint is evidenced by the modest staffing of its Bankruptcy Division and by the limited supervision the division exercises over the bankruptcy courts. The entire bankruptcy system is served from Washington by a division consisting of only five attorneys, one auditor, and five secretaries. Its duties, briefly summarized, are to make recommendations to the Judicial Conference on bankruptcy laws and procedures, number of referees and locations of offices, referees' pay, fees to be charged, and the annual budget; and to audit bankruptcy courts and investigate complaints.[3] Some service is rendered the bankruptcy courts by other divisions of the Administrative Office: tabulating of statistics by the Division of Procedural Studies and Statistics, routine personnel processing by the Division of Personnel, and aid in budget formulation and cost studies by the Division of Business Administration. Referees and judges look primarily to the Bankruptcy Division, however, for help and information.

The staff of the Bankruptcy Division is so small that visits to bankruptcy courts for surveillance and advice are infrequent. Trips are scheduled mainly to courts where a referee's term is soon to end, where an increase in staffing has been requested, or where complaints have been made. While visiting such districts a staff member will sometimes visit other districts nearby. As of October 1969, 112 referees' offices (51 percent) had not been visited for two years. In Washington, the Bankruptcy Division's main work priorities are staff work for the Judicial Conference (particularly studies of the need for personnel in referees' offices), studies of proposed legislative changes, issuance of administrative instructions and standard procedures, and complaints both from and about the courts of bankruptcy.

Staff members audit reports of closed bankruptcy cases to verify that amounts paid to the Referees' Salary and Expense Fund are correct, that excessive fees are not being charged, and that no districts are permitting monopolies in trusteeships. A monopoly is defined as any one trustee serving in more than 20 percent of the cases in a district. Such a standard is doubly unsound: first, because 20 percent of the cases in some districts would amount to thousands; and second, trustees' fees are limited to statutory percentages, and it is more important to be concerned about the compensation of attorneys for trustees, on which there is no limit.

3. For a more detailed listing, see Administrative Office of the U.S. Courts, "Manual for Referees in Bankruptcy: Administrative Procedures and Regulations" (processed), pp. xix–xx (rev. February 1969).

When the present study began, audits were made only of straight bankruptcy asset and nominal-asset cases. Audit of Chapter XI cases was not begun until 1966; in March 1967 the Judicial Conference ordered studies of administrative costs in Chapter XIII cases. The Bankruptcy Division also reviews reports of cases that have been open for eighteen months or longer and matters that referees have had under advisement for more than sixty days.

The division chief and his men are clearly on good personal terms with referees and are familiar with the strong and weak spots in the bankruptcy courts. Their attitude is consistently constructive, and they are able to resolve many problems at an early stage. Nevertheless the tradition of judicial independence is strong, and the division's staff is small in relation to the scope of the bankruptcy system. Hence the referees, judged by normal governmental standards, receive little professional leadership, procedural review, or routine surveillance from the Administrative Office. This minimal supervision is understandably acceptable to the district judges and referees, all of whom, when interviewed, commended the work of the division.

DEPARTMENT OF JUSTICE EXAMINATIONS

The courts of bankruptcy, like other federal courts, are inspected periodically by examiners from the Office of the Assistant Attorney General for Administration. These examiners must be attorneys, and they are often recruited right out of law school. No other qualifications are required except ability to deal with people. They are asked to serve at least three years, an objective not always achieved, although some have done this work for decades.

An examiner typically spends four to five months inspecting a district, devoting ten days of this period to bankruptcy. He follows a prescribed outline and checklist in reviewing compliance with the law, procedural rules, and local bankruptcy rules. The outline instructs the examiner to "report matters of major importance and general practices rather than individual instances of deficiencies."[4] Yet it also prescribes detailed reviews of personnel practices, procedures for custody of funds, and other fine points of bankruptcy administration. The checklist requires the examiner to make findings

4. U.S. Department of Justice, "Outline of Examination, Referees in Bankruptcy" (Aug. 20, 1969; processed), p. 2.

ranging from details of procedure ("Dividend checks are mailed by trustees by regular mail") to difficult professional judgments ("Compensation awarded officers of the estate appeared commensurate with work they performed," or "The appraisal of the property of the estate appears to have been real, not perfunctory").[5]

The examiners tend to concentrate on the more detailed aspects of their work. They naturally feel more secure reporting on verifiable minutiae than on matters requiring professional discrimination —particularly if the examiner is inexperienced.

On both large and small matters the examiners are handicapped by lack of authority. They are instructed to report and persuade, not to insist:

> The principal function of the examiner with respect to bankruptcy matters is to determine and report on the extent of compliance with the Bankruptcy Act, General Orders of the Supreme Court of the United States, Federal Rules of Civil Procedure where applicable, and recommended procedures. The examiner also reviews controls over operations and resources to determine whether they are functioning effectively and as intended. If possible, the referee should be persuaded to correct deficiencies before the examiner leaves the district. If, however, a referee does not agree to bring a practice into compliance with the law, General Orders, or the recommended procedures, the examiner has fulfilled his function if he discusses the matter with the referee (and the judge) and reports their reactions along with a description of the condition and recommended corrective action.[6]

This limitation makes the examiners' work frustrating. They may report procedural errors or ethically questionable practices with the realization that nothing may be done about their findings. Following are some examples brought up by examiners in the bankruptcy session of their 1966 conference:

Unavailability of bank statements and canceled checks in closed files;

Use of collection agencies owned by trustees to collect accounts receivable due estates in bankruptcy;

Use of excessive numbers of banks as depositories;

Handling of cash by referees' offices (contrary to policy).

The examining staff cannot possibly do an adequate job of in-

---

5. Department of Justice, "Examiner's Work Sheet for Bankruptcy Case Review," Form No. AD-325 (ed. 2-2-61).

6. Department of Justice, "Outline of Examination," p. 1.

specting bankruptcy courts. For the task of examining the ninety-two district courts there were only four examiners out of an authorized complement of fourteen on duty as of September 30, 1969, and one of these was a trainee not yet admitted to the bar; there were also three auditors. The staff is severely limited by budget and even more by difficulty in recruiting lawyers willing to travel most of the time.

Although the examiners' objective is to visit each district every two years, they have been working on a schedule that takes them to each one every four years. As of August 30, 1969, examinations of referees' offices had been completed (that is, final reports completed) as follows:

Years	Percentage of the districts
Within 1	15
Within 1½	28
Within 2	40
Within 3	67
Within 4	98

In each referee's office examiners are expected to study a minimum of ten cases with assets of $1,000 or more. Ten cases every three or four years is hardly an adequate basis for evaluating a referee's work.

This thin coverage is reflected in the replies of judges and referees in the eight districts studied to questions about the work of the examiners. For the most part they indicated lack of any contact, with other answers scattered and largely favorable. In a few instances judges spoke resentfully of what they considered unwarranted criticisms and recommendations by examiners.

In general, the examining program by its very existence exerts some pressure for compliance with procedures and for honesty in handling funds, but it can make only a modest contribution to the integrity and efficiency of the bankruptcy system.

OTHER AUDITING CONSIDERATIONS

The lack of adequate federal government audit of bankruptcy estate funds has led the Judicial Conference to adopt a policy requiring that referees "cause a thorough audit to be made of all

accounts of receivers and trustees."[7] In June 1969, representatives of
the General Accounting Office began auditing district court records
after reaching agreement with the Administrative Office to do so.
The GAO's audits were limited to general revenue funds and moneys
entering or leaving the Referees' Salary and Expense Fund. More
recently, these audits have been extended to a few trustees' accounts.

INVESTIGATION OF BANKRUPTCY CRIMES

Investigation and prosecution of fraud and other crimes are additional means by which the Department of Justice exercises some
check on bankruptcy activities. More often than not such crimes
consist of concealing or diverting assets or of falsifying records. Information about possible violations of law must be brought to the
attention of U.S. attorneys by referees, trustees, receivers, or other
attorneys. Possible wrongdoing by referees, trustees, and others may
be reported by creditors or by officials of the Administrative Office.

The number of criminal matters related to bankruptcy that are
actually investigated and prosecuted is extremely small, as Table
8-1 shows. If these figures are related to the total numbers of bank-

TABLE 8-1. *Number and Outcome of Bankruptcy Matters Investigated and*
Prosecuted by Department of Justice, Fiscal Years 1964-69

Description	1964	1965	1966	1967	1968	1969
Bankruptcy cases filed	171,719	180,323	192,354	208,329	197,811	184,930
Matters investigated[a]	300	331	292	365	298	211
Matters terminated without indictment	249	265	230	293	223	174
Criminal cases filed	51	66	62	72	75	37
Criminal cases terminated	46	57	68	65	63	67

Sources: Administrative Office of the U.S. Courts, "Tables of Bankruptcy Statistics" (1969;
processed), p. 1; records of Fraud Section, Criminal Division, Department of Justice, and interview with Fraud Section representative.
a. Estimated.

ruptcy cases filed in those fiscal years, they show that there is
roughly one matter investigated formally for every 500 to 900 bankruptcy cases filed. One criminal case is filed for every 2,500 to 5,000
bankruptcy cases filed.

7. *Reports of the Proceedings of the Judicial Conference of the United States, Held March
1962*, p. 67.

Why so few investigations? A number of explanations are possible, listed in what seems to us order of probability:

Inadequate incentive for creditors and trustees to develop and report evidence of improprieties.

Pressures of higher priority or more attractive workload on the U.S. attorneys and the Federal Bureau of Investigation. (Referees and attorneys complained to us about inaction by U.S. attorneys on bankruptcy complaints.)

Close personal and professional relations that have developed over the years among trustees, receivers, attorneys, and referees.

Availability of lesser sanctions in the bankruptcy process (for example, denial of discharge).

PETITIONS FOR REVIEW

The appeal process is another little-used means of overseeing the bankruptcy courts. Referees' decisions are reviewed by judges when petitioned by debtors, creditors, trustees, or receivers. Such reviews are not new trials, and judges must accept referees' findings unless clearly erroneous. Although judges mentioned reviews as their principal means of judging the quality of a referee's work, such judgments would be based on very little experience. Petitions for review were filed in only 2 to 3 percent of asset cases, according to a complete count of all petitions filed in fiscal years 1964 and 1965 in the eight districts studied. The percentage was higher in Southern New York (14 percent in 1964, 10 percent in 1965), where a larger proportion of bankruptcies were business cases, many with extensive assets. There were far more reviews in Chapter XI cases—such petitions were filed in about one-third of the cases. (See Appendix Table c-17 for a full count.)

Two factors contribute to the infrequency of petitions. Few of the matters on which referees rule are actually contested, and even when they are, the stakes are generally not high enough to justify the time and expense. The system of review is part of the traditional, adversary judicial process, which does not function when there are no substantial adverse interests. Another deterrent (to an attorney) is that the referee will be making future decisions about him—approving fees or making appointments. Two quotations from interviews with attorneys who frequently serve as trustees

illuminate this point. Said one: "I am bright enough to know that
it is a better tactic to settle any controversy I might have than to
take a review of a formal ruling." Less subtly, another said, "I will
not go against my own referee." It is significant that 64 percent of
the straight bankruptcy trustees we interviewed had *never* petitioned
for review of a referee's ruling.

Once a petition is filed, the referee must prepare a summary of
the evidence and his findings, as well as a statement of the issue
presented by the appeal. These are forwarded to the district court
judge for consideration. The length of time it took to perform this
routine function varied markedly from one district to another. Action is by far the slowest in Southern California, where more than
two months elapsed between filing and certification in about one-
third of the petitions filed. It is also slow in Southern New York (15
to 60 days in about 60 percent) and Northern Ohio (8 to 31 days
in about 60 percent). It is most rapid in Maine (90 percent within
two weeks), Oregon (all within two weeks, 60 percent within one
week), and Western Texas (about 60 percent within two weeks).

The grounds on which petitions for review were filed in 1964 and
1965 in the eight districts studied cover familiar sources of controversy in bankruptcy. They are listed here in order of frequency:[8]

Grounds of petition	Number of times cited
"Abuse of discretion"	49
Validity of security	46
Excessive or inadequate fees or allowances	34
Allowance of claims	32
Turnover orders	30
Preferences or transfers	30
Restraining orders	23
Jurisdiction of court	22
Reclamation of property	17

8. Multiple replies were possible. In tabulating these grounds, it was observed that
there were variations in the number and degree of specificity of the reasons cited in the
petitions. These variations resulted partly from the preferences of the attorneys filing
the actions and partly from the care and detail with which petitions for review were
reported by the court clerks. Under these circumstances, analyzing the grounds for
review by districts or by chapters of the Bankruptcy Act, or attempting other more re-
fined studies, seemed unproductive.

Discharge improperly granted or denied	17
Validity of a contract	15
Timeliness of filing (any documents)	13
Exemptions	12
Validity of priority	10
Confirmation of Chapter XI plan	10
Dismissal (or refusal to dismiss) proceedings	10
Adjudication	9
Approval of compromise	8
Disapproval or removal of trustee or receiver	8
Misrepresentation	7
Vesting of property in trustee	7
"Findings of fact and law" (no more detailed reason)	7
Allowance for administrative rent	4
Attachment or garnishment	3
Superiority or subrogation of claims	3
Provisions of Chapter XIII plans	3
Provisions of Chapter XI plans	2
Foreclosure	2
Petition to sell denied	2
Section 21a examination	1
Abandonment of property	1
Distribution of estate	1
Decision not to proceed with suit	1
Other	25

The outcome of the reviews usually supported the referees—a result that might be expected from the burden placed on the petitioners to demonstrate error on the part of the referees, from the judges' lack of familiarity with and interest in bankruptcy law and procedure, and from the judges' natural inclination to back up persons they had appointed. Referees were affirmed in two-thirds of the cases on which reviews were held (see Appendix Table c-18). In 23 percent of the cases decided by district courts the litigants went on to the courts of appeal. The latter courts, as shown in Appendix Table c-19, showed a strong tendency to affirm both the decisions of the district courts and the original decisions of the referees. Eleven cases out of 379 were carried on to the Supreme Court—one was withdrawn, and the Court declined to hear the rest.

It is evident that, while the review and appeal process provides safeguards against extremes of error against debtors and creditors who can finance appeals, there are strong incentives to discourage them and their attorneys from appealing and to encourage judges to support the judgments of the referees. We emphasize that it is an unusual and unwholesome practice to have judges sitting in review of their own appointees.

PERSONNEL

Bankruptcy cases are managed partly by public officers and employees (referees in bankruptcy and their clerks), partly by officers elected or appointed in court (trustees and receivers), and partly by the attorneys for the debtors and creditors. We consider now the methods by which these participants are chosen, used, and paid.

REFEREES IN BANKRUPTCY

Before the 1940 report by the Attorney General's Committee on Bankruptcy Administration and the consequent enactment of the Referees' Salary Act of 1946, referees were employed on a different basis than now. Although appointed by district judges, as at present, referees were far more numerous (470 on December 31, 1939); mainly part-time (378 on that date);[9] paid out of the estate in each case on a fee basis; and appointed for a two-year term. The committee stressed the advantages of establishing a corps (a more expert, less distracted corps) of referees, and as a result the act stipulated that referees be salaried officials, appointed for a renewable six-year term. They have tenure of a sort, that is, they may be dismissed during a term only for cause. As of June 30, 1969, there were 183 full-time referees, 35 part-time, and 7 vacant positions. When workload increases in bankruptcy courts, part-time referee positions are converted to full-time.

Selection of referees. The Bankruptcy Act imposes only modest qualification requirements (unless the first one is interpreted rigorously) to guide district judges in choosing referees. An appointee is required (1) to be competent to perform the duties of a referee; (2) not to hold paid office in federal, state, or local govern-

9. *Administration of the Bankruptcy Act*, Report of the Attorney General's Committee on Bankruptcy Administration, 1940 (1941), p. 64.

ment (with some exceptions); (3) not to be related to a district or appellate judge; (4) to be a resident of his district; and (5) to be a member of the bar of his district. There is no requirement, statutory or other, that he be experienced in bankruptcy or that his qualifications and character be investigated.

When a full-time referee position is created or becomes vacant, a part-time referee is sometimes appointed to it. During the period July 1, 1947, through June 30, 1966, 24 percent of the full-time referee appointments were made in this way (58 out of 238). At the time of their conversion to full-time status, these referees had served a median of eight years part-time.[10]

Most of the referees were in their forties and fifties when first appointed.[11] A special study of their previous occupations (see Table 8-2) showed that more than half of the full-time referees had been in private practice. Approximately one-third had been in federal service.

TABLE 8-2. *Positions Held by Referees in Bankruptcy before First Appointment, as of June 30, 1969*[a]
In percent

Position	All districts	Eight districts in study
U.S. Attorney's office	13	15
Clerk to federal judge	9	4
Other federal office	9	17
State or local judge	1	2
Other state or local office	7	4
Private practice	57	52
Other	1	0
Unknown	2	4

Source: Calculated from files in the Administrative Office of the U.S. Courts. Percentages do not add to 100 because of rounding.
a. Includes appointments to both part-time and full-time positions. There were 167 referees in all covered by this calculation; 46 in the eight districts under consideration.

When referees in the eight districts were asked how they were chosen, most of them said they had known a district judge for some time or had impressed him in some way. Of the 53 referees we inter-

10. From a special study made for this project by the Administrative Office of the U.S. Courts.
11. *Bankruptcy Legislation 1967*, Hearing before a Special Subcommittee of the Senate Committee on the Judiciary, 90 Cong. 1 sess. (1967), p. 23.

viewed, 46 percent were professionally known to the judge (in other ways than those now to be listed); 25 percent were recommended by political party officials; 21 percent "applied for the job"; 19 percent worked in the U.S. Attorney's office; 15 percent practiced bankruptcy law and thus came to the notice of the judge; 10 percent were recommended by another referee; 8 percent clerked for the judge; and 4 percent were recommended by a bar group.[12]

In Northern Illinois, referee appointments were formerly handled as matters of personal judicial patronage, each referee being selected by one of the judges and normally holding office only as long as the judge did. This practice changed in 1966, however, to provide for selection of each referee by a majority of all the judges, as required by the Bankruptcy Act.

Training. Since many of the referees were inexperienced in bankruptcy when appointed, they had to learn on the job from colleagues in those courts where there is more than one referee. Since 1964 the learning process has been aided by a series of seminars for new referees conducted by a "faculty" of experienced referees. Seminars are encouraged by the Judicial Conference and are held on official time at government expense. Each seminar lasts a week and includes discussion of the philosophy, background, and ethics of the bankruptcy process, as well as details of procedures. As in most types of training conferences, the participants are likely to learn from one another during meals and social gatherings as well as in the formal sessions.

Pay and benefits. Full-time referees are paid $30,000,[13] about the same as officials of the executive branch in grade GS-16, the third highest civil service pay grade. It is well below the $40,000 paid district judges but above the salaries paid clerks of courts.

The Bankruptcy Act places referees under the provisions of the Civil Service Retirement Act. Legislative efforts to give them the preferred treatment accorded congressmen and legislative branch employees—larger annuities for shorter periods of service—were opposed by the Civil Service Commission and not enacted. Referees do not earn annual or sick leave, as civil service employees do. Their pay continues during periods of vacation or illness, when their caseloads are handled by neighboring referees.

12. Multiple replies permitted.
13. Except for five with limited workloads, who receive $25,000.

Tenure and reasons for termination. Referees expect to be reappointed at the expiration of their six-year term, and frequently are; over half of the full-time referees have served more than six years. We found that full-time referees' tenure was shorter in 1969 than in 1940, although one of the purposes of the 1946 act was to make their positions more secure. Full-time referees in 1940 had median tenure of 9.8 years whereas in 1969 their median tenure was 8.2 years (for details, see Appendix Table c-20).

Retirement and death were found to be the most frequent reasons for termination of full-time referees. Resignation was the most common reason for part-time referees (see Appendix Table c-21). It is not known what part of the retirements or resignations were due to unsatisfactory performance, personality conflicts, or patronage.

Referees' own attitudes. Referees interviewed for this study appeared to be knowledgeable (except those newly appointed) and constructively interested in their work. In our judgment their competence varied widely. Understandably, nearly all of them gave affirmative answers to the question, "Should any changes be made with respect to the status or job security of referees?" Some of the suggestions dealt with their power: 49 percent said that they should have the title and powers of judges, and 12 percent thought they should be authorized to cite for contempt of court. Other ideas were concerned with their perquisites and status: 45 percent wanted longer terms; 16 percent mentioned that they should wear robes (some already do); 14 percent wanted higher salaries or expense allowances; 8 percent wanted to be under a merit system; and 4 percent desired presidential appointments. Despite these comments, they expressed general satisfaction with their jobs. Some said that they had welcomed their appointment either as an economic improvement or as a relief from the pressures and more irregular working hours of other types of legal work.

CLERKS AND SECRETARIES

Work on correspondence, forms, and files in the referees' offices is done by about 850 clerks and secretaries, paid at various levels between $6,000 and $12,000.[14] They are not under civil service regulations governing selection and salary, nor do they have tenure.

14. As of July 1971.

They do, however, have the same leave and retirement privileges as regular civil service employees. They are hired by the referees, but their titles and pay grades are determined on the basis of difficulty of work by the Personnel Division of the Administrative Office, which thereafter gives them minimal attention. It is difficult to see why these employees should not be fully under civil service.

RECEIVERS, TRUSTEES, ATTORNEYS, AND OTHERS

We have already discussed (in Chapters 5 and 7) the election or appointment of receivers and trustees, noting that when a referee chooses a receiver, he often continues the same person as trustee. Of the referees interviewed, 43 percent said that they chose trustees from a list of five or less; 22 percent used one "standing" trustee (this was the invariable practice in Northern Illinois at the time of the field research);[15] 20 percent chose from a list of ten or less, and other replies were fragmentary. In general, therefore, trustees tend to come from a small group known to the referee or to the creditors' attorneys.

The trustees interviewed were experienced, devoting a major portion of their time to bankruptcy. Asked how long they had been serving as trustees, 83 percent of elected and 93 percent of appointed trustees said they had served from two to more than five years. Of the time spent on bankruptcy, the typical trustee devotes between 80 and 90 percent to trustee duties, though many spend less. Being attorney for other trustees or attorney for debtors or creditors is likely to occupy the remaining time.

Chapter XIII trustees. In wage earner cases, trustees function largely as collectors and disbursing agents. By Supreme Court rule, they may be standing trustees. They need not be lawyers; in fact, no qualifications are prescribed. When referees were asked what qualities they seek in appointing them, the most frequent answers were (in this order): honesty, knowledge of accounting, administrative ability, sympathy for debtors, diligence, and knowledge of bankruptcy procedure. Most of the trustees interviewed had some acquaintance with their referees or judges before they were appointed. Most were experienced in their work: nine of the sixteen

---

15. This is a practice contrary to frequently stated policies of the Judicial Conference and to rules of the Supreme Court (General Order 14).

interviewed had served five years or more, and five had served two to five years. Six spent nearly all their time on bankruptcy work; the rest, widely varying amounts of time.

Appraisers, auctioneers, and accountants. The use of persons in these categories depends on the size and complexity of the cases. In our straight bankruptcy sample, they were used in the following percentages of the cases:

	Asset	Business	Former business	Non-business	All
Appraisers	41	42	16	6.0	13.0
Auctioneers	14	18	3	0.3	3.0
Accountants	7	10	0	0.0	1.5

Interviews showed that all except two (accountants) had had long association with bankruptcy matters, some of them for thirty, forty, or even sixty years. Most did *not* spend a major portion of their time on bankruptcy cases. Nearly all said their appointments had been suggested by the receiver or trustee.

Attorneys. The dominant influence exerted on the bankruptcy process by attorneys has been brought out in earlier chapters. Most trustees, many receivers, and all attorneys for creditors' committees are chosen from among attorneys for creditors, so many lawyers play more than one part. There is clearly a specialized "bankruptcy bar" in the districts studied. Its existence was acknowledged by all but one of the federal judges interviewed and by most of the attorneys, and was evident to the Brookings research staff in their interviewing and visits to bankruptcy courts. When judges and attorneys were asked about the repute of the "bankruptcy bar," replies were inconclusive, but at least a quarter of each group interviewed commented on the low esteem in which bankruptcy lawyers are held.

Earlier chapters have shown the indifferent quality of guidance given to personal bankrupts by attorneys. In our judgment it is entirely feasible for many debtors in personal bankruptcies to do without attorneys. (Many taxpayers take up problems with the Internal Revenue Service without the aid of counsel.) Debtors whose cases are such that they should stay out of bankruptcy could be advised and helped on budgeting, refinancing, and working out repayment plans by disinterested nonprofit credit counseling agencies[16] or by a suitable government office. A proposal for such service can be found in Chapter 10.

COMMENTS ON PERSONNEL

Looking at the interrelations of all these people as a personnel system, we draw some unfavorable conclusions. Referees, selected by judges on a personal-political patronage basis, try to bother the judges as little as possible with bankruptcy matters—which is the way the judges want it. Referees can grant favors to attorneys or withhold them. Attorneys, either as individuals or as the organized bar, can by their behavior and their comments affect the referees' reputation and future. Trustees, and their attorneys, must perform in a way that will at once remunerate them satisfactorily, keep creditors reasonably satisfied, and fit the referees' policies and methods. Appraisers, auctioneers, accountants, and others employed to help liquidate estates must satisfy the trustee and referee.

This system runs by means of a series of mutual accommodations, exchanges of favors, and resolutions of pressures. Each of the participants behaves in a way that will enhance his own security and maximize his gains. Fortunately, some of the pressures are conducive to reasonable competence in performance and maintenance of tolerable ethical standards. Publicized instances of criminal behavior or of gross incompetence may cause reactions from the judiciary, bar associations, Congress, and the public. There are opposing pressures, however, that result in slack performance or that work against the best interests of debtors, creditors, and the general public. Debtors' attorneys could doubtless work out many composition or extension agreements or common-law assignments; in wage earner cases they could challenge many shaky liens or overvalued items of collateral, but they would have to do more work with little likelihood of return. Trustees could be dispensed with in many low-asset cases—but then who would take care of the trustees?

In short, a philosophy of "don't rock the boat" or "let's take care of one another" prevails. There are few incentives in the present situation for high standards of performance, and resources for supervision and inspection are too scanty to achieve significant change.

16. Such assistance is less likely to be helpful if the agency is dominated by creditors.

PROCEDURES AND FORMS

In earlier chapters we noted inadequacies in records and delays in procedures. The total bankruptcy system is generally inefficient from the standpoint of paperwork procedure. This system, which processes some 200,000 cases a year, most of them with many routine, repetitive elements, at a total administrative cost of over $37 million,[17] offers many unrealized opportunities for speeding up, routinizing, and standardizing the work. What are the reasons for this backwardness, and what does it consist of?

First, bankruptcy cases are handled as if they were adversary proceedings. Although this gives all interests an opportunity to be heard in court and to bring in evidence, it becomes a sham in tens of thousands of routine cases where creditors neither appear nor are represented, and where debtors' attorneys are either absent or silent. Almost every one of the bankruptcy cases observed or analyzed by the research staff could have been handled with more speed and equal justice as administrative proceedings, with recourse to the courts available in disputed matters.

Second, the various courts have issued rules reflecting differences in their operating policies and in practices of the bar in their vicinity. This results in a proliferation of local forms and in local variations of the official forms approved by the Supreme Court.

Third, the general policy of judicial independence has contributed to neglect of effective paperwork management. Reluctance to tell judges how to run their business, as noted earlier, has held the Administrative Office back, both in its own staffing and in developing an aggressive approach to red-tape matters in the bankruptcy courts. Yet judges, in the words of former Chief Justice Earl Warren, "no longer have the time or even the competence to play the role of administrator."[18] Nor do referees or clerks of the court have such time or competence. (The chief justice noted that the clerks "still operate much as they have throughout our history.")[19]

For the management problems of the judicial branch as a whole, the new Federal Judicial Center offers some hope for future im-

17. Sum of Referees' Salary and Expense Fund obligations plus costs of administration paid from estates in fiscal year 1968.
18. Address at sesquicentennial banquet, Harvard Law School (Sept. 23, 1967; processed), p. 14.
19. Ibid., p. 4.

provement. This center is governed by a high-level judicial board comparable to the Judicial Conference and chaired by the chief justice. Its director ranks with federal judges. The center's task is to improve judicial administration through research, administrative recommendations, and education and training. The governing board is instructed to, among other things, "study and determine ways in which automatic data processing and systems procedures may be applied to the administration of justice in the courts of the United States."[20] Several studies of court caseload, work measurement, data processing, and general systems analysis have been undertaken.[21]

It is already clear, however, that bankruptcy administration will have a low priority in the work of the center. A questionnaire "aimed at eliciting the views of the judiciary on the most critical areas of judicial administration" was sent to all federal judges in December 1968. The judges were asked to indicate their interest in and view of the importance of twelve topics, one of which was "training of referees in bankruptcy," designed in part "to bring about the use of standard forms and procedures." When the results were in, this item ranked next-to-last in both priority and interest.[22] The center should not be regarded, therefore, as the salvation of the administratively defective bankruptcy process.

ADMINISTRATIVE OFFICE FORMS AND PROCEDURES

The mishmash of paperwork involved in a typical small-asset bankruptcy is shown in the following actual example. The case took nearly two years, cost the estate $80 in fees and expenses,[23] and brought the creditors $67. The estate consisted of $147 in nonexempt wages. The file contained the following forms, affidavits, and letters, shown in the order in which they appeared in the file (note that some documents are undated and some are out of order):

Sept. 13, 1961 (form): Debtor's Petition
Sept. 13, 1961 (form): Statement of Affairs with Schedules

20. 28 U.S.C. 623.
21. See *The Third Branch: A Bulletin of the Federal Courts*, Vol. 1 (July 1969), and subsequent issues.
22. "Report on Responses of Federal Judges to Questionnaire on Program for Federal Judicial Center" (1969; processed).
23. In addition, the bankrupt had previously paid his lawyer $150.

Dec. 8, 1961 (typed): Amendment to Schedule A-2

Undated (form): Referee's Certified Record of Proceedings

Sept. 13, 1961 (typed): Poverty affidavit concerning inability to pay filing fees

Oct. 9, 1961 (form): Order for First Meeting of Creditors

Oct. 9, 1961 (form): Notice of First Meeting of Creditors

Oct. 9, 1961 (form): Certificate of Mailing

Undated (typed): Letter to debtor's attorney to have debtor present at first meeting

Oct. 25, 1961 (form): Order Approving Appointment of Trustee

Oct. 25, 1961 (form): Order Allowing Claims

Oct. 25, 1961 (form): Referee's Record of Examination

Oct. 25, 1961 (form): Order for Payment of Filing Fees in Installments

Oct. 25, 1961 (form): Bond of Trustee

Oct. 26, 1961 (form): Order Approving Bond of Trustee

Oct. 25, 1961 (form): Trustee's Report of Exempt Property

Dec. 8, 1961 (typed): Application to Amend Petition

Undated (typed): Order Authorizing Bankrupt to Amend Schedule A-2

Undated (typed): Notice to Creditors Omitted from Original Schedule

Feb. 23, 1962 (form): Precipe for Subpoena [on bankrupt's former partner]

Feb. 15, 1962 (typed): Order on Bankrupt to Appear for Further Examination

Undated (typed): Application for Turnover Order [wages]

March 6, 1962 (typed): Order to Show Cause [on above application]

June 5, 1962 (form): Order Fixing Time for Objections to Discharge

June 5, 1962 (form): Notice of Order Fixing Time for Objections to Discharge

June 5, 1962 (form): Certificate of Mailing

Sept. 11, 1962 (form): Discharge of Bankrupt

May 29, 1963 (form): Order Allowing Claims

June 10, 1963 (form): Notice of Meeting of Creditors

June 10, 1963 (form): Certificate of Mailing

Undated (typed): Trustee's First Report and Application for Compensation

Undated (typed): Affidavit concerning additional work performed by trustee

June 24, 1963 (typed): Order Approving Reports and Allowing Fees and Expenses

June 24, 1963 (form): Order for trustee to pay fees and expenses

June 24, 1963 (form): Order for Payment of Dividends

Undated (typed): Trustee's Final Report

July 5, 1963 (form): Notice of Final Meeting of Creditors

July 5, 1963 (form): Certificate of Mailing

May 28, 1963 (mimeo.): Referee's Work Sheet

July 16, 1963 (form): Order Approving Trustee's Report of Exemptions

July 16, 1963 (form): Order Approving Account, Discharging Trustee, and Closing Estate

This much-ado-about-little mass of papers was used in a relatively brisk and straightforward proceeding. A case with substantial assets may take double the time and triple the paperwork.

The degree of pointless effort in some cases becomes both pathetic and humorous. The following documents, all listing the same basic information, were used in another case, where a junk automobile was sold for ten dollars:

Trustee's petition for sale of personal property;
Referee's order for sale;
Trustee's report of sale;
Referee's order confirming sale.

Each paper was separately typed, signed, and filed.

Yet some work has been done to plan bankruptcy paperwork. The Administrative Office has designed and prescribed a series of forms needed to determine the nature, progress, and status of a case, and to audit it when closed. Instructions for the use of such forms appear in the "Manual for Referees," and the forms are stocked in the Administrative Office for requisitioning by referees and clerks of the court.

One report (called "JS-19") has been part of a long-term problem. This form is the source of the annual statistics published by the Administrative Office on volume, dollar value, and costs. The office has encountered difficulty for years in getting referees to submit this report promptly, completely, and accurately. Referees in turn have trouble getting trustees to submit complete reports. The problem has led to the issuance of increasingly detailed instructions by the Administrative Office.[24]

Other documents, known as "Official Forms" and approved by the Supreme Court, are stocked by the Administrative Office for use by the bankruptcy courts. These forms cover the most common steps in a bankruptcy case from beginning to end. Some of them are voluminous and difficult to use, like the schedules appended to the debtor's petition. (These are prepared in triplicate and must be notarized in several places, and every copy of every page must be signed by the debtor.) Most of the forms, being legal communications, are in the format of orders, notices, and pleadings. Routine or repetitive information is typed again and again in spaces whose

24. "Manual for Referees," pp. 702.01–702.13 (rev. August 1969) and pp. 702.14–702.15 (rev. August 1970).

placement is dictated by phraseology rather than clerical efficiency. The bankrupt's name, address, occupation, case number, and date of filing may be typed scores, even hundreds, of times in a case.

In fiscal year 1967 an electronic computer using magnetic tape was installed in the Administrative Office for processing bankruptcy caseload and cost statistics as well as for other purposes. Before this machine can be used to full advantage the basic procedures and source documents need to be redesigned.

One example shows that small procedural shortcuts of the most obvious type can result in impressive savings of effort and money. Public Law 89-166, approved September 2, 1965, rescinded a requirement that filing fees must be paid in full before the court could fix a time for the filing of objections to discharge. This made it possible to combine the notice of first meeting with the notice of the time limit for filing discharge objections. Elimination of the latter resulted in a saving of $150,000 annually, according to an estimate by the chief of the Bankruptcy Division.

BANKRUPTCY FILES

When a bankruptcy case is opened a "traveling file folder" is prepared by the clerk of the court. All documents pertaining to the case are required to be fastened into the file in chronological order. Our project staff, abstracting data from more than 1,600 files in the eight districts, found that the files were seriously deficient in two ways.

First, and less important, they were clerically sloppy in most of the districts. The instruction to put papers in chronological order was not followed with any precision, many files contained useless duplicate copies of documents, and entries on forms were often illegible.

Second, and more important, much information was missing and some was too grossly presented. It was difficult to tell what happened (surely one purpose of keeping files) in several stages of many cases.

Some examples of information most frequently missing are:

The age and basis of the debts;

The nature of property claimed as exempt;

Identity, numbers, and categories of creditors present or represented at first meetings and subsequent proceedings;

Information about examinations of a bankrupt: who was examined, who participated, what subjects were covered, what the result was;

Circumstance of sales: public or private; who participated; who bought; appraised values of property sold;

What happened to property securing debts;

Detailed information about property sold, repossessed, or abandoned (such cursory entries as "inventory and equipment, $50,000" were not uncommon);

The outcome of motions, applications, and petitions filed;

Numbers and amounts of claims of different classes proved and allowed.

These omissions occur largely because debtors' and creditors' attorneys "can't be bothered." The lawyers tend to do the minimum necessary to get the case completed, distributions and administrative costs paid, and the debtor discharged. Higher standards are not enforced by referees, who are under pressure from the Administrative Office to keep cases moving. They are required to report reasons for cases taking more than eighteen months and to report on matters that they themselves have had under advisement for more than sixty days. They and the attorneys, therefore, push cases through with only modest regard for completeness, accuracy, and intelligibility of records.

Despite this emphasis on speed, the bankruptcy courts have not been able to make their total processing of cases more rapid over the years. In fiscal years 1958 through 1969 pending cases were around 90 percent of new filings, ranging from 83.7 percent in 1959 to 96.6 percent in 1969.[25]

WHAT CAN BE DONE

The main tribute that can be paid to the procedures of the bankruptcy courts is that they are not backlogged. Processing begins when petitions are filed. After that, procedures slow down, as shown in Chapters 5 and 7. Excessive amounts of time are allowed

25. Administrative Office of the U.S. Courts, "Tables of Bankruptcy Statistics" (1969; processed), p. 12.

for proving claims, discovering and liquidating property, ordering discharges, and making final accountings and distributions. Thus, assets are tied up unnecessarily and the status of debtors kept unresolved for too long. Nevertheless, the situation is far more favorable than that in many state and federal courts, where civil litigants must wait years for their cases to be heard.[26]

Time and manpower are clearly wasted by the archaic paperwork procedures of the bankruptcy courts. Even if the courts should retain all their present functions (see Chapter 10), the paperwork system should be completely redesigned. The basic procedures are so standardized that they could readily be adapted to modern data processing and storage equipment. The systems of the Social Security Administration and the Internal Revenue Service could serve as partial models.

The data in the original petitions, statements of affairs, and schedules could be prepared on standard, precoded forms, punched, and entered at once in a computer tape (or disc) file maintained either in a central data processing facility for the Administrative Office or in a regional computer. (Servicing by the equipment of another government agency might be arranged.) The file could be kept up to date by the submission of precoded card forms reporting claims proved, assets realized, discharges granted, and allowances and distributions approved. Notices, reports, and payments to creditors, debtors, tax authorities, and courts could be printed out by machine. Statistical reports, current to within a few days, could be produced on any desired schedule to show counts of cases by category, time consumed in administration, debt structure, realizations, costs, distributions, and any other data. Such information not only would expedite the processing and reporting of cases but would have other management values. Sources of delay or error could be caught. Personnel could be assigned promptly to deal with overloads. Such a systems redesign would force the Judicial Conference to make difficult decisions about the extent of procedural standardization to be required.

Some starts have already been made toward a more modern bankruptcy processing and information system. Chapter 5 mentioned the automated procedures for Chapter XIII cases in Bir-

26. See examples in Joseph D. Tydings, "A Fresh Approach to Judicial Administration," *Judicature*, Vol. 50 (August–September 1966), pp. 44–45.

172   BANKRUPTCY

mingham, Alabama, and Kansas City, Kansas. As of October 1969, the Kansas City facility was handling a total of 15,911 active straight bankruptcy and Chapter XIII cases for twenty-seven referees in twenty-six different locations.[27] It has developed programs for sending notices of first meetings to creditors and for preparing lists of creditors' claims and the record of the proceedings.

In Lexington, Kentucky, a pilot project for automated processing of straight bankruptcy no-asset cases was begun in November 1967, with excess costs underwritten by the Administrative Office. Data are prepared on punched paper tape in the referee's office, then fed into a local commercial computer for processing. Another experiment in Chattanooga, Tennessee, was begun in fiscal 1970 under a similar funding arrangement.

CONCLUSION

The tone of disparagement running through this administrative analysis may surprise or irritate readers who are accustomed to the operating methods of the judiciary. The bankruptcy system, however, is in most cases not a genuine judicial enterprise. It is a large-scale example of routine administrative machinery. As such it is appallingly archaic and ineffective, and its location in the courts imposes special conditions and difficulties. Bankruptcy is not unique in this respect, for probate, guardianship, and other court duties could also be considered administrative functions of the judiciary.

Even if the present bankruptcy procedures served some useful purpose—a condition on which Chapters 5 and 7 cast doubt—the system is substandard. Operating authority has been liberally decentralized to referees who are not chosen by reason of merit, who receive little training and virtually no supervision, and whose work is rarely, and then only superficially, reviewed. Paperwork procedures are antiquated and wasteful. Such a combination is intolerable, and a thorough reorganization is needed.

27. Letter from Claude L. Rice, bankruptcy attorney and a proprietor of Electronic Processing, Inc., Kansas City, Oct. 7, 1969.

9

---·◈·---

Financing the Bankruptcy System

What does it cost to administer bankruptcy cases? Who pays? These have been controversial questions over the years. Most of the controversy is over how much of the estate is taken for trustees, attorneys, and others, and how much is left for creditors. There are other features to be treated, however, in any review of bankruptcy costs. Such costs are financed in four ways: first, from general revenues of the United States government; second, from the Referees' Salary and Expense Fund (which receives payments both from filing fees and from estates); third, by payments from estates in bankruptcy; and fourth, by direct payments from debtors and creditors to their attorneys or, as part of debtors' filing fees, to trustees and court clerks.

COSTS FINANCED FROM GENERAL REVENUES

Smallest of these categories is bankruptcy costs financed from the Treasury. The largest segment is the salaries and expenses of the Bankruptcy Division and of other parts of the Administrative Office. For fiscal year 1969 these expenses were about $2 a case closed, or around $380,000 altogether. (For earlier years, see Appendix Table c-22.) This amount is a minor fraction—less than 0.5 percent—of total estates in bankruptcy.

173

In the district courts the salaries and most of the expenses of the judges, the clerks of the court, and their staffs are also financed from general revenues.[1] It is very hard to judge what part of these costs should be attributed to bankruptcy. A district judge, for example, may spend a negligible amount of his time on bankruptcy in one year—review a few reports, approve a few fees, or decide two or three cases on petition for review. In the next year he may be tied up for months in a complex reorganization or a hotly contested liquidation. Since judges only recently started keeping time records, it has not been possible to determine what part of their salaries and expenses are properly bankruptcy costs. Another group of hidden expenses consists of space costs (heat, light, cleaning service, and so forth) when bankruptcy courts are located in federal buildings.

Better estimates can be made in the offices of clerks of the court because some employees spend all of their time (or a major portion of it) on bankruptcy. In six of the districts researched the clerks (emphasizing that they were estimates) provided the following figures for fiscal year 1967:

	Bankruptcy case costs	Cost per case filed
Southern New York	$23,000	$22
Maine	10,000	6
Northern Alabama	21,000	3
Northern Ohio	29,000	3
Oregon	12,000	3
Southern California	35,000–40,000	2

COSTS FINANCED FROM THE REFEREES' SALARY AND EXPENSE FUND

The Referees' Salary and Expense Fund, established by the 1946 amendments to the Bankruptcy Act, is fed by a portion of the filing fees in all types of cases, plus percentage charges in asset and nominal-asset cases and special relief chapter cases (see Appendix Table c-23 for details).

Congress appropriates from the Fund to pay the salaries of ref-

1. As an exception to this rule, however, clerks receive a portion of filing fees to help pay their expenses: $3 (formerly $8) in straight bankruptcy cases, $3 in Chapter XIs, and $5 in Chapter XIIIs.

erees and their clerks, plus benefits, travel, supplies, and equipment. The accumulated surplus in the Fund was $1.5 million on June 30, 1970. In fiscal year 1970 $11.0 million was received and $15.6 million obligated, the fifth consecutive deficit year.[2] The deficits continued despite an effort to bring receipts and expenditures into balance through legislation that turned over to the Fund an additional $5 of the filing fees in straight bankruptcy, Chapter XI, and Chapter XII cases.[3]

Costs paid out of the Fund in the eight districts in the present study are shown in Appendix Table c-24. The average of such costs per case terminated for the eight rose 40 percent from 1964 to 1969, from $45 to $63 a case.

COSTS PAID FROM ESTATES

By far the largest share of administrative expenses comes from the estates in bankruptcy. This category accordingly receives the greatest attention of the Administrative Office, the courts, and the bar.

NOMINAL-ASSET CASES

By definition nominal-asset cases are those in which costs of administration use up all of the estate. Such cases have been running 11 to 15 percent of the number of straight bankruptcy cases in recent years.[4]

The lion's share in these cases went to the trustees, who received 44 percent of disbursements in all districts, according to the official statistics. In the districts we studied, trustees received 75 percent in Maine, 58 percent in Northern Ohio, and less in the others.[5] (Appendix Table c-25 provides the details of these and other variations in practice among the districts.) As another example, attorneys for

2. *Reports of the Proceedings of the Judicial Conference of the United States* and *Annual Report of the Director of the Administrative Office of the United States Courts* (1970), p. 201.

3. P.L. 90-161, Nov. 28, 1967.

4. Computed from "Tables of Bankruptcy Statistics" (1964–68), Table F 4a. Dismissed cases were excluded from the computations.

5. The dollar figures for average total expenses and the percentages shown for trustees' commissions *do not include* the $10 statutory fee for trustees paid as part of the filing fee. This sum is not considered part of the estate.

bankrupts received 46 percent in the sample cases from Oregon, but not more than 20 percent in any of the other sample districts. Expenses are shared among more different participants in the bankruptcy process in Northern Illinois and in Southern New York than in the other districts, where most of the money goes to trustees, bankrupts' attorneys, trustees' attorneys, and the Referees' Salary and Expense Fund.

ASSET CASES

Asset cases (which number about 11 to 13 percent of straight bankruptcies[6]) vary enormously in size and complexity. A similar variation is found in the amount, proportion, and makeup of costs of administration. In the smallest cases, resulting in payment of a few dollars to a tax collector or a zealous store, administrative expenses take a very large part of the estate and consist mainly of fees to trustees and attorneys. There would be more such high-cost, low-distribution cases if it were not for the pressure exerted by the Judicial Conference and the Administrative Office to keep cost percentages down. (Numerous interviewees spoke of 25 percent of estates as a rule-of-thumb applied by judges and by the Administrative Office for the expenses of administration.) If a referee sees, for example, that a case with an estate of $400 would show $320 in costs and $80 in distributions to creditors, he has an incentive to pay out the entire $400 in costs (thus turning it into a nominal-asset case), rather than report it as an asset case with administrative costs of 80 percent.

In the largest cases costs may be a smaller fraction of the estate but may include sizable payments to receivers, trustees, attorneys, appraisers, auctioneers, court reporters, landlords, and others.

On the average, costs of administration throughout the United States are about 25 percent of the amounts brought into the estates. During fiscal years 1964 through 1968, they ranged from a low of 22.8 percent in 1967 to a high of 26.6 percent in 1964, according to the official statistics. For the eight districts in the present study costs were closer to 30 percent, on the basis of both government statistics and those of this study. Government figures for fiscal year 1964

6. Computed from "Tables of Bankruptcy Statistics" (1964–68), Table F 4a. Dismissed cases were excluded from the computations.

TABLE 9-1. *Costs of Administration in Bankruptcy Asset and Chapter XI Cases as a Percentage of Estates, by District, Fiscal Year 1964*

	Costs	
District	Bankruptcy asset	Chapter XI
Northern Illinois	52.1[a]	15.0
Northern Ohio	35.9	12.1
Oregon	31.5	—[b]
Southern New York	30.4[c]	26.8
Maine	30.0	20.5
Western Texas	24.5	—[b]
Southern California	19.4	29.4
Northern Alabama	17.4	9.8
Average	29.3	24.9

Source: File sample of business, personal, and Chapter XI cases.
a. This unusually large figure results from the inclusion of operating costs in a large Chapter XI case, later adjudicated. Adjustment to eliminate this factor reduces the Northern Illinois average cost to 30.5 percent and the overall average of asset cases to 25.8 percent.
b. There were no Chapter XI cases in this district.
c. Business asset cases only.

show costs of administration for all districts to be 26.6 percent, and for the eight districts studied here, 30.5 percent.[7] Costs for the asset and Chapter XI file cases in our sample are shown in Table 9-1.

In straight bankruptcies, the largest share of these costs, 5.7 percent of estates, went to attorneys for trustees.[8] Next were trustees, 4.1 percent, and auctioneers, 2.4 percent. The entire list appears in Appendix Table c-26. Attorneys generally receive the greater part of the money spent for administrative costs. Auctioneers, accountants, appraisers, and others receive significant shares of estates only in the larger (and usually more complex) straight bankruptcy cases.

CHAPTER XI CASES

We found costs to be lower in Chapter XI cases than in straight bankruptcies in almost every sample district (see Table 9-1).[9]

7. "Tables of Bankruptcy Statistics," Table F 7, for the years concerned.
8. Not counting 7.7 percent in a category labeled "other." This was principally costs of business operation for Chapter XI cases in Northern Illinois (including one particularly large one) which were later adjudicated. Such costs could of course have been reduced by earlier adjudication.
9. The Administrative Office does not publish data on fees and expenses in Chapter XIs despite the fact that these cases tend to be larger and more expensive (in dollars) than straight bankruptcies.

There are three reasons. First, estates are usually large. Second, attorneys and others who might be entitled to allowances (which would be recorded as expenses of administration) may waive their allowances in order to speed up confirmation and free their cases from court control. (They are then paid directly by the debtors and creditors.) Third, in those cases in which the debtor is left in possession of the business there are no payments to a receiver or trustee or to their attorneys.

Nonetheless, attorneys' fees and expenses made up the greater part of these costs, notably 10.2 percent of estates to debtors' attorneys and 3.0 percent to attorneys for creditors' committees (see Appendix Table c-27 for full list of cost components).

CHAPTER XIII CASES

In wage earner cases cost-of-administration percentages were generally smaller than in straight bankruptcies, except in Southern California:[10]

	Percent
Northern Ohio	24
Western Texas (two cases)	22
Southern California	21
Northern Illinois	20
Northern Alabama	16
Oregon	16
Maine	15
Seven districts	17
Excluding Northern Alabama	22

These costs consisted almost entirely of payments to trustees (7.4 percent), debtors' attorneys (5.4 percent), and the Referees' Salary and Expense Fund (3.7 percent).[11]

CHAPTERS XII AND X

We can supply only a few examples of administrative cost payments in cases under these two chapters. The Chapter XIIs tend to provide for payments over extended periods of time. As a result,

10. Only business cases were considered in Southern New York.
11. Bases for these percentages and those in the table above are total amounts of estates in cases in which payments were made to creditors.

amounts paid to creditors upon confirmation were comparatively small. For instance, in the cases mentioned on pages 109 and 115, administrative expense totaled $2,100 when creditors of the construction business received $7,800; $19,500 (most of which was for operating expense during the case) when creditors of the doctor's ranch received $12,000; and $8,000 when creditors of the motel received $59,000.

Administrative expenses in the General Stores proceeding under Chapter X, however, totaled $380,000—still only 12 percent of the estate. Among those paid were:

The trustee and his attorney—$182,000;

The trustee for secured creditors—$117,000 (largely for management of the two drug subsidiaries during the proceedings);

The debtor's attorney—$32,000 (in addition to $12,500 paid directly by the debtor before the petition was filed);

Attorneys for stockholders—$12,800 (they initiated move to transfer from Chapter XI to Chapter X);

The attorney for another stockholder—$12,000 (after stockholder provided the $3,200,000 to finance plan).

FEES AND EXPENSES RECEIVED BY TRUSTEES AND ATTORNEYS

Before total costs of administration are summed up and evaluated, we should analyze further the amounts of fees and expenses paid to trustees and attorneys and the ways these amounts are determined.

TRUSTEES' COMPENSATION

Fees and expenses paid to trustees in straight bankruptcy cases were small, as might be expected from the prevalence of small cases. In 34 percent of the sample cases in which trustees were paid they received less than $50; in 54 percent, less than $100; in 82 percent, less than $200; and in 94 percent, less than $500.[12] These small pay-

---

12. These amounts do not include the $10 trustees receive from the debtor's filing fee.

ments are sometimes ludicrous. One Oregon trustee, for example, received a total of $36 for four cases; another, $132 for six. Fortunately they had other means of support. Other trustees handled more lucrative cases, like one in Western Texas, who received $2,738 for seven cases, or a Southern California trustee who was paid $4,283 for five cases. High-volume, routinized straight bankruptcy trusteeships were observed in several districts, notably Northern Illinois, where one trustee handled twenty-seven of the cases in the Brookings sample, receiving $2,303, and another administered seventeen for $1,834.[13] Each of the Northern Illinois referees appointed "his own" trustee, who did all, or nearly all, of the trustee work for that referee.

Under the Bankruptcy Act (Section 659), trustees in Chapter XIII cases are paid "actual and necessary costs and expenses" and commissions of not more than 5 percent of amounts paid out. It became apparent years ago that trustees could earn large incomes from commissions alone, and the project staff learned of two cases of income between $40,000 and $50,000. (If a trustee handled a thousand cases a year disbursing $80 a month on the average, his commissions at 5 percent could amount to $48,000.) Such high fees were anomalous when referees were receiving a maximum of $22,500, so the Judicial Conference in September 1963 decreed that Chapter XIII trustees' compensation should not exceed referees' compensation (now $30,000).

Expense money is paid in different ways within and among the eight districts. Most trustees received a percentage (from 3 to 7 percent) of amounts paid out to creditors. One trustee was paid $1.50 a month for each case; another received $25 every time he made a group of disbursements to creditors, there usually being five such payments. Three districts reimbursed trustees for actual itemized expenses.

Trustees tempted to make money on these expenses are inhibited by several safeguards: audit of their accounts; a requirement that referees certify expenses; questioning of doubtful expenses by the Bankruptcy Division; and issuance of comparative studies that "point the finger" at high-cost trustees.

When expenses are added to commissions, costs per case still tend

13. All of these trustees received considerably more because they served and were paid as receivers in some of these cases.

to be low. In our sample, median payments to Chapter XIII trustees for fees plus expenses were:[14]

Southern California	$130
Oregon	87
Maine	74
Northern Illinois	53
Northern Alabama	41
Northern Ohio	33
Median, six districts	45
Median, excluding Northern Alabama	84

In 55 percent of the cases in which trustees were paid, they received less than $50; in 78 percent, less than $100; in 93 percent, less than $200; and in 98 percent, less than $300.

ATTORNEYS' COMPENSATION

Fees allowed the various categories of attorneys were the subject of many of our interview questions and tabulations. In analyzing attorneys' compensation, we refer *both* to payments from estates and to payments from debtors and creditors. No data were gathered, however, on fees charged by creditors' attorneys, and estimating what they received is difficult. Creditors' attorneys are paid on any of three bases: fee for services, contingency, or retainer. No matter how paid, the fee for the bankruptcy proceedings may be inextricable from fees for collection efforts or for representation in state courts. All this remuneration is *in addition to* what creditors' attorneys may receive from the estate for serving as receiver, trustee, attorney for receiver, attorney for trustee, attorney for petitioning creditors, or for some other service. In large, complex business cases, creditors' attorneys may earn fees in four or five figures. In small cases they will earn little. In personal bankruptcies, the attorney for one creditor (such as a finance company or department store) may appear in court in several cases at once and will have developed an economical office routine for filing claims. This makes it possible for him to charge each creditor a relatively low fee.

Judgments on fee setting. The Bankruptcy Act requires referees to

14. Western Texas is omitted because there were too few cases to be significant. The average cost a case for all trustees in the country was $54 in fiscal 1967, a weighted average computed from cost study tables prepared by the Bankruptcy Division.

rule on the reasonableness of attorneys' fees.[15] Referees and attorneys for debtors and creditors were asked what factors should be, and are, considered by referees in approving fees. Both emphasized the quantity and quality of work done, rather than fixed scales or percentages. Most named productivity, assets brought into the estate, time spent, amount and difficulty of the work, and skill exhibited in handling the case, in roughly that order. A few based fees on a percentage of the estate or on the bar association fee schedule. There were various other responses, including "personal relationship between referee and attorney." About one-quarter of the referees said they authorized only nominal fees for debtors' attorneys, since otherwise they would in effect be paid by creditors.

Efforts to apply these factors inevitably result in wide differences in judgment among referees. This was convincingly demonstrated in a practice exercise at one of the seminars held for new referees. The thirty-seven referees present were asked to set fees in each of twenty-two hypothetical cases in which work performed by attorneys was described. The results in four cases of different sizes are shown in Table 9-2. Recall that the enormous discrepancies were all based on the same sets of facts and were all the work of incumbent (though recently appointed) referees in bankruptcy.

TABLE 9-2. *Variations in Attorneys' Fees Set by Thirty-seven Referees in Four Hypothetical Cases*
In dollars

Ranking of fees set	Case 1	Case 2	Case 10A[a]	Case 14B
Highest	2,000	8,650	1,150	10,300
Tenth	900	3,500	400	7,000
Nineteenth	750	2,000	200	5,500
Twenty-eighth	650	1,268	100	3,725
Lowest	350	600	50	1,500

Source: Exercise papers from seminar for new referees. The numbering of the cases is as it appeared in the exercise.
a. Only thirty-three referees set fees in this case.

The referee, whether his judgment is consistent or scattered, severe or lenient, cannot always get the truth about the amount of time actually spent by an attorney. He may suspect that a request

15. He decides on fees paid from the estate to various attorneys. He *may* rule on fees paid outside the estate to debtors' attorneys on his own initiative and is required to do so if requested by the bankrupt, the trustee, or any creditor.

for allowance is "padded," but cannot prove it.[16] Thus he must base his decisions on a combination of personal impressions and observed results in relation to the size of the estate. All this adds up to a chaotic and indefensible way of setting pay for performance of an important public function.

Most of the debtors' attorneys interviewed certainly did not feel that review of their fees by the courts was zealous or excessive. Asked "What has been your experience in having your compensation reviewed by the bankruptcy court?" 47 percent said, "Never happens"; 22 percent said, "Very little experience"; 12 percent said, "Always reviewed"; 5 percent, "Larger fees critically reviewed"; and 14 percent gave miscellaneous replies.

Attorneys administering straight bankruptcy estates. According to the court files we reviewed, attorneys for receivers were paid in only 2.6 percent of the straight bankruptcy cases. The median amount they received for fees and expenses was $326; the mean, $924. Payments to attorneys for receivers were largely (87 percent) below $1,000. The need for such attorneys' services varies more with the nature of the case than with the size of the estate.

Attorneys for trustees were paid more often (in 10.3 percent of the cases). Here again most of the fees were small: 80 percent below $1,000; 66 percent below $500; and 42 percent below $200. The median was $303; the mean, $1,252.

Debtors' attorneys. Our interviews with sixty-eight attorneys and four hundred debtors showed that debtors' attorneys are paid according to various arrangements that depend on their own wishes and on their clients' circumstances. In about two cases out of five the lawyers require payment in full at the start of a proceeding. More often there is some form of periodic payment, either "cash down, balance in installments," "monthly or weekly payments," or whenever the debtor can pay something. If the debtor uses Chapter XIII or Chapter XI, his attorney is often paid through the court, along with the creditors.[17] Less frequently, attorneys are paid in full at the end of each case.

16. One surprisingly candid attorney spoke of such practices as reporting two hours for fifteen minutes of work and reporting work on different cases aggregating forty hours in one day.

17. Debtors' attorneys were paid from estates in 84 percent of the cases in our Chapter XIII file sample, and in 31 percent of the Chapter XI sample.

Attorneys often complained, without stating amounts, that debtors and bankrupts did not pay in full. Of our 400 interviewed debtors, 12 percent acknowledged that they still owed their lawyers
something. The amounts due ranged from $25 to $300, with a
median of $72.

How much were debtors' attorneys paid? This is shown in various
ways in Table 9-3: what the case files say the attorneys charged and
were paid; what the attorneys we interviewed said they charged;
and what the debtors interviewed said they paid.[18] Note that the
median amount paid, according to the case files, was $145, though
nearly $200 was charged. The median amount paid from the estate
(and this occurred in 13 percent of the straight bankruptcy asset
cases in our sample) was $130. Debtors interviewed, however, said
that they paid their attorneys a median of $161. Fees were largest in
Southern New York (where only business cases were studied) and
Western Texas (where there were few personal bankruptcies). In
the remaining districts fees charged were considerably higher in
Northern Ohio and Northern Illinois than in the other districts.
Remember that Chapter XIIIs made up 74 percent of the cases
in Northern Alabama, where it is customary to charge only $25 or
$50, with additional fees for debts later added to the plans.[19] In all
districts, Chapter XIII debtors paid their lawyers less than straight
bankrupts did, even though Chapter XIIIs normally require more
work: preparing the original plan and modifications and challenging claims.

When straight bankruptcy fees paid are analyzed according to
whether they are in business or personal (nonbusiness or former-
business) cases, the averages are:

18. The reader will recall that the files are of cases closed in fiscal year 1964 and
that attorneys and debtors were interviewed in 1966. He should also know that some
attorneys do not report advance payments from clients in straight bankruptcy cases,
and referees do not insist that they do so. Also, the amounts shown in the table do not
include fees paid for other legal services occasioned by financial difficulties that pre-
ceded bankruptcy: defense in state court suits, action on attachments and garnishments,
and other advice and help.

19. The median fee levels discussed in this section are somewhat understated because
of the way fees for spouse filings were treated. When one fee was paid for two petitions,
the fee was divided in half for tabulation because there was no clear indication of how
much was paid for the husband and how much for the wife. In reality it is common
practice to charge more for the first petition than for the second (for example, $200 for
the husband, plus $100 for the wife).

TABLE 9-3. *Fees Charged by and Paid to Attorneys for Debtors, by Type of Case and District*
In dollars

District	Straight bankruptcy			Chapter XIII			
	Median fee charged[a]	Median fee paid[b]	Commonest fee of attorneys interviewed[c]	Median fee charged[a]	Median fee paid[b]	Commonest fee of attorneys interviewed[c]	Median fee paid, according to debtors[d]
Southern New York[e]	750	625	—	—	—	—	—
Western Texas	347	238	250	200	200	200, 350	187
Northern Illinois	242	143	300	243	109	300, 325	262
Northern Ohio	234	102	250	119	91	125, 200, 225	197
Southern California	173	167	250	221	180	200, 275	144
Northern Alabama	157	149	100	46	46	100	37
Maine	146	138	150, 200	84	82	75, 100	128
Oregon	138	127	150	133	119	150, 200	131
Eight districts	196	145	—	—	—	—	—
All except Southern New York	195	143	150, 250	54	51	100, 200	161[f]

Sources: Cols. 1, 2, 4, and 5—bankruptcy and Chapter XIII case files; cols. 3 and 6—Brookings staff interviews with debtors' attorneys; col. 7—interviews by Chilton Research Services with bankrupts and debtors.

a. Payments from debtor, plus payments from estate, plus amounts still owing.
b. Payments from debtor, plus payments from estate.
c. Modes. Personal bankruptcies only.
d. Personal straight bankruptcies *and* Chapter XIIIs.
e. Business bankruptcies only.
f. Plus median of $72 still owing.

Cases	Median	Mean
Nonbusiness	$129	$141
Former business	139	156
Business	299	570

(Note the effect of the larger cases on the means.) For the relatively few Chapter XI cases in the file sample, fees were scattered in a wide range from under $500 to over $250,000, with a median of approximately $3,000.[20]

In each district some attorneys were interviewed or observed in court who had a high-volume practice of no-asset or low-asset cases. They had reduced these to a routine, using standard forms filled out by their office clerks. At a charge of $200 a case, such attorneys can gross $50,000 a year on 250 cases—about one each working day —or $100,000 on two a day. Since several of these attorneys had more clients than that, or charged more, they could easily gross $200,000 or more annually. (Not all fees, of course, are paid in full— see Table 9-3.)

The "monopoly" question. Concern has been expressed by the Judicial Conference and critics of the bankruptcy system about the concentration of lucrative bankruptcy practice in the hands of relatively few law firms. To throw light on this question, a special analysis of payments to attorneys in cases in the Brookings sample was made. With some exceptions, the results are not conclusive.[21]

In all eight districts there were numerous firms each of which handled only one case in the Brookings sample, generally as attorneys for bankrupts or for Chapter XIII debtors. Examples are:

District	Number of cases studied	Number of firms handling only one case
Southern California	337	119
Oregon	250	74
Northern Ohio	195	88

20. This covers only the cases in which debtors' attorneys were paid from estates— about one-third of the sample.

21. In this discussion the term "firm" is used to denote either a law firm or an individual attorney or a combination of firms or attorneys who worked as a unit on a particular case. For sampling reasons, the findings here are illustrative or indicative rather than fully representative of practice in the districts studied. The sampling process was based on types of cases (for example, straight bankruptcy nominal asset or Chapter XIII dismissed) within districts and did not take account of certain other variables. Some firms, for example, work only in certain cities, some accept only substantial business cases, and others specialize in representing small debtors.

Generally such firms were used in small cases and earned small or average fees. A few, however, received high payments: one in Los Angeles made $3,627, one in Chicago, $10,000, and one in San Antonio, $1,250, for instance.

Our sample contains no conclusive evidence of "monopoly" of cases except in Cleveland, Ohio. There one combine of firms (in varying groupings) earned $65,994 from 38 cases in the sample of 203. In some of these cases attorneys from the group served in several different capacities: attorney for the debtor, receiver, distributing agent, and attorney for the receiver. In other cases it was not unusual for one attorney from the group, having been appointed trustee, to have his partner named attorney for the trustee. The group accepted bankruptcy cases of all sizes in its practice.

Aside from this instance there was no clear pattern of concentration of large-fee cases in certain firms. In Northern Ohio and in the other districts there were instances of a firm's handling only one large-fee case (defined for this purpose as $1,000 or more) in the sample. Others worked on two, three, four, or more. Some of the firms mixed small and medium-sized cases with the large ones; some did not. Some instances from the sample include:

Southern California	Firm A	5 cases	$ 3,500 (Chapter XI)
			361
			91 (nominal asset)
			200
			2,500
	Firm B	1 case	5,325
Western Texas	Firm A	2 cases	4,485
			10,163
	Firm B	3 cases	200 (nominal asset)
			1,250
			1,000
Northern Illinois	Firm A	2 cases	11,075
			12,575
	Firm B	3 cases	310
			536
			1,405

We do not say that undue concentration of large-fee cases is uncommon, only that our sample shows little of it.

Large-volume, small-fee firms have been mentioned above. One in Chicago worked on nine cases for $2,562. A firm in Portland,

188   BANKRUPTCY

Oregon, received $1,776 for twenty-two cases; one in El Paso, $2,028 for nine; one in Santa Ana, California, $4,752 for twenty-nine. A firm in Birmingham, Alabama, received $2,316 for work on fifty-one cases, all Chapter XIII.

In general, the distribution of both number of cases and size of fees among law firms is so diverse as to be meaningless. Because of the relative scarcity of large-fee cases, a definitive analysis of the problem would require larger samples, designed for this purpose and representing a longer period of time.

PAYMENTS TO OTHERS

Appraisers' fees and expenses tended to be small (78 percent under $50) because so much of their work consisted of appraising automobiles and household goods. The median payment from the estate was $32. Auctioneers, who are generally not used in small cases but who earn commissions in liquidating substantial businesses, earned a median of $518 from estates. Twenty-nine percent of the payments were under $100; 37 percent between $1,000 and $5,000. Accountants' fees and expenses varied greatly in amount around a median of $599.

RECAPITULATING STRAIGHT BANKRUPTCY COSTS

All these costs and payments are varied and complex. It may be helpful to simplify the summary by listing costs of administration of a typical straight bankruptcy and the share paid by each party to the proceeding (see Table 9-4). The case is assumed to be the median straight bankruptcy asset case in the Brookings sample, with an estate of $549,[22] closed in fiscal year 1964. From the estate itself, $175 (or 32 percent) is paid for salaries and expenses of the referee's office and payments to personnel who administer the estate. Outside the estate, an additional $116 is paid by the debtor for filing fees and attorneys' services. On the assumption that this amount would otherwise be part of the estate, the total cost is $291 (or 44 percent) out of a total available amount of $665 ($549 estate plus $116 out-

22. This figure has not been used earlier in this book because it was computed from both personal and business bankruptcy cases. Median estate figures for each category appear in Chapters 5 and 7, respectively.

TABLE 9-4. *Recapitulation of Costs in a Median Asset Case Closed in Fiscal Year 1964*

Component of cost	How paid	Who pays	Cost[a] (dollars)
Portion of salaries and expenses of referees and their clerks paid from estate	Referees' Salary and Expense Fund	Creditors	14 (2.6%)
Fees and expenses of receivers, trustees, debtors' attorneys, and others paid from estate	From estate, as approved by referee	Creditors[b]	161 (29.3%)
Total costs paid from estate			175 (31.9%)
Remainder of estate			374 (68.1%)
Total estate			549 (100.0%)
Portion of salaries and expenses of referees and their clerks not paid from estate	Referees' Salary and Expense Fund[c]	Debtor	32[d] (27.6%)
Clerk of court	Portion of filing fee	Debtor	8[e] (6.9%)
Trustee	Portion of filing fee	Debtor	10 (8.6%)
Fee to debtor's attorney	Direct obligation	Debtor[f]	66 (56.9%)
Total costs paid outside estate			116 (100.0%)
Total available amount (line 5 + line 10)			665 (100.0%)
Total costs paid (line 3 + line 10)[g]			291 (43.8%)

Source: File sample of business and personal bankruptcy cases.

a. Numbers in parentheses are percentages of the base amounts shown for each category.

b. If it is assumed that this is money creditors would otherwise receive and that the estate would have been conserved equally well without receivers, trustees, and so forth.

c. The Fund keeps portions of filing fees in all cases (see p. 174 and Appendix Table C-23).

d. Since changed to $37.

e. Since changed to $3.

f. $196 (median fee charged; see Table 9-3) less $130 (median amount paid from estate; see p. 184). The $196 is a low figure because it includes charges in no-asset and nominal-asset as well as asset cases. Charges would be higher in asset cases but were not tabulated separately.

g. Excluding expenses of federal courts, paid by taxpayers, of approximately $2, and fees or retainers of unknown amount paid attorneys by creditors.

side). Approximately $2 is spent from general revenues for expenses of the federal courts, most of which goes to the Bankruptcy Division. And there are direct payments by creditors for attorneys' services in an unknown amount.

GENERAL EVALUATION OF COSTS AND FINANCING

Two important and difficult questions may be asked about the costs of bankruptcy. Are they at an appropriate level—too high, about right, or too low? And are they properly assessed as to benefits, obligations, and incentives?

LEVELS OF COST

Are bankruptcy costs too high? The question is difficult because there is no good standard of comparison. The answer lies somewhere between "Probably yes" and "It all depends." Most of the participants in the bankruptcy process—judges, referees, attorneys, trustees, and even debtors and creditors—did not criticize costs as being too high. Some had an interest in the present system; others had no basis for suggesting anything else. When costs are judged as percentages of estates (whether one uses the 32 percent paid from estates or the 44 percent that includes other costs[23]) the answer is still not clear.

We tried to get cost data from other federal organizations engaged in acquiring and liquidating property under conditions roughly comparable to those of the bankruptcy courts, but the results cannot be relied on. The Veterans Administration, selling real estate acquired through the loan guaranty program, had an average cost of 15 percent in fiscal year 1966, but agency overhead costs were not included. The Federal Housing Administration, selling real estate acquired by foreclosure from 1961 to 1967, had costs of about 20 percent, but many questions could be raised about the cost factors included. The Small Business Administration spends about 10 percent of the gross selling price on preserving and selling property acquired after a loan goes bad, but this does not include foreclosure costs. All these organizations deal only with their own claims and do not have to locate other property or be concerned about proof

23. See Table 9-4.

of other claims, as bankruptcy courts do.[24] So bankruptcy costs may or may not be high for a government operation.

It may be more appropriate to consider that 33 percent is the typical contingent fee received by attorneys in damage suits. Lawyers take many such cases and receive nothing. Similarly, in over 70 percent of bankruptcy cases there is nothing available for compensation but $10 from the filing fee. Thus the pay of those who administer the system must come from estates in the rest of the cases. By this standard bankruptcy costs are not high. We simply point out that it is an odd and inequitable way to help finance a large-scale, nationwide government processing operation.

Costs must certainly be high if the judgment is based on organization and efficiency factors. Cost levels are not critically reviewed by Department of Justice examiners and not reviewed at all by congressional committees or by the General Accounting Office.

Only two types of pressure help keep costs as low as they are. First, admonitions are addressed to judges and referees by the Judicial Conference and the Administrative Office. This pressure is mainly hortatory; referees' courts where costs are rising or relatively high are identified in cost studies distributed throughout the system, and the referee is visited or written to. A referee who wants his record of costs to look good can help himself in various ways. He can, as we noted earlier, turn a high-cost low-asset case into a nominal-asset case. He can also allow exemptions so generous that a case becomes no-asset. More straightforwardly, he can hold down allowances and commissions, can hold sales in court instead of using auctioneers, and can insist on genuinely competitive bidding for assets.

Second, zeal and pressure by creditors to receive distributions should help control costs. As earlier chapters demonstrated, however, creditor control is more make-believe than real. Bankruptcy cases are controlled by the bankruptcy bar and by referees. The former have strong incentives to keep costs up; the latter have only

24. Other even less comparable figures were obtained from the Office of Alien Property (insolvencies not involved); the Federal Deposit Insurance Corporation (assets are very liquid); and the Tennessee Valley Authority (sale of federal lands). Unsuccessful efforts were also made to get comparable cost figures from the General Services Administration, the Federal Savings and Loan Insurance Corporation, the Farmers Home Administration, and the Farm Credit Administration.

mild incentives to keep them down. And the obsolete paperwork methods detailed in Chapter 8 are a further barrier to cost reduction. Expenses of administration could be reduced or better service given to debtors and creditors for the same price. Some proposals will be outlined in Chapter 10.

WHO SHOULD PAY?

Bankruptcy costs are paid mainly by debtors and creditors— debtors paying the largest part in small cases and creditors carrying the load in large cases. (The taxpayer, as reported above, makes a very modest contribution to governmental overhead expenses.) Creditors are able to pass their share on to their other customers and, by deducting bad debts from business expenses, to taxpayers.

One defect of the present self-supporting system is that the large cases are paying in some degree for the small cases. Trustees in small cases are poorly paid for their time, but they recoup when serving as trustees or particularly as attorneys for trustees in large ones. This may lead referees to make or approve appointments on a remedial rather than a merit basis. The solution to this problem is the use of public officials, selected in accordance with merit principles, instead of trustees. As for filing fees and payments from estates to the Salary and Expense Fund, in our judgment small cases are *not* being carried by the larger ones. Each small case brings in at least $37 to the Fund. Most of them require only a few minutes of the referee's office and court time.

The clear intent of the Bankruptcy Act is that most of the costs be paid by the parties. The apparent rationale is that other citizens are not involved in the proceeding. In this respect bankruptcy is comparable to state probate proceedings, whose expenses (except for judges' salaries in most states) are paid out of decedents' estates.

But here rationality ends, at least in the financing of federal judicial proceedings. Bankruptcy alone among such proceedings is self-supporting of salaries and other administrative expenses. In ordinary civil cases a filing fee of $15 is charged. Thus bankruptcy cases are financed by insolvent debtors and by creditors who are losing assets, yet one great corporation can sue another at a cost of $15.[25]

25. Plus other minor costs (for example, for service of papers) paid by the losing party to the suit.

The general pattern of financing court proceedings in the United States since about 1800 has been to have the public assume the costs of maintaining the courts and to have litigating parties pay their own attorneys' fees. Little scholarly work has been done on the legal and economic theory of financing litigation, and none of it is useful in the present context. We can only conclude that, as long as bankruptcy is a judicial process and as long as other judicial processes are conducted at public expense, it is manifestly unfair for the parties in bankruptcy to bear the costs.

If bankruptcy is instead regarded as a governmental process comparable to other processes carried on by federal adjudicative or service agencies, there is still no clear guidance. Consistency of principle, though not of practice, obtains in the executive branch, where "user charges" are assessed under government-wide law and regulations. A Bureau of the Budget circular states: "Where a service (or privilege) provides special benefits to an identifiable recipient above and beyond those which accrue to the public at large, a charge should be imposed to recover the full cost to the Federal Government of rendering that service."[26] Under this authority federal agencies charge or fail to charge fees for a large variety of services—health, recreation, transportation, use of natural resources, and others. Each decision about such fees, whether it is a legislative or executive decision, requires a balancing of private interests against the public interest.

Finding patterns of practice that are applicable to the bankruptcy process is difficult. Among the regulatory agencies there is a growing tendency to charge fees for licenses, authorizations to do business, or certifications of various kinds. Such fees are imposed by the Federal Power Commission, the Federal Communications Commission, the Securities and Exchange Commission, the Interstate Commerce Commission, the Civil Aeronautics Board, and the Federal Aviation Administration. In most of these agencies higher fees are charged for more complex findings, but it is not claimed that the fees fully support the cost of the government service.[27]

Some other government services that may help prevent or help resolve disputes are supported by the taxpayers. The Federal Medi-

26. Circular No. A-25 (Sept. 23, 1959), p. 1. For the governing law, see 5 U.S.C. 140.
27. However, costs of administering Part 1 of the Federal Power Act are borne by licensees.

ation and Conciliation Service does not charge fees; nor do the National Labor Relations Board and the Board of Veterans Appeals. The Tax Court of the United States charges only a $10 filing fee.

The assessment of fees and other costs to parties in bankruptcy proceedings may be defended on the ground that they are receiving special services not provided other citizens. Under this argument, the debtors' discharges and the creditors' distributions from the debtors' estates can be considered special benefits. Such an assessment may also be defended by a more severe philosophy: to the extent that bankruptcy cases result from imprudent credit transactions, the costs should be borne by the parties to such transactions. (Of course, prudent transactions are also reflected in bankruptcy debt schedules.)

The gist of the opposing argument is that bankruptcy proceedings should, like other government remedies provided for citizens in trouble and citizens in disagreement, be financed by all taxpayers. This argument maintains that people in bankruptcy courts are merely unfortunate victims of a credit system from which all citizens benefit and that therefore all citizens should pay for the process.

We conclude that the bankruptcy process should be financed through tax funds. In the vast majority of bankruptcies (no-asset or low-asset cases) a service is performed that gives relief to citizens in difficulty. This is an appropriate function to carry out at public expense. The less frequent cases in which disputes between debtors and creditors are resolved should, like other controversies decided by courts or administrative agencies, be financed by the public also.

THE REFEREES' SALARY AND EXPENSE FUND

Even if the bankruptcy system should remain self-supporting, it does not follow that the Salary and Expense Fund is necessary. The Fund was expedient in the transition from paying referees on a fee basis to paying them a salary, but this device is no longer required. Fees and charges could now be paid to the U.S. Treasury and treated as miscellaneous receipts without going into a special revolving fund. (Many other types of fees are treated in this way, for example, charges paid to the Public Health Service by immigrants for medical examinations.) Such receipts would, as now, be factors considered in making appropriations for expenses of administration. A surplus in the Fund has been defended on the ground that it assures money to maintain the bankruptcy system in periods when filings might decline (as they did in 1968–69) and fees and charges are too low to support the courts.

Such a defense is not persuasive. It is the duty of Congress to appropriate annually at a suitable level for any needed court or agency. The maintenance of the Salary and Expense Fund simply causes unnecessary bookkeeping in both the Treasury and the Administrative Office. The Fund should be abolished as part of any revision of provisions for financing the bankruptcy system—or sooner. The Judicial Conference has recommended legislation to this end, and the matter is under consideration by Congress.

10

Toward a More Serviceable System

Bankruptcy is bad by definition—a negative concept connoting failure and broken agreements. Bankruptcy is bad for the debtor: he loses property (if he has any nonexempt property); he may feel stigmatized; and he has difficulty obtaining low-cost credit. It is bad for the creditor, who loses money he presumably expected to collect. It is bad for governments and taxpayers: losses are written off and potential revenues unrealized. The term has even become a metaphor for ruin or unpleasant finality—"the mayor's political career is bankrupt." The Gallup survey (see Appendix A, section 4) gives further evidence of this cultural attitude.

But the results of bankruptcy are not necessarily all bad for all creditors and debtors. Creditors have anticipated bad-debt losses in their pricing, and they receive the tax advantages of write-offs. Debtors get rid of their unsecured debts—unless they revive them— and are occasionally rehabilitated under the provisions of Chapters X, XI, XII, and XIII.[1]

On balance, however, the high tide of bankruptcies has properly been viewed as unfortunate. The losses of property and income are aggravated by costs of collection efforts and later of bankruptcy

1. Throughout this chapter we will continue to use such terms as Chapter X, XI, XII, or XIII for the sake of brevity and clarity. Obviously, if the Bankruptcy Act is repealed and completely rewritten, the numerical citations would be changed. Also note that this study does not deal with the rarely used Chapter IX and Section 77 of the Bankruptcy Act.

196

proceedings. The social and emotional costs are also significant: frustration, fear, mistrust, anger, broken relationships.

Yet we have seen that bankruptcy is inevitable and necessary. The process ends a deteriorating but unresolved situation so that those involved can make a fresh start. As long as there is a large volume of credit, some credit will go bad and formal remedies will have to be sought. Any nation whose trade is based on credit, even in part, must provide for legal recognition of insolvency.

THE GENERAL PROBLEM AND ITS SOLUTION

The total bankruptcy system gets its job done according to the literal requirements of the law, but it is a dreary, costly, slow, and unproductive process. Compared to what the system might be doing, the present reality is a shabby and indifferent effort. The research reported in earlier chapters shows:

Baffling inequities from one state to another, one court to another, in what gets a debtor into court, what form of relief he is given, what property is taken from him, what he pays, and how well he is protected afterward.

Casual representation of debtors by attorneys disinclined to examine the validity of liens or the valuation of security, or to protect the debtor after bankruptcy, and who handle the bankruptcy process without imagination.

Inadequate incentives for creditors to be provident in extending credit or to participate in bankruptcy proceedings when such credit goes bad.

Use of the adversary procedure for matters in which there is little or no adversary interest.

Business bankruptcy cases usually managed without significant help from or benefit to the creditors.

Management by a coalition of referees, trustees, and the bankruptcy bar which is of little benefit to debtors, creditors, or the public. Management characterized by loose supervision, infrequent field examinations, little concern for qualifications of personnel, archaic procedures, high costs, and unwarranted delays.

These shortcomings are a natural result of using a judicial system to try to solve problems that are by nature administrative. The judicial system relies on adversary procedure and on judges who are for the most part not highly skilled in the supervision of bankruptcy matters or in the selection of expert referees.

We grant that most participants in the bankruptcy process are honest, that most referees acquire competence in their work, that many have labored long and earnestly to remedy inequities to both debtors and creditors, that the Administrative Office strives constantly for improved performance, and that the referees' offices are not backlogged. Things could be worse, but we must focus on how they can be made better.

Modest improvements have been made in the years since World War II, and more could be done within the present system. The Bankruptcy Act could be amended, for example, to require that referees be chosen competitively and tested on their knowledge of bankruptcy before they are appointed, and that all estates be administered by standing trustees of proven expertness, chosen competitively and supervised rigorously. The Judicial Conference could adopt policies requiring referees to provide for detailed scrutiny of all claims and liens; it could require more stringent limits on costs of administration. There could be more thorough standardization of procedures from one court to another and modernization of the total paperwork system. Appropriations could be increased to permit a larger staff for the Administrative Office and more Department of Justice examiners.

Such changes would increase the efficiency of the work and of the service given both debtors and creditors. Yet they would not alter materially the supremacy of the district courts over the bankruptcy process, their lack of interest in it, their independence, their habituation to patronage, and their resistance to coordination, standardization, and procedural change. Nor would such approaches alter the fact that use of adversary procedure by private practitioners is a grossly inefficient way to administer estates in bankruptcy.

So widespread and so ingrained are the shortcomings of the present system that radical rather than incremental change is necessary. Tinkering with the Bankruptcy Act or with the budget of the bankruptcy courts will not do the job. Each minor change would need its own justification, attract its own opposition, encounter its own delays—all without challenging the approaches and tenets of the present system. Thorough innovation is needed: new incentives, new relationships, new organization, new statutory provisions, new procedures.

We recommend a completely new bankruptcy statute that will authorize or prescribe the major changes needed in the whole bankruptcy system: organization, financing, policy, and procedure. Only the principal points will be presented here. Refinements of language and procedure will have to be worked out by appropriate officials of the Department of Justice and by staffs of congressional committees. The new law should assure the greatest possible comprehensiveness yet ease of reference.

The policies, organization, and processes of the new system have been planned to achieve several objectives. First, it would encourage debtors and creditors to settle problems of insolvency outside the bankruptcy system; second, it would provide practical incentives and methods for insolvent debtors to pay their debts; third, it would deter creditors from extending improvident and unconscionable credit and yet afford them maximum returns on just and proper debts; fourth, it would make procedures speedy, economical, and resistant to error and fraud; and fifth, it would resolve controversies fairly in accordance with the law. Such objectives should be summarized in the preamble to the law. (There is no statement of purpose in the present Bankruptcy Act.)

ORGANIZATION OF A BANKRUPTCY AGENCY

The statute would authorize the President to establish a bankruptcy agency within the executive branch. This organization would do essentially the work now done by the courts of bankruptcy, plus the work of trustees, receivers, appraisers, accountants, auctioneers, and other auxiliary personnel.

AN EXECUTIVE AGENCY

Why an agency and why in the executive branch? Why should bankruptcy not be kept in the courts? Retention of this function by the judicial branch is defensible only if bankruptcy is regarded as primarily a judicial function—arranging for, making, and implementing decisions on disputed issues of fact or law between contending parties. We have seen, however, that bankruptcy problems are in most cases problems of guidance and management. The major need is for speedy, discriminating, understanding processing of about two hundred thousand small, largely uncontested cases each year. This is an administrative function rather than a judicial function, and it should be performed by a staff selected on a merit basis and aided by the most modern records management and data processing methods.[2]

The judicial branch, moreover, emphasizes the independence of the several courts and consequently de-emphasizes central management and services. Patronage (political or personal) is securely established in the judiciary as a method of personnel selection. Scrutiny of judicial branch functions by Congress and by the General Accounting Office has been extremely restrained. The agency is more likely to have efficient, well-controlled administration in the executive branch, where it would be under pressure (as are the present departments and agencies) to make good progress both in program development and in effective management and where it would receive help from the Office of Management and Budget, the Civil Service Commission, and other staff agencies. In the judicial branch the agency would be insulated from (and perhaps resistant to) such pressures and help.

INDEPENDENT STATUS

It is much easier to make a case for establishing the agency in the executive branch than to find a home for it among the departments there. We believe it should be independent, first, because its program should be given visibility and emphasis, and second, because none of the existing executive departments is a logical place to put it. Both the Department of Labor and the Department of Health, Education, and Welfare are concerned with wage earners and consumers, but neither department is a logical place for business bankruptcies. Another possibility is the Treasury, no stranger either to credit problems or to financial difficulties of individual citizens.

2. In the field of probate, which is comparable to bankruptcy in some respects, serious consideration is being given to use of administrative determinations in uncontested matters. See "Uniform Probate Code," *Law Quadrangle Notes* (Fall–Winter 1967–68), pp. 5–6. See also National Conference of Commissioners on Uniform State Laws, "Uniform Probate Code" (Chicago, 1967; processed.)

However, the bureau most familiar with such difficulties, the Internal Revenue Service, is involved as creditor in many bankruptcy cases, so there would be a conflict. The Department of Justice already examines bankruptcy courts and prosecutes bankruptcy crimes, but these are subsidiary interests, and it too represents the government as creditor. The Department of Commerce is more oriented to business than to individual citizens and hence could have (or be accused of) a creditor bias. We conclude that the agency should have independent status, as do agencies such as the Federal Deposit Insurance Corporation and the Small Business Administration.[3]

HEADQUARTERS ORGANIZATION

To concentrate authority and responsibility, the agency should be headed by a single director rather than several commissioners. This is an operating agency, not a regulatory agency, which might appropriately be a commission. The agency should also be highly decentralized, with all possible decisions made at or near the place where the bankruptcy petition is filed. The headquarters would provide overall management planning, staff guidance, and review of fieldwork. The director should be free to plan his organization as he judges best. Some such headquarters organization as this might be suitable:

Director and Deputy Director, to be responsible for the general direction of the agency.

Program Guidance Division (specialists in property management and liquidation, business management, and accounting), to be responsible for the preparation of guidance materials for field offices; assistance on bankruptcy legislation and rules; and expert advice to field offices as needed.

Field Operations Division (attorneys and credit specialists with management competence), to be responsible for general appraisal and inspection of field offices; trouble shooting; and supervision of office managers.

3. If the reorganization plan transmitted by President Nixon to Congress on March 25, 1971, should be enacted, the proposed bankruptcy agency could appropriately be placed in the recommended department of economic affairs. See President's Advisory Commission on Executive Organization, *Papers Relating to the President's Departmental Reorganization Program: A Reference Compilation* (March 1971).

Records and Systems Division (specialists in systems design and data processing), to be responsible for planning and maintaining a complete records system for the agency, including accounts and payments in Chapter XIII and XI cases. Would manage or have access to a data processing facility.

Administrative Division (specialists in budgeting, personnel administration, auditing, and office services), to be responsible for budget, personnel management, mail, supplies, equipment, and internal audit program.

Information and Reports Division (specialists in statistics, report preparation, and public relations), to be responsible for analysis of trends and preparation of statistical and narrative reports on the work of the agency.

Legal Division (attorneys), to be responsible for legal advice to the director and other headquarters officials; general guidance and problem solving for attorneys in field offices; drafting of bankruptcy legislation and rules; and representation of agency in necessary litigation.

Office of Hearing Examiners, to conduct field hearings as needed.

Board of Appeals (highly qualified hearing examiners), to decide contested matters appealed from examiners.

Office of Special Investigations, to investigate complaints and internal ethical problems.

Headquarters divisions should be small but staffed with highly qualified experts. The hearing examiners and the board of appeals would be independent of the director and other staff in their decision-making power. As noted later, decisions could be appealed to the circuit courts of appeal.

FIELD ORGANIZATION

The location, size, and precise duties of the various field offices would have to be decided after analyses had been made of the workload of all the present bankruptcy courts, with adjustments to reflect the new law and policies. Offices should be readily accessible to debtors and creditors so that both may be given the greatest possible protection and quickest possible service. The following general pattern of organization comprising three types of offices should be considered:

Centers. Ten or more relatively large offices staffed by a variety of specialists and located in cities (such as Chicago and Los Angeles) with a large volume of bankruptcies, including business bankruptcies of substantial size (estates of at least $50,000). Each center would have as many hearing examiners, estate managers, attorneys, accountants, financial counselors, interviewers, appraisers, hearing reporters, and clerks as its workload justified. Available on a part-time basis would be auctioneers and specialists in particular kinds of businesses. A center would also be a logical headquarters for members of the agency's internal audit and investigative staffs stationed in the field. The center's staff could maintain their own data processing facility, prepare source data for a facility in the headquarters, or be served by another federal facility.

Offices. Fifty or more smaller organizations located in cities with a fairly high volume of less complicated, largely uncontested cases (for example, Chattanooga, Tennessee; Madison, Wisconsin). Most consumer and small business cases would be concluded at that location. An office would be much smaller than a center. It would need a hearing examiner and financial counselor but would probably not require a full-time accountant.

Suboffices. Twenty or more offices located in cities where caseload is small but sufficient to justify minimum service on the basis of distribution of population and distance from other offices (examples are Charleston, South Carolina, and Pendleton, Oregon). Suboffices would be satellites of *offices* and would perform very limited functions: meeting with debtors to answer questions, advise on remedies, receive petitions, and prepare source documents for the records system. Each suboffice would be headed by a bankruptcy representative (interviewer-counselor), assisted by clerks. It would be visited as necessary by staff members from the nearest offices to conduct financial counseling, to liquidate estates, or to make decisions on confirmations, dismissals, discharges, and lesser contested matters.

PERSONNEL AND FINANCING

The agency's personnel would *not* be exempted from civil service, except for (1) its director and deputy director, who would be presidential appointees; (2) attorneys (who would be employed and compensated on the same basis as elsewhere in the executive branch, that is, subject to the Classification Act, but not to competitive appointment procedures); and (3) specialized experts needed intermittently, such as auctioneers, experts in particular fields of business, and consulting economists. Hearing examiners would be recruited and assigned by the Civil Service Commission, as in the case of other administrative agencies.

Expenses of administration would be financed from general appropriations. Any effort to estimate the agency's costs is necessarily speculative, but some gross estimates are presented in Appendix B, section 7. More specific, accurate "pricing" must depend on provisions of the law establishing the agency and on conditions prevailing at the time it is set up. The Referees' Salary and Expense Fund would be abolished. Fees for trustees, receivers, attorneys, and others would be eliminated because such work would be done by salaried agency personnel. Specialists employed intermittently would be paid on a per hour or per diem basis in accordance with the usual practice of executive agencies. Debtors and creditors who used their own attorneys would pay them outside the bankruptcy proceedings.

HOW THE AGENCY WOULD WORK

The agency director would be authorized by the new law to make those decisions now made by referees in bankruptcy. He would delegate much of the authority for day-by-day operations to appropriate field officials. The procedures of the agency would have much in common with those of the present referees' offices, but there would be extensive changes to increase speed, efficiency, equity for both debtors and creditors, and where possible, rehabilitation.

CHOICE OF PERSONAL BANKRUPTCY PROCEEDINGS

The debtor seeking relief would go in person to the nearest field office.[4] He might be accompanied by an attorney or the attorney might appear for him, but in the typical case he could be unrepresented. He would be interviewed by a trained bankruptcy rep-

4. Here we describe voluntary bankruptcy procedure. It would still be possible for creditors to file involuntary bankruptcy petitions at any office as they now do in courts of bankruptcy. See p. 212, below, for treatment of involuntary business cases.

resentative. If the debtor had enough information about his assets and debts with him, the bankruptcy representative would fill out a worksheet showing the debtor's situation: debts secured and unsecured; judgments, attachments, garnishments; property owned; family situation; family income; and other relevant information. If the debtor did not have the information he would be given an instruction sheet listing the types of information needed and asked to return it later. The representative, with or without complete information, would explain to the debtor possible courses of action, and their advantages and disadvantages: working out a solution with creditors without filing a bankruptcy proceeding; filing in straight bankruptcy; or filing a Chapter XIII petition. The representative would not choose the remedy but would advise the debtor, using guide materials developed by the agency staff.

If it seemed feasible to work out the problems without filing, the representative would suggest a course of action to the debtor—a rough budget and possible repayment plan. He should also suggest wherever possible a means of continuing aid through appropriate local agencies. The representative would not attempt detailed tactical guidance of the debtor (for example, "Better pay the bank first, then see if the appliance store will wait a month"). Debtors who stalled or wanted prolonged "nursing" would be advised of the gravity of their situation and the necessity for making a decision and following it up. If the debtor decided to file, the financial counseling services of the agency would be available as long as the case was pending.

STRAIGHT BANKRUPTCY

If the debtor's situation required, and if he selected, straight bankruptcy, his right to a discharge would continue. The representative would have advised him of the problems and consequences he might face: possible repossession of property covered by secured debts, efforts to get him to revive debts, difficulty in obtaining credit from high-quality, low-cost sources, and attempts to collect debts discharged.

The debtor would be required to pay a nominal filing fee (we suggest $15) or take a pauper's oath that he had no money for the fee. His petition would then be typed by an agency clerk on a standard form that could be easily coded for data processing. The information would be coded, punched, and fed into the agency's data system.

Appraisal. The case would then be turned over to a bankruptcy analyst, roughly equivalent to a trustee. (Such other titles as "bankruptcy officer" or "liquidator" might be considered.) He would study the case, investigate the bankrupt's assets (both exempt and nonexempt), and have all property claimed as exempt, as well as all collateral for secured claims, promptly appraised by a salaried appraiser. This provision would assure fairer administration of exemption provisions. A creditor would be treated as secured only to the extent that his claim actually *was* secured. When a secured creditor had already foreclosed on the collateral and obtained a deficiency judgment, the agency would determine the value of the collateral and allow the deficiency claim only in the amount by which the indebtedness exceeded the value of the collateral or the sale price, whichever was higher.[5]

Exemptions. These would be determined on the basis of a uniform, nationwide provision in the new law designed to permit the bankrupt to continue his occupation and to maintain a standard of living reasonably consistent with his occupation and previous history. Exemptions would include a homestead allowance up to a stated dollar limit (perhaps $20,000), plus another dollar limit (perhaps $3,000) covering clothing, household goods, tools of his trade, cash value of life insurance, a vehicle, and cash. To compensate for inflation, dollar amounts specified in the exemption provisions could be adjusted by the director of the bankruptcy agency in accordance with changes in the consumer price index. The agency would be empowered and expected to administer exemptions in such a way as to prevent the debtor from retaining luxury items. Exemptions would be approved as claimed by the debtor unless challenged by the bankruptcy analyst or creditors and reduced or disallowed by an examiner. This proposed exemption provision is more generous than those now in effect in most states, and would probably result in a higher proportion of no-asset cases.

5. This provision is among those recommended by the National Bankruptcy Conference. If a creditor had already received a determination in a nonbankruptcy court of record as to the amount of his deficiency, such a determination would of course be honored.

Notice to creditors. Next, a notice would be sent to creditors to tell them that (1) the petition had been filed; (2) the standard exemption would be allowed; (3) there appeared (or did not appear) to be assets that would enable some payments to be made on creditors' claims; (4) they were ordered to refrain from proceeding against the bankrupt's property or wages; (5) if they wished to examine the bankrupt's petition and submit written questions about their claims, they would have to do so within one week of receipt of the notice; (6) in the absence of objections the bankrupt would receive a discharge, and such discharge would be a bar to postbankruptcy collection actions;[6] and (7) any proofs of claims should be filed within thirty days of the date of the notice, unless there appeared to be no assets, in which event the notice would advise that creditors need not file claims. If assets were produced later in the proceeding, creditors would again be notified and would have thirty days in which to prove their claims.

The new statute would reduce from six months to thirty days the time allowed for creditors to prove claims, with exceptions to be granted by an agency examiner only in cases where special operating circumstances made it impossible to submit proof within the thirty days. This provision would help speed up the processing of cases.

Liquidation. The analyst would then abandon or liquidate nonexempt assets as appropriate. He might hold sales in the agency office or make arrangements with a local reputable auctioneer, depending on the nature of the property and the anticipated selling costs. (Auctioneers would be paid according to a fee schedule prescribed by the agency.) When it was necessary to order property into the estate, the analyst would have the order prepared and signed by a hearing examiner (unless there had already been a hearing before the examiner). Actions to void prebankruptcy transactions prohibited by the statute would be brought by the analyst, represented by an attorney from the legal division. Such actions would be heard by the hearing examiner unless the defendant demanded a jury trial before the federal district court.

Allowance of claims. In the absence of significant nonexempt assets, most creditors would not file claims. If no nonexempt assets

6. See discussion below, p. 210.

were found and no claims filed, the whole procedure would be shortened, and the notice of discharge could be sent out as soon as the thirty-day period had elapsed.

Claims that *were* submitted would be reviewed by the bankruptcy analyst if assets were sufficient to produce a distribution to creditors. He would review claims to determine the proper amount and class of debt, as at present. He would also, under new statutory provisions, determine whether a debt was unconscionable or whether extension of the credit to the particular debtor at the particular time was clearly improvident. If the analyst found unconscionability or improvidence, the case would go to a hearing examiner for decision on reduction or disallowance of the claims concerned. Such a decision could be based either on written presentations by the debtor or creditor or on a hearing. All parties would have access to guideline materials on unconscionability and improvidence prepared by the agency staff in consultation with experts in personal finance. These new provisions would help deter some outrageous debts that lead to bankruptcies and would help assure fair treatment for debtors and for their more ethical creditors.

Exceptions from discharge. Under the new law fewer types of claims would be excepted from discharge: only those for alimony and support and unscheduled debts of creditors who had had no notice of the proceeding. This would mean discharge of several kinds of debts now excepted: taxes not already dischargeable; debts resulting from false statements by the bankrupt; claims for willful or malicious injury; claims resulting from seduction, breach of promise, or adultery; claims resulting from fraud or embezzlement; wages earned by employees within the three months before the bankruptcy; and claims for moneys posted with the bankrupt to secure performance by an employee. Where the intent of such exceptions is to punish the debtor for his conduct (as for fraud or sexual irregularities), there are more appropriate sanctions and penalties available elsewhere in the laws. Where the intent is to prefer certain types of claims (as for taxes and wages), we submit that such provisions negate the purposes of bankruptcy proceedings. If an arrangement was feasible, these debts would be paid along with others. If the debtor's situation required a straight bankruptcy discharge, his "fresh start" would be impeded by the existence of such claims.

Denial of discharge. If creditors filed objections to discharge, they would be resolved by the hearing examiner. The new statute would provide that a discharge be denied only on the grounds of (1) fraud and uncooperativeness in the bankruptcy proceeding and (2) the debtor's having been granted a bankruptcy discharge within six years. (Confirmation of a composition arrangement would *not* be grounds for denying a discharge.) These changes would mean that prebankruptcy dishonesty or crime of any kind would no longer be grounds for denial of discharge. The debtor or bankrupt can be punished by more appropriate means under other federal and state laws. Discharge would be automatic unless challenged by the bankruptcy analyst or creditors and denied by an examiner.

Distribution. Once liquidation was completed, claims allowed, and dischargeability questions resolved, the analyst would prepare a distribution document on a standard form designed for use in the agency's data system. The data system would then prepare and address checks for creditors and a notice of discharge both to them and to the bankrupt.

Priorities in distribution would be changed by the new law. Administrative expenses would be paid out of general appropriations, and the statute would amend distribution priorities to exclude tax claims, claims due the federal government for matters other than taxes, and landlords' claims, leaving priority only for wage claims. This change would rectify inequities among creditors in the present priority provisions. A debtor's physician, grocer, or fuel dealer should have the same rights of recovery as his tax collector and landlord. The sovereignty of any level of government is insufficient reason for putting government claims ahead of other debts. If the reason for tax priorities is fairness to other taxpayers, this too is insufficient. Furthermore, the taxes collected under the priority rule are of no great value to the government, as pointed out in Chapter 7.

We recommend retention of wage priorities on the ground that employees, particularly at lower pay levels, have no real opportunity to appraise the employer's financial situation and thus need more protection than other creditors. But there should be no requirement that wages must have been earned within the three months before bankruptcy to be given priority. Instead, wages should have priority without time limit up to $1,500, which would be subject to changes in the consumer price index. (This increases the $600 limit now in Section 64a(2) of the Bankruptcy Act, as amended in 1938, by the same percentage as the rise in the consumer price index since that year.)

Postdischarge protection. The notice of discharge would also warn creditors against attempting postdischarge collection actions. The debtor's copy would explain that his discharge was a defense against efforts to collect debts scheduled in his bankruptcy proceeding and would encourage him to call on the agency for assistance if such efforts were made.

This procedure would be grounded on other new provisions of law: that a creditor who had notice of the proceeding must raise any objection to the discharge of his claims before the bankrupt's discharge is granted; that it shall be unlawful for such creditors to bring a subsequent action on discharged claims; and that the director of the bankruptcy agency may bring action to recover, for the debtor's (or bankrupt's) benefit, double the amount of the claim involved.

CHAPTER XIII

The new statute would broaden the scope of Chapter XIII by making it available to any noncorporate debtor, not merely wage earners. Many self-employed persons might readily pay their debts under a Chapter XIII arrangement.

If the debtor (employed or not) decided to submit a Chapter XIII petition, the procedure would be like that for straight bankruptcy in many respects. The petition would contain a proposed plan of repayment, worked out by the debtor and the bankruptcy representative. As soon as the petition was completed, the agency would appraise any collateral and value the security to aid in preparing the plan. The difference between the value of the security and the original claim would be treated as an unsecured debt.

The debtor would pay the same filing fee as a straight bankrupt. The notice to creditors would contain much the same information, too, but with these differences. First, it would include the proposed plan and state that the plan would be confirmed unless objected to in writing by a majority (in number and amount) of all creditors, and unless an examiner found that objecting creditors could not reasonably expect to receive the fair value of their claims. (Objecting creditors would be included in the plan unless this finding was made.) Second, creditors with secured claims would be allowed the fair value of their security. (The agency, as in the case of straight bankruptcies, would have authority to reduce or disallow claims on grounds of unconscionability, improvidence, or other invalidity.) Third, only wages or other income would be subject to the plan, and there would be no need for allowance of exemptions. Fourth, the debtor would receive a discharge upon successful completion of the plan or upon decision that his failure to complete it was due to circumstances beyond his control.

The preparation and confirmation of the plan under the new law would be made more equitable by several changes. The proceeding would (1) include claims secured by real estate for the purpose of rectifying defaults and meeting payments that became due during the proceeding; and (2) allow confirmation of a plan if there was a finding that it adequately provided for payment to creditors of the value of their claims and that it provided equal treatment for each creditor of the same class.[7] Change (1) would provide more complete coverage of the debtor's affairs by the plan. Change (2) would prevent a single secured creditor or a majority of a class of unsecured creditors from blocking confirmation of what might be a feasible plan.

After the plan was confirmed, the agency would do the work now done by Chapter XIII trustees. The local office or suboffice would receive money from the debtor or his employer. Payments would be recorded there, and the information would be fed into the agency's data processing system, which would keep the accounts, issue periodic and final statements to the debtor and creditors, prepare checks for the creditors and the notice of discharge, and supply data for reports.

Counseling would be available to the debtor to help him comply with the plan. If he nevertheless fell behind in his payments, the data processing system would produce a notice that one or more payments had been missed. This would come to the attention of the bankruptcy analyst for appropriate follow-up action with the debtor. If the reason for the default (such as serious illness or uninsured loss)

7. This provision was also proposed by the National Bankruptcy Conference.

made resumption of the plan impossible, the analyst could recommend an immediate discharge. Before such a discharge was granted, creditors would be notified and given an opportunity to be heard. Otherwise, the analyst might recommend dismissal, adjudication,[8] substantial revision of the plan, or perhaps merely a short extension. If within a year, a second default occurred, indicating the debtor's inability to manage his finances and meet his commitments to the plan, dismissal (or adjudication if the debtor consented) would follow. This procedure should reduce the time during which debtors struggle with proceedings that have turned out to be an inappropriate solution to their problems. Creditors would also be aided by having the debtor's status resolved promptly.

BUSINESS BANKRUPTCY PROCEEDINGS

Business cases would follow the same general process as that outlined for personal bankruptcies.[9] The bankruptcy representative would refer the matter to the analyst immediately if the debtor either had a plausible arrangement to propose or wanted advice about an arrangement. We assume that most business debtors would already have lawyers advising them.

In voluntary liquidation cases the bankruptcy analyst would first ensure that the property was safeguarded, employing a custodian if necessary, and would dispose of perishable inventory. He would then follow the procedure outlined above for personal bankruptcies to liquidate the estate.

In the rare instance of an involuntary bankruptcy case, the petition would be referred immediately to a hearing examiner, who would order the debtor to submit the necessary information in writing and would decide whether the debtor's estate should be liquidated under the law. If so, the bankruptcy analyst would do so in the usual manner.

REHABILITATIVE CASES

If the bankruptcy analyst believed that the case might be a Chapter X, he would consult an attorney in the agency. If the attorney agreed, the petitioner would be advised to file in federal district

8. As at present, the debtor would not be adjudicated bankrupt without his consent.

9. Except for Chapter X cases, which would be filed in district courts, as at present. (See below.)

court, for the bankruptcy agency would not be staffed to manage these infrequent, complex, and time-consuming cases.[10]

The agency would accept Chapter XI cases, which would be referred immediately to an analyst. If the analyst concluded there was no chance of rehabilitation, he would recommend liquidation to the examiner. The debtor would be entitled to a hearing on that issue.

If the analyst concluded that rehabilitation was possible and that a promising plan had been submitted, the same procedure as that for Chapter XIII would be followed: notice sent to creditors that would include the plan and a statement that the plan would be found feasible and confirmed unless objected to in writing by a majority (in number and amount) of all creditors, and unless an examiner found that such objecting creditors could not reasonably expect to receive the fair value of their claims. (Objecting creditors would be included in the plan unless this finding was made.) The law would be changed to include secured claims in the proceeding, and creditors with such claims would be allowed the fair value of their security. (The plan might provide for different treatment for different classes of creditors.) Objections would be considered at a hearing leading to confirmation, adjudication, or dismissal. Confirmation under the new law would be contingent on a positive finding by the examiner not only that the plan was feasible, but that continuation of the debtor's business after confirmation was also feasible. Examiners' findings on feasibility would *not* be based primarily on there being no creditors' objections, but on appropriate data about the debtor's ability to pay and to continue in business. Guidelines for examiners' use would be prepared by the agency staff.

If no plan (or no feasible plan) had been proposed and the analyst concluded that rehabilitation was possible, he would ask a consultant in the debtor's line of business to examine the problem with the debtor. Supplemental advice could also be obtained from local credit organizations, bankers, or the Small Business Administration. As in personal cases, every effort would be made to solve the prob-

10. We recommend that a change which has been of interest to a few bankruptcy professors and practitioners not be made. This is known as "Chapter X and a half"—a proposed provision for reorganizing medium-sized corporations whose securities are publicly held without following the existing stringent and time-consuming requirements of Chapter X. These safeguards in the current law are essential and appropriate for the protection of investors in such corporations.

lem outside the formal bankruptcy system. If the consultant and the debtor agreed that a successful arrangement was feasible within the bankruptcy system, they would prepare a plan. Such success, however, would probably be exceptional. (Our interview results and case analyses indicate that most businesses that can be saved with creditor cooperation have been salvaged before Chapter XI proceedings are filed.) The study of the debtor's problems would frequently result in a conclusion that prompt liquidation was the wisest solution.

If a plan was prepared and confirmed, however, the agency would retain jurisdiction of the case until the debtor (1) completed the payments under the plan; (2) defaulted and had the case dismissed or consented to an adjudication; or (3) if unincorporated, received a discharge because the default was caused by circumstances beyond his control.

As in Chapter XIII cases, the agency would receive payments from the debtor, keep necessary records, and make payments to the creditors.

No Chapter XII remedy would be needed under the new bankruptcy system because Chapter XIII would include real estate debts, and Chapter XI, secured debts.

IMPROVED REPORTS

Since all its transactions would be recorded and processed through a modern integrated data system, the agency could issue more complete, frequent, and analytical reports than are possible at present. For example, the system could produce information:

Showing personal and business (and former-business) bankruptcies separately;

Correcting data for filings by spouses or partners of bankrupts;

Presenting frequency distributions of cases by size of estates, amounts distributed to creditors, and other significant measures;

Demonstrating the extent and nature of creditor activity in cases of various types.

None of this information is reported at present.

The agency would make periodic reports of its operations to the President and to both houses of Congress.

PROCEDURES AND REVIEWS

Our discussion of how the agency would work has stressed speed, expertness, and sympathetic, equitable service to all parties. The proposed bankruptcy agency would, however, adhere to the provisions of the Administrative Procedure Act. Contested matters would be heard and adjudicated by hearing examiners in full compliance with the act. Nevertheless, our emphasis on speed and informality in the early stages and in uncontested proceedings is consistent with the policy of other administrative agencies, such as the Veterans Administration, the Interstate Commerce Commission, and the Social Security Administration.[11]

In the event that contested issues were not satisfactorily resolved by examiners, appeals would go first to a central appeals board in the agency and then, if necessary, to the circuit courts of appeals. The new bankruptcy law would specify the principal agency actions assigned to hearing examiners and subject to review, such as disallowance of claims and of exemptions, findings on the validity of liens, discharges, and feasibility of rehabilitative plans.

Provision would also be made for review in another sense: constructive scrutiny of the agency's program by both creditors and the public. First, the new statute would establish a creditors' advisory council to the director of the bankruptcy agency to review trends, comment on major policies, draw attention to procedural problems, suggest deterrents for improvident and unscrupulous actions by debtors, and in other ways bring creditors' interests effectively into the policy-determining process. Second, the law would provide for critical reevaluation of the work of the bankruptcy agency by a commission of knowledgeable citizens no less often than once every five years.

THE EFFECT OF OUR RECOMMENDATIONS

How would the implementation of our recommendations affect the groups and institutions most involved?

Creditors in asset cases and in cases under Chapters XI and XIII

11. For a brief, readable discussion of precedents and opportunities for informal processes that are acceptable under the Administrative Procedure Act, see Peter Woll, *Administrative Law: The Informal Process* (University of California Press, 1963), particularly Chaps. 1, 2, 5, and 6.

could expect higher returns because none of the assets would be used up in expenses of administration. Creditors would benefit also from more effective rehabilitative proceedings, which would keep their customers in business with them. Some creditors would have claims scaled down or eliminated as unconscionable or improvident, and some secured claims would be reduced to the value of the security, but other creditors would benefit from these actions. Creditors in no-asset cases would be in the position they are now in, except that there might be more such cases. Creditors in what are now nominal-asset cases would get either small recompense or nothing (as they do now), depending on the effect of the uniform exemption provisions. In part, the increase in no-asset cases caused by higher exemptions would be offset by the elimination of administrative expenses. Finally, all creditors would benefit from more efficient processing of the cases.

Debtors under the proposed new bankruptcy system would receive more effective aid in choosing a remedy. In rehabilitative cases they would benefit from having unconscionable or improvident debts scaled down or eliminated and from having secured claims reduced to the value of the collateral. In straight bankruptcy they could expect to receive their discharges more promptly since the whole process would be quicker, and they would be better protected from postdischarge collection efforts. In some cases debtors could obtain relief without retaining attorneys; in others, the attorneys would be relieved of so much work that fees should be greatly reduced. The new exemption provisions would help the debtors live and work at a more desirable level.

Attorneys for creditors are not likely to be affected by the change to the new system because they would have about the same amount of work in representing their clients' interests. Those who now serve as trustees or as attorneys for trustees would lose work to the new agency. They could, of course, seek employment there if they were interested and qualified. Attorneys for debtors would certainly lose some business, but in most instances bankruptcy work is only a small part of their practice.

Referees in bankruptcy would be supplanted, but some of them would probably be employed by the bankruptcy agency as examiners or analysts.

The federal judiciary would be relieved of the administrative burdens of the bankruptcy system. This has been a light load for most judges. Some would welcome the relief; a few might deplore the loss of function and appointments. The courts would also have fewer contested bankruptcy matters to decide because most issues would be settled by the examiners and the board of appeals in the bankruptcy agency.

All parties (at least, all well-motivated parties) to the present bankruptcy system would gain from the tighter system of administration, which would discourage errors, ethical slippages, and waste. The taxpayer would pay a higher bill for the bankruptcy system as a result of reduced filing fees and the use of appropriated funds to pay administrative expenses. He would benefit, however, to the extent that rehabilitated debtors and creditors with lower bad debt losses would pay more in taxes. Governments as creditors would lose their priority status, and taxes would now be dischargeable debts, but the total fiscal effect of these changes would be negligible.

The new agency would be "under the gun"—and should be. Its performance under the new law would be watched closely by the judiciary, by Congress, by the General Accounting Office, by the Office of Management and Budget, and by the interest groups—the credit industry, consumer interests, bar associations, and the recommended citizens' commission. The work of the present bankruptcy system is much less visible and is given relatively low priority attention by judges, Congress, and other governmental and private interests.

The principal threat to the success of the new system is the possibility of dilatory, mediocre performance. Creditors, debtors, and citizens in general would be no better off if the agency's examiners made a slow, costly "federal case" out of every relatively minor bankruptcy decision, if exceptions to deadlines were granted too generously, if debtors' and creditors' inquiries were dealt with unsympathetically or routinely, or if personnel of poor quality were employed. In particular the agency would have to guard against "overjudicializing" its administrative process. Hearing examiners should not take as long as, or longer than, referees do now in scheduling and deciding issues. They should get the facts and decide.

However, there is far less danger of such bureaucratic performance under the recommended system than under the existing system. All personnel would be chosen on a merit basis, and their careers would depend on their performance. Figures on the speed, economy, and effectiveness of operations would be watched by appropriations subcommittees, by the judiciary committees, and by the Office of Management and Budget. Specific details would be audited by the General Accounting Office. Failures of any kind could be dealt with by the appropriate authorities.

The big difference between the current system and the proposed system is one of motivation. The present bankruptcy process is run by the referees, trustees, and debtors' and creditors' attorneys. They have achieved an accommodation of interests under which scandals and spectacular errors are minimized; the rewards are kept high, but not high enough to provoke severe controls; and their security is not threatened. They are motivated primarily to keep the process as it is, and neither the judges nor the Administrative Office is rocking the boat.

Officials of the proposed bankruptcy agency would also be motivated by a desire for professional survival, but this would be conditioned on high performance—effective guidance of debtors, maximum return to creditors, rapid and inexpensive processing of cases, and production of valuable information about insolvencies.

The legal profession, the judges, and other officials of the federal government have no cause for pride in the present bankruptcy law and system. Revision of the law, the process, and the structure would be a memorable achievement both for jurisprudence and for public administration.

APPENDIX A

Methodology

This appendix presents information, particularly statistical data, about study methodology too detailed for inclusion in the main text of the book but of interest to close students of the bankruptcy process. Methodology is summarized in the final section of Chapter 1 and is mentioned briefly as appropriate elsewhere.

GENERAL BACKGROUND

The project staff began its work by reviewing bankruptcy statutes and rules, related state laws, academic and periodical literature on the subject, statistical compendia, and reports of other studies (listed below). Further background was supplied by interviews with officials of the Administrative Office of the United States Courts and of the Department of Justice and with a few bankruptcy attorneys. Staff members also attended meetings of the National Association of Referees in Bankruptcy and of the National Bankruptcy Conference.

Work planning was done during this same period. Elements of a model system for dealing with insolvency were drafted, sample districts were selected for study, sample cases drawn, and questionnaires put together. Actual field research began in December 1965.

EARLIER STUDIES

The staff, particularly at the outset of this project, reviewed other studies of bankruptcy processes and problems. These included:

Administration of the Bankruptcy Act, Report of the Attorney General's Committee on Bankruptcy Administration (1941)

Edward W. Reed, "Personal Bankruptcies in Oregon" (University of Oregon, Bureau of Business and Economic Research, 1967; processed)

George M. Stabler, "The Experience of Bankruptcy" [Rockford, Illinois] (Consumer Credit Association of Rockford, 1966; processed)

Robert O. Herrman, *Causal Factors in Consumer Bankruptcy: A Case Study*
[Sacramento, California] (University of California, Institute of Governmental Affairs, 1965)

Dori Jacobs, "The Family in Financial Crisis" [Southern District, Arizona] (master's thesis, University of Arizona, 1965)

John J. Brosky, *A Study of Personal Bankruptcy in the Seattle Metropolitan Area* (Retail Credit Association of Seattle, 1965)

Robert Dolphin, Jr., *An Analysis of Economic and Personal Factors Leading to Consumer Bankruptcy* [Flint, Michigan] Occasional Paper No. 15 (Michigan State University Graduate School of Business Administration, Bureau of Business and Economic Research, 1965)

George Allen Brunner, "Personal Bankruptcies in Ohio" (Ph.D. dissertation, Ohio State University, 1965)

Grant L. Misbach, *Personal Bankruptcy in the United States and Utah* (University of Utah Press, 1964)

Wesley D. Harms, "Some Aspects of Business Policies and Procedures in Relation to Personal Bankruptcy in the Wichita Area" (master's thesis, University of Wichita, 1961)

Samuel L. Myers, "The Consumer Bankrupt in Maryland" (Morgan State College, 1961; processed)

George L. Schaber, "Voluntary Bankruptcy—A Growing Consumer Bankruptcy Problem" [Western District, Kentucky] (University of Virginia, School of Consumer Banking, 1959; processed)

Herbert Jacob, *Debtors in Court* (Rand McNally, 1969)

Shirley Suzanne Matsen, "Selected Characteristics of Personal Bankruptcy Petitioners in Portland, Oregon" (master's thesis, Oregon State University, 1967)

H. Lee Mathews, *Causes of Personal Bankruptcies* (Ohio State University, Bureau of Business Research, 1969)

Harry H. Haden, "Chapter XIII Wage Earner Plans—Forgotten Man Bankruptcy," *Kentucky Law Journal*, Vol. 55 (1966–67), pp. 581–84.

1. STAFF INTERVIEWS

The Brookings staff interviewed 607 persons in various categories in the eight court districts chosen for study. Table A-1 gives details.

2. CASE FILE ANALYSES

At the time these interviews were being conducted, the research staff also sampled and abstracted 1,675 bankruptcy cases. Table A-2 shows the

TABLE A-1. *Officials and Other Persons Interviewed by the Brookings Research Staff, by District, 1966*

Category	Northern Ohio	Northern Alabama	Maine	Northern Illinois	Oregon	Western Texas	Southern New York	Southern California	Total
District judges	6	3	1	8	2	4	5	14	43
Referees	9	6	2	9	5	2	4	16	53
Trustees and receivers	12	8	7	9	5	9	5	22	77
Chapter XIII trustees	3	3	2	1	2	1	0[a]	4	16
Debtors' attorneys	7	6	10	13	8	8	2	14	68
Creditors' attorneys	8[b]	9	10	11	10	10	4	18	80
Creditors (nonbusiness debtors)	8	8	11	12	4	9	1[a]	19	72
Creditors (business debtors)	0	0	4	0	8	3	3	4	22
Employers	3	4	4	7	6	4	0[a]	6	34
Welfare authorities[c]	4	4	6	8	3	6	0[a]	9	40
Appraisers[b]	1	0	2	3	2	0	1	3	12
Auctioneers[b]	2	0	2	3	1	0	1	3	12
Accountants[b]	1	0	1	2	2	2	0	5[d]	13
Business debtors	1	0	5	12	8	4	0	20	50
State court judges[b]	2[e]	2[f]	5	1	1	2	0	2	15
Total	67	53	72	99	67	64	26	159	607

a. Personal bankruptcies were not studied in Southern New York. Interview with creditor of nonbusiness debtors did not pertain to Southern New York cases but to nationwide business.

b. Interview results in these categories were hand tabulated.

c. The general term "welfare authorities" is used to cover officials of welfare agencies (both public and private), counseling agencies, legal aid offices, and union officials.

d. Includes one interview with an "adjuster."

e. Includes one interview with a municipal court trustee.

f. Includes one interview with a clerk of court.

TABLE A-2. *Bankruptcy Cases Concluded in Fiscal Year 1964 That Were Analyzed by the Brookings Research Staff, by District and Type of Case*

District	Type of case	Number analyzed	Base[a]	Sampling rate	Multi-plier
Northern Ohio	Straight bankruptcy				
	No asset	30	6,106	1–204	68
	Nominal asset	33	1,231	1–37	37
	Asset	104	1,210	1–11	11
	Chapter X	2	2	1–1	—[b]
	Chapter XI	6	7	1–1	1
	Chapter XII	0	—	—	—
	Chapter XIII				
	Arranged	21	23	1–1	1
	Dismissed	7	147	1–21	21
Northern Alabama	Straight bankruptcy				
	No asset	30	1,001	1–33	11
	Nominal asset	12	56	1–4	4
	Asset	30	154	1–5	5
	Chapter X	0	—	—	—
	Chapter XI	3	4	1–1	1
	Chapter XII	2	3	1–1	—[b]
	Chapter XIII				
	Arranged	87	3,094	1–36	36
	Dismissed	60	2,490	1–42	42
Maine	Straight bankruptcy				
	No asset	25	325	1–13	4
	Nominal asset	24	372	1–16	16
	Asset	76	326	1–4	4
	Chapter X	0	—	—	—
	Chapter XI	2	3	1–1	1
	Chapter XII	0	—	—	—
	Chapter XIII				
	Arranged	44	135	1–3	3
	Dismissed	34	297	1–9	9
Northern Illinois	Straight bankruptcy				
	No asset	60	12,412	1–219[c]	73[c]
	Nominal asset	32	280	1–9	9
	Asset	90	420	1–5	5
	Chapter X	0	1	—	—
	Chapter XI	28	28	1–1	1
	Chapter XII	0	—	—	—
	Chapter XIII				
	Arranged	40	81	1–2	2
	Dismissed	32	281	1–9	9
Oregon	Straight bankruptcy				
	No asset	51	1,879	1–37	12

TABLE A-2 *(continued)*

District	Type of case	Number analyzed	Base*	Sampling rate	Multiplier
Oregon	Nominal asset	57	916	1–16	16
(continued)	Asset	98	989	1–10	10
	Chapter X	0	—	—	—
	Chapter XI	0	—	—	—
	Chapter XII	0	—	—	—
	Chapter XIII				
	Arranged	25	25	1–1	1
	Dismissed	19	37	1–2	2
Western Texas	Straight bankruptcy				
	No asset	32	92	1–3	1
	Nominal asset	15	15	1–1	1
	Asset	34	41	1–1	1
	Chapter X	0	1	—	—
	Chapter XI	0	—	—	—
	Chapter XII	0	—	—	—
	Chapter XIII				
	Arranged	1	1	1–1	1
	Dismissed	2	2	1–1	1
Southern New York	Straight bankruptcy				
	No asset	0	—	—	—
	Nominal asset	0	—	—	—
	Asset	31	210	1–7	7
	Chapter X	3	3	1–1	—b
	Chapter XI	18	94	1–5	5
	Chapter XII	0	—	—	—
	Chapter XIII	0	—	—	—
Southern California	Straight bankruptcy				
	No asset	99	14,775	1–149	50
	Nominal asset	40	1,207	1–30	30
	Asset	117	1,437	1–12	12
	Chapter X	0	—	—	—
	Chapter XI	33	42	1–1	1
	Chapter XII	4	4	1–1	—b
	Chapter XIII				
	Arranged	54	268	1–5	5
	Dismissed	27	452	1–17	17

Source: Administrative Office of the U.S. Courts, "Tables of Bankruptcy Statistics" (1964; processed), Tables F 4a and F 4b. This source applies to *Base* column only.

a. The bases for straight bankruptcy cases include adjudicated Chapter X, XI, XII, and XIII cases.

b. Chapter X and XII cases were not analyzed statistically.

c. After the statistical tabulations were run and the analyses completed, it was discovered that, for straight bankruptcy no-asset cases in Northern Illinois, the sampling rate should have been 1–207, and the multiplier, 69. Substituting 69 for 73 in the tables as run produced no significant difference in the percentaging.

number of cases of each type analyzed in each district, with sampling rates and the multipliers used to correct for differences in sampling rates in interdistrict comparisons.

3. INTERVIEW STUDY OF FOUR HUNDRED DEBTORS AND BANKRUPTS

In seven of the sample districts, 400 individual debtors and bankrupts (plus 9 persons in the eastern district of Pennsylvania interviewed in the pretest phase of this survey) were located and interviewed for this research project in the summer of 1966 by representatives of Chilton Research Services of Philadelphia. Interview questionnaires were drafted by Chilton on the basis of specifications supplied by Brookings, revised after comment by Brookings research staff members, pretested, and revised again for field use.

Interviews were conducted in the following cities and their adjacent commuting areas:

Northern Ohio	Akron, Canton, and Cleveland
Northern Alabama	Anniston and Birmingham
Maine	Bangor and Portland
Northern Illinois	Chicago
Oregon	Corvallis and Portland
Western Texas	El Paso and San Antonio
Southern California	Los Angeles and Santa Ana

The code for analyzing responses was drafted by Brookings, tested on a portion of the completed questionnaires, then revised for use on all questionnaires. Coding was done by Chilton, occasionally in consultation with Brookings. Tabulation was done by Chilton, following specifications prepared by Brookings. There was a 100 percent reliability check on the coding of the first 25 percent of the questionnaires; a 10 percent check and a count of punched card columns on questionnaires was made thereafter.

The actual number of persons interviewed in each district is shown in Table A-3, with sampling rates and the multipliers used to correct for differences in sampling rates in interdistrict comparisons.

The Chilton staff were given all the names and addresses that could be determined from the case files of individual bankrupts and debtors in the Brookings sample. As addresses were verified and efforts made to locate interviewees, the number proved to be insufficient. More were obtained by random sampling from docket records of individual cases closed in fiscal year 1964 in the sample districts, and these were sent by Chilton to

TABLE A-3. *Individual Bankrupts and Debtors Interviewed in Chilton Survey, by District*

District	Number	Base[a]	Sampling rate	Multi-plier
Northern Ohio	58	7,920	1–137	34
Northern Alabama	77	7,637	1–99	25
Maine	61	1,389	1–23	6
Northern Illinois	45	12,773	1–284	71
Oregon	60	3,577	1–60	15
Western Texas	28	116	1–4	1
Southern California	71	16,833	1–237	59
Eastern Pennsylvania[b]	9	347	1–39	10

a. No satisfactory base reflecting a mixture of employee bankrupts and debtors and small business bankrupts was readily available in official statistics. Our bases were computed as follows. In each district a percentage was computed on the basis of 1963 filings in which the dividend was the number of nonbusiness filings plus one-half of the merchants' filings, and the divisor was the total number of voluntary filings. (The year 1963 was used because more of the Chilton interview cases were filed in that fiscal year than in any other.) This percentage was then applied to the total of cases closed in that district in 1964, excluding Chapter X, XI, and XII cases.

b. Used only in all-district figures.

the appropriate post offices for verification. Next, letters were sent to prospective interviewees indicating they would be called on, and the interviewers began efforts to see them. The difficulty of locating and interviewing the respondents is shown in these figures for the seven districts:[1]

Total names received from bankruptcy files	3,596
Insufficient addresses	−488
Addressees outside prescribed interviewing areas	−170
Duplicate names (probably spouse or partnership cases)	−31
Post offices reported addresses unknown	−1,145
Addresses verified or new addresses reported by post offices	1,762
Letter returned marked "addressee unknown"	−134
Respondent moved	−480
Respondent ill or deceased	−21
Respondent temporarily absent during interviewing period	−119
Refused; too busy; not interested	−132
Not interviewed for other reasons (such as error in identity, broken appointment)	−86
Possible interviewees	790
Completed interviews	−400
Not necessary to contact	390

1. Excluding Eastern Pennsylvania and Southern New York. City-by-city figures are available in the Brookings files.

Of the 400 completed interviews, 125 were bankrupts or debtors in the Brookings case file samples, and 275 were others.

Interviewees were not compensated for their participation.

4. INTERVIEW STUDY OF THE GENERAL POPULATION

A sample of the general United States public was interviewed by the Gallup Organization, Inc., of Princeton, New Jersey, in May 1966 about knowledge of and attitudes toward bankruptcy. Gallup describes the sample as follows:

The design of the sample is that of a replicated probability sample down to the block level in the case of urban areas, and to segments of townships in the case of rural areas.

After stratifying the nation geographically and by size of community in order to insure conformity of the sample with the latest available estimate of the Census Bureau of the distribution of the adult population, about 160 different sampling locations or areas were selected on a strictly random basis. The interviewers had no choice whatsoever concerning the part of the city or county in which they conducted their interviews.

Approximately 10 interviews were conducted in each such randomly selected sampling point. Interviewers were given maps of the area to which they were assigned, with a starting point indicated, and required to follow a specified direction. At each occupied dwelling unit, interviewers were instructed to select respondents by following a prescribed systematic method and by a male-female assignment. This procedure was followed until the assigned number of interviews was completed.

. . . this sampling procedure is designed to produce a sample which approximates the adult civilian population (21 and older) living in private households in the U.S. (that is, excluding those in prisons and hospitals, hotels, religious and educational institutions, and on military reservations) . . .

The characteristics of the persons interviewed are shown in Table A-4.

Seven questions about bankruptcy were asked as part of the usual type of Gallup survey interview on public issues and political opinions. A total of 1,523 persons were interviewed.

The questions were drafted and pretested and the code prepared by Brookings. Coding and tabulating were done by Gallup. Results are presented in Appendix B, section 1.

5. CREDIT BUREAU SURVEY

The Associated Credit Bureaus of America, Inc., obtained information from its member bureaus, at no charge to the Brookings study, concerning the credit status of sample bankrupts and debtors, both at the time they filed petitions and subsequently. Brookings supplied ACBA with questions to be asked about all noncorporate debtors and bankrupts in the Brookings

TABLE A-4. *Characteristics of Interviewees in Gallup Survey of Bankruptcy Attitudes*

Description	Number of interviews	Percentage of sample
Sex		
Male	741	48.7
Female	782	51.3
Race		
White	1,424	93.5
Nonwhite	99	6.5
Education		
College	316	20.7
High school	834	54.8
Grade school	366	24.0
Undesignated	7	0.5
Occupation of chief wage earner		
Professional and business	336	22.1
White collar	163	10.7
Farmer	113	7.4
Manual worker	614	40.3
Not in labor force	276	18.1
Undesignated	21	1.4
Age		
21–34 years	379	24.9
35–49 years	489	32.1
50 years and over	632	41.5
Undesignated	23	1.5
Region of country		
East	434	28.5
Midwest	445	29.2
South	425	27.9
West	219	14.4
Income		
$10,000 and over	323	21.2
$7,000–$9,999	335	22.0
$5,000–$6,999	295	19.4
$3,000–$4,999	249	16.3
Under $3,000	299	19.6
Undesignated	22	1.5
Respondent's contact with bankruptcy proceedings		
No contact	1,240	81.5
As debtor	33	2.2
As creditor	55	3.6
As stockholder	19	1.2
As friend or relative	155	10.2
Other	21	1.3

TABLE A-5. *Noncorporate Bankrupts and Debtors Reported on by Credit Bureaus, by District and Type of Case*

District	Type of case	Number[a]	Base[b]	Sampling rate	Multiplier
Northern Ohio	Straight bankruptcy	200	8,547	1–43	11.0
	Chapter XI	1	7	1–7	7.0
	Chapter XIII	11	170	1–15	7.5
Northern Alabama	Straight bankruptcy	52	1,211	1–23	6.0
	Chapter XI	3	4	1–1	1.0
	Chapter XII	2	2	1–1	1.0
	Chapter XIII	160	5,584	1–35	18.0
Maine	Straight bankruptcy	97	1,023	1–11	3.0
	Chapter XI	2	2	1–1	1.0
	Chapter XIII	89	432	1–5	2.5
Northern Illinois	Straight bankruptcy	153	13,112	1–86	22.0
	Chapter XI	14	28	1–2	2.0
	Chapter XIII	64	361	1–6	3.0
Oregon	Straight bankruptcy	114	3,784	1–33	8.0
	Chapter XIII	39	62	1–2	1.0
Western Texas	Straight bankruptcy	42	148	1–4	1.0
	Chapter XIII	1	3	1–3	1.5
Southern New York	Straight bankruptcy	5	210	1–42	10.0
Southern California	Straight bankruptcy	190	17,419	1–92	23.0
	Chapter XI	33	42	1–1	1.0
	Chapter XII	5	5	1–1	1.0
	Chapter XIII	82	720	1–9	4.5

a. Numbers exclude cases that could not be identified by a chapter of the Bankruptcy Act.
b. Straight bankruptcy figures include adjudicated chapter cases.

case file samples. These were transmitted to the bureaus concerned on forms designed by ACBA. Copies of completed returns from the bureaus were shipped to Brookings without editing or interpretation. Results were hand-tabulated by Brookings staff. The rate of return was approximately 80 percent.

Table A-5 shows the numbers of debtors reported on by credit bureaus, with sampling rates and multipliers.

6. TRIAL ATTORNEYS

The Brookings staff sent a questionnaire to a sample of trial attorneys to find out the extent to which defendants in negligence suits went bankrupt (or threatened to go bankrupt) to avoid paying damages. Table A-6 presents some statistical detail about the methodology of this substudy. Its results are presented on pages 48–49.

TABLE A-6. *Number of Questionnaires Sent to Trial Attorneys by Authors, and Returned, by District*

District	Number sent	Number returned	Rate of return (percent)	Base	Sampling rate	Multiplier
Northern Ohio	147	49	33	592	1–4	4
Northern Alabama	96	38	40	111	1–1	1
Maine	127	38	30	149	1–1	1
Northern Illinois	173	42	24	517	1–3	3
Oregon	109	34	31	336	1–3	3
Western Texas	114	30	26	133	1–1	1
Southern New York	154	36	23	615	1–4	4
Southern California	137	54	39	1,093	1–8	8
Unknown (district not identifiable in return)	—	11	—	—	1–3[a]	3
Total and average	1,057	332	31			

a. Assumed.

APPENDIX B

Explanatory Memoranda

This appendix presents further information about certain characteristics of bankruptcy and about our study which again were too detailed for inclusion in the text.

1. AMERICANS' IDEAS ABOUT BANKRUPTCY

Background information bearing on popular knowledge of bankruptcy and reactions to bankrupt persons and businesses was acquired for this study through a nationwide survey of bankruptcy attitudes. Professional interviewers from the Gallup Organization talked to a representative sample covering a wide spread of ages, occupations, educational levels, income levels, occupational types, and geographical areas. (See Appendix A, section 4, for methodological detail.)

Although one person out of every thousand in the United States files a petition in bankruptcy, the survey shows that one out of every five (19 percent) had some direct personal contact with bankruptcy proceedings. More than half of these (10 percent) were friends or relatives of a person involved in bankruptcy; 4 percent were involved as creditors.

With or without any such direct contact, American citizens understand the elementary purposes and features of bankruptcy. They realize that a bankrupt gets rid of his debts and that his credit may be impaired. They say they would be ashamed of going bankrupt themselves and would be reluctant to deal with a person or business that had been bankrupt. Despite the stigma they attach to bankruptcy, they associate it less with crookedness than with poor management of business or personal affairs. In all levels and in all areas they have a generalized distaste for bankruptcy.

These general attitudes emerged in specific answers to questions about both the nature and impact of bankruptcy. The 1,523 interviewees were asked, for example, "Suppose a person (or business) did go bankrupt, what would you, personally, think about doing business with him (the business) in the future?" Only 9 percent said "Don't know." Of the rest, the "would not's" and the "reluctant's" outnumbered the "would's" by a wide margin (percentages are rounded):

Negative or cautious replies	*Percent*
Would not do business with him	26
Would be reluctant, cautious, hesitant, leery; prefer to do business elsewhere	26
Depends on whether he was honest; on whether bankruptcy was his fault or not	20
Would do business *for cash only;* would not give him credit	3
Depends on whether I was buying or selling; on whether he sells something I want	2

Positive replies	
Would do business with him; wouldn't care if he had gone bankrupt	10
Would do business with him to give him a chance	5

Respondents were then asked an equally important question: "Suppose you, yourself, got into a very difficult financial situation—how would you feel about going bankrupt?" The replies showed that the element of distaste grew stronger (percentages rounded):

	Percent
Would go bankrupt only as a last resort; try everything else; try other ways out	33
Would *not* go bankrupt; rather die; simply wouldn't	20
Would feel badly; terrible; disgraced	18
It would be OK if I had to	8
Inconceivable that I could go bankrupt; never considered the possibility	5
Actually went bankrupt; had to go bankrupt	1
Would want to go bankrupt; it would be an advantage	1
Don't know	15

Citizens' sensitivity to bankruptcy was tested further by the question: "What do you think others—your friends or co-workers—would think of you if you went bankrupt?" This query stopped a quarter of the interviewees; that is, 25 percent said "Don't know." Of the rest, more responded negatively than positively or neutrally.

The most frequent among the negative answers were the generalized type—like the New England ice-cream maker who said, "Somehow or other I don't think they'd have a good impression of me." Next came "poor manager" replies like "They would think we were living a little too high on the hog" (an Ohio truck driver). Only 6 percent mentioned dishonesty.

In general, then, the American public is familiar with the basic elements of bankruptcy and views them with some distaste and anxiety.

2. ESTIMATES OF AGGREGATE LIABILITIES SCHEDULED AND DISCHARGED IN BANKRUPTCY CASES

In attempting to update to 1968 the figures showing average return to creditors, we began by estimating the claims of creditors as roughly $2 billion for cases closed in 1968. This is derived as follows. Total liabilities in straight bankruptcy asset and nominal-asset cases and special relief ("chapter") cases amounted to $1,081 million for cases closed in fiscal year 1968:

Straight bankruptcy asset	$ 418,700,919
Straight bankruptcy nominal-asset	527,129,861
Chapter XI (arranged cases only)	112,807,402
Chapter XIII	22,358,939
	$1,080,997,121

After rounding this to $1,081 million, we add to it the estimated liabilities for no-asset cases. Such liabilities were not reported in the Administrative Office of the United States Courts' annual "Tables of Bankruptcy Statistics" after fiscal year 1964. However, a reasonable projection, on the assumption that the amount of debt was proportionate to the numbers of cases concluded, would be $1,279 million for fiscal year 1968. Adding this to the total above gives a grand total of $2,360 million in liabilities.

We estimate that $960 million of this total was in personal bankruptcies. This is derived by multiplying a median of $5,000 a case (see Appendix Table c-3) by 192,000 nonbusiness cases filed in 1967. Most of these cases were probably closed in 1968, if our analysis in Table 5-6 of the average time taken is correct.

This figure of $960 million must now be reduced by 20 percent to correct for duplicate filings by spouses. This is a conservative percentage: our interviews with individual bankrupts showed that 32 percent of spouses had also filed (Chapter 4, note 33); in our file sample at least 40 percent of the former-business and 22 percent of the nonbusiness debt was scheduled by petitioners whose spouses had also filed (page 57). This 20 percent (of $960 million) reduction equals $192 million, which we deduct from the grand total above, leaving $2,168 million in liabilities.

Now, how much did creditors get?

Straight bankruptcy asset cases	$ 65,934,107
Chapter XI	43,987,697
Chapter XIII	21,262,098
	$131,183,902

The estimate for Chapter XI is generous because it assumes full payment of sums provided for in confirmed Chapter XI plans without deducting for subsequent defaults. Figures are from "Tables of Bankruptcy Statistics" (1968), Tables F 6 and F 11. The "Tables" do not include distributions in closed Chapter X or XII cases.

In addition, perhaps $51 million in debts were reaffirmed by personal bankrupts (based on the assumption that one-third of them, after the 20 percent reduction above, reaffirmed an average of $1,000 of debts, as suggested by our interviews reported on page 61).

All in all, then, we estimate that bankruptcy petitioners owed $2,168 million and that creditors received $182 million. Thus "losses" to creditors amounted to $1,986 million.

It is difficult to determine how much of this discharged debt was in personal bankruptcies, but the figure approaches $700 million:

		Millions of dollars
Estimated liabilities, personal bankruptcies		960
Less: 20 percent to correct for spouse filings	192	
Debts reaffirmed	51	
Paid in Chapter XIII cases	21	−264
		696

less an unknown but small portion of the $66 million paid to creditors in straight bankruptcy asset cases.

3. COMPARING RATES OF INCREASE IN THE PERSONAL BANKRUPTCY RATE AND DEBT–INCOME RATIO

Because the personal bankruptcy rate is so sensitive to the country's prosperity, it is difficult to make any real comparison between the increase in the rate from one year to the next and the simultaneous increase in the aggregate debt–income ratio. So we constructed a five-year moving average of the two series to smooth out the irregularities introduced by temporary economic conditions. The series appear in columns 1 and 2 of

Table B-1. Each number in the series is an average of the personal bankruptcy rate or the debt–income ratio over five consecutive years. Thus the entries for 1947 are an average of the bankruptcy rates in fiscal years 1945 through 1949 (one-fifth of the sum of the five rates) and an average of the debt–income ratios on December 31 of the calendar years 1945 through 1949.

The third and fourth columns of the table contain five-year rates of increase in the personal bankruptcy rate and debt–income ratio computed from the numbers in the first two columns. Thus the entries for 1952 are the ratios of the five-year average of bankruptcy rates centered on 1952 to the average bankruptcy rate in 1947, computed in the same way, minus one (to measure the increase in the rate, not the rate itself, as a fraction of the earlier figure), and a similar computation for the debt–income ratio. Between 1947 and 1952 the personal bankruptcy rate grew by 137 percent, while the debt–income ratio grew by 58 percent.

The last column contains a comparison of the rates of growth of the two series. Each entry is the ratio of the increase in the personal bankruptcy rate over the rate of five years before (the entry in column 3) to the same increase in the debt–income ratio, except that the increase in the second of these series is computed over a five-year period that begins one year before the five-year period for the personal bankruptcy rate. For example, the entry in column 5 for 1952 is the ratio of the number in column 3 for 1953 to the number in column 4 for 1952. The debt–income series is lagged by one year because it is computed for calendar years whereas the other series is computed for fiscal years.

The numbers in column 5 show that early in the postwar period, when the debt–income ratio was low, a given increase in that ratio was accompanied by a smaller increase in the personal bankruptcy rate than accompanied the same increase in the ratio later in the period, when the debt–income ratio was high. This result conforms to the explanation in Chapter 3 of why the increase in the personal bankruptcy rate throughout this period should have been considerably higher than the increase in the debt–income ratio that was related to it. The numbers in the column form an increasing sequence between 1952 and 1962 (apart from a slight dip in 1960), just the pattern we might have expected. The series turned down in 1963 and declined again in 1964, but in both years the numbers still are larger than they were throughout most of the earlier part of the period. The series has not been extended beyond 1964, because the pronounced decline in the debt–income ratio that began in 1967 would be reflected in the moving average for 1965 and later years, and would inflate the column 5 figures for 1965–68.

TABLE B-1. *Five-Year Computations of Personal Bankruptcy Rate and Debt–Income Ratio, 1947–68*

Year[a]	(1) Personal bankruptcy rate[b] (percent)	(2) Debt as a percentage of income[c]	(3) Five-year increase in bankruptcy rate[d] (percent)	(4) Five-year increase in debt–income ratio[e] (percent)	(5) Ratio of increase in bankruptcy rate to increase in debt/income[f]
1947	13.12	20.4	—	—	—
1948	15.79	23.4	—	—	—
1949	19.49	25.7	—	—	—
1950	22.89	27.8	—	—	—
1951	26.55	30.1	—	—	—
1952	31.15	32.2	137.4	57.8	2.18
1953	35.67	34.5	125.9	47.4	2.23
1954	40.07	37.2	105.6	44.7	2.30
1955	46.40	39.6	102.7	42.4	2.51
1956	54.78	41.8	106.3	38.9	2.59
1957	62.64	43.9	101.1	36.3	2.71
1958	70.76	45.6	98.4	32.2	3.44
1959	84.48	47.2	110.8	26.9	3.99
1960	96.13	48.9	107.2	23.5	3.96
1961	105.80	50.8	93.1	21.5	4.00
1962	116.48	52.5	86.0	19.6	4.04
1963	126.82	53.9	79.2	18.2	3.16
1964	133.07	54.7	57.5	15.9	2.99
1965	141.75	55.1	47.5	12.5	—[g]
1966	147.11	54.7	39.0	7.7	—[g]
1967	147.60	53.9	26.7	2.7	—[g]
1968	147.94	52.7	16.7	−2.2	—[g]

Sources: Col. 1—"Tables of Bankruptcy Statistics," issued annually by the Administrative Office of the United States Courts, plus population estimates by age groups, *Economic Report of the President, February 1971,* Table C-21, p. 221; col. 2—*Economic Report of the President, February 1971,* Tables C-58 and C-60, pp. 266 and 268.

a. Bankruptcy rates (col. 1) are for fiscal years; debt–income ratio (col. 2) for December 31 of calendar years.

b. Five-year moving average; equal in year t to average of personal bankruptcy rates in fiscal years $t - 2$ through $t + 2$. Personal bankruptcy rate expressed as number of filings of personal bankruptcy cases per hundred thousand persons in population aged 20 or over at beginning of fiscal year.

c. Five-year moving average; equal in year t to average of debt–income ratios in years $t - 2$ through $t + 2$. See definition of debt–income ratio in notes c and d, Table 3-1.

d. Equal in year t to (entry in col. 1 in year t minus entry in col. 1 in year $t - 5$)/(entry in col. 1 in year $t - 5$).

e. Equal in year t to (entry in col. 2 in year t minus entry in col. 2 in year $t - 5$)/(entry in col. 2 in year $t - 5$).

f. Ratio of col. 3, year $t + 1$, to col. 4, year t.

g. Not computed; see p. 234.

4. EXEMPTIONS FROM GARNISHMENT OF WAGES
AND PERSONAL BANKRUPTCY RATES OF STATES

To test whether state bankruptcy rates are related to the amount of a person's wages that are exempt by state law from garnishment, we carried out a statistical test on two sets of data using rank correlation analysis. All the states but Arkansas plus the District of Columbia were ranked twice—once according to the number of personal bankruptcy cases filed within each state in fiscal 1967 per hundred thousand residents, and again according to the size of the wage exemption from garnishment that each state allows, expressed as a fraction of a person's wages. Each state was assigned two numbers corresponding to the state's position in the two rankings. If low wage exemptions are associated with high bankruptcy rates and high exemptions with low bankruptcy rates, high numbers in one ranking should be associated with low numbers in the other.

Even if the size of a state's wage exemption really had no effect on its personal bankruptcy rate, one would expect on ranking fifty jurisdictions to find some with low bankruptcy rates and high wage exemptions, and vice versa. And chances are that in other states both the bankruptcy rate and the wage exemption would be high, or both low. These results would appear by the normal operation of the laws of chance, even if no actual relation existed between the two parameters, much as such combinations turn up when a pair of dice are rolled many times.

If wage exemptions and personal bankruptcy rates are not related, it should not happen too often that when one of them is low the other is high, and the reverse; or that both are either low or high. If it does happen often, it probably means that the two parameters are indeed related. Rank correlation analysis is little more than a method of giving a precise meaning to the words "often" and "probably."[1]

Table B-2 presents a listing of all the states except Arkansas plus the District of Columbia arranged in descending order by size of their personal bankruptcy rate in fiscal 1967. Arkansas was omitted when it proved impossible to reduce the state's wage exemption to a single number. Column 3 in the table gives the size of each state's wage exemption from garnishment expressed as a percentage of earnings, and column 4 shows the state's position in a descending order ranking by size of wage exemption. Ties were decided by giving each of the tied states the median ranking that the group as a whole was entitled to; thus if two states were tied for fifth position, both were given a ranking of 5.5 and the next state was ranked

---

1. It is something more than this in that it also includes the method of organizing the data to display whatever relation is apparent between the parameters, and of measuring that relation by the rank correlation coefficient. The coefficient is evaluated by consulting a set of standard tables to determine whether it is "too high" or "too low."

TABLE B-2. *Personal Bankruptcy Rates and Wage Exemptions, by State, Fiscal Year 1967*

State[a]	Personal bankruptcy rate[b]	Rank by bankruptcy rate	Wage exemption from garnishment (percent)	Rank by wage exemption
Nevada	301	1	50.0	33
Alabama	288	2	75.0	22.5
Tennessee	260	3	24.1	49
Oregon	246	4	50.0	33
Colorado	223	5	70.0	25
Arizona	209	6	50.0	33
California	197	7	50.0	33
Maine	183	8	32.2	48
Ohio	178	9	75.5	20
Georgia	166	10	58.4	27
Oklahoma	155	11.5	75.0	22.5
Utah	155	11.5	50.0	33
Washington	154	13	37.6	43
Kentucky	151	14	50.0	33
Kansas	143	15	90.0	9.5
Indiana	136	16	91.2	7
Idaho	135	17	50.0	33
Illinois	125	18	85.0	14
Wyoming	124	19	50.0	33
New Hampshire	123	20	21.9	50
Missouri	119	21	90.0	9.5
Virginia	112	22	37.5	44
New Mexico	103	23	80.0	18
Michigan	95	24.5	34.3	46
Minnesota	95	24.5	50.0	33
Wisconsin	94	26	75.0	22.5
West Virginia	90	27	80.0	18
Montana	88	28	50.0	33
Nebraska	79	29	90.0	9.5
Vermont	78	30	50.0	33
Louisiana	77	31	80.0	18
Iowa	69	32	33.2	47
Rhode Island	57	33	46.5	40
Hawaii	53	34	85.8	13
Alaska	49	35	47.9	39
Connecticut	47	36	40.4	42
Mississippi	44	37	75.0	22.5
New York	36	38	90.0	9.5
North Dakota	34	39	63.6	26
Massachusetts	27	40	46.3	41

TABLE B-2 *(continued)*

State[a]	Personal bankruptcy rate[b]	Rank by bankruptcy rate	Wage exemption from garnishment (percent)	Rank by wage exemption
South Dakota	25	41	100.0	3.5
Florida	19	42	100.0	3.5
New Jersey	18	43	36.4	45
Delaware	11	44	80.7	16
Pennsylvania	9	45	100.0	3.5
District of Columbia	8	46	82.0	15
Maryland	7	47	87.6	12
North Carolina	5	49	100.0	3.5
South Carolina	5	49	100.0	3.5
Texas	5	49	100.0	3.5

Sources: Col. 1—"Report on 1967 Nonbusiness Bankruptcies by States" (Washington: National Consumer Finance Association, 1967; processed); col. 3—Commerce Clearing House, *Handbook on Assignment and Garnishment of Wages* (Chicago: CCH, 1966).
a. Arkansas is omitted since its wage exemption cannot be reduced to a single percentage figure.
b. Number of personal bankruptcies in fiscal 1967 per 100,000 population.

seventh; if three were tied for fifth position, each was ranked sixth and the next state was ranked eighth.

The rank correlation analysis that we carried out on these data strongly supports the idea that bankruptcy rates are inversely correlated with the wage exemptions in state garnishment laws; that is, the higher the wage exemption is, the lower—usually—the bankruptcy rate, and vice versa. There is less than one chance in a hundred that the pattern we found in the data appeared by chance and that bankruptcy rates and wage exemptions bear no relation to each other.

The rest of this discussion will be devoted to explaining how we ranked states by the size of their wage exemption when the exemption was expressed in other ways than as a percentage of individual earnings, or when a condition was attached to the exemption. No such problem arose in comparing the states' bankruptcy rates, for there the basis of the ranking was a single, known number. But wage exemptions from garnishment often depend on a variety of conditions, such as whether the debtor is a resident of the state, the character of his employment, his family status, the purpose for which the debt was contracted, and whether the garnishment is before or after judgment. Clearly, we had to make some simplifying assumptions. In all cases, for example, we compared only the exemptions to which residents of the states were entitled. We assumed that our debtor was a married man with two dependent children; that the writ of garnishment was served after judgment; that the debt had been incurred "for the common necessaries of life" whenever that affected the size of the exemption; and that the debtor was not entitled to a larger than normal exemption by reason of his employment.

In some states a higher exemption is available if the debtor can show that he needs the increment for the support of his family. We generally followed the practice of using the highest exemption that could be awarded, unless no upper limit was given and it was left to the discretion of the court to fix the exemption; in that case we simply used the highest stated exemption. But we departed from this rule in cases where it seemed that a lower exemption was specifically ordained if the debt was incurred "for the common necessaries of life."

Many times a state's wage exemption is expressed as so many dollars a day (or week or month) instead of as a fraction of earnings; or dollar amounts are mixed with fractions, as when the exempt amount is a certain percentage of earnings, but in no case more than a specified number of dollars a day (or less than another number of dollars a day, or both). In other states a schedular exemption is provided: in Hawaii, for example, 95 percent of the first hundred dollars that a man earns each month is exempt from garnishment, then 90 percent of the next hundred dollars, and 80 percent of everything above that. At least two states express their exemptions simply as a fixed number of dollars, omitting any reference to the length of time the employee has worked to earn the wages his employer now owes him.

In all these cases, putting the exemptions on a consistent basis in all states required converting dollar amounts into fractions of earnings. This we did with the help of data compiled by the Department of Labor on the wages paid workers in different states. As the base in each state to which to apply the stated exemption, we used the average weekly earnings of workers in manufacturing industries for 1967.[2] Thus for Georgia, where average earnings were reported to be $17.95 a day, and the wage exemption from garnishment was $3.00 a day plus 50 percent of a man's daily earnings in excess of $3.00 we computed a wage exemption of 58.4 percent. A similar procedure was followed in other states. Occasionally, to interpret dollar exemptions that omitted any reference to an earnings period, we had to make some assumption about the frequency with which a man was paid before we could compute the exemption. In this instance, we assumed that he was paid biweekly and that each payment was for work performed during the two weeks immediately preceding the payment. Thus a writ of garnishment served on the employer would find him owing an average of one week's wages to his employee, to which the exemption would apply.

2. U.S. Bureau of the Census, *Statistical Abstract of the United States: 1968* (1968), Table 334, p. 232.

At no time did we take account of the different ways that states define the wage base to which their exemption applies. Two states that exempt the same fraction of earnings will have different exemptions if the courts in one state interpret the exemption as applying to a man's gross income, before the deduction of such items as taxes, while the courts in the other state apply the exemption to a man's disposable income. States do differ in this respect, and reading their statutes is often of little help in determining which procedure they follow.

Finally, we usually—though not always—ignored the important practical question of what portion of a debtor's earnings owed him by his employer are affected by a writ of garnishment. This differs from state to state. In some states it seems to be the wages the employee has earned, but has not yet been paid, up to the date when the writ was served; in others, his unpaid earnings up to the date when the employer answered the writ; in still others, not only the earnings that his employer already owes him, but all his future earnings from that employer as well. A few states make a nice distinction between wages that are merely "due" an employee and those that are "due and payable," only the second being subject to garnishment. All these distinctions determine how much money can be collected in a garnishment action and so presumably affect a creditor's willingness to institute such an action. Similarly, creditors may be deterred if a statute allows only one levy at a time.

The excuse in all cases for ignoring these other features of the garnishment laws is that there appeared to be no way of summarizing their diversity in a single number by which we might rank states according to the ease or stringency of their garnishment laws. In defense of these omissions, it may be said that the value of the analysis we carried out is not much weakened by our focusing on wage exemptions alone unless it can be shown that leaving out these other important features has seriously biased the data we worked with. The key word here is "biased." A bias would be imparted if the features of each law that we ignored tended generally to work against the effects of the wage exemptions; that is, if most of the states with high exemptions had laws that were tougher than average in other respects and most of the states with low exemptions had laws that were less strict than average in other respects. But if there are few consistent differences between the garnishment laws of the states with high wage exemptions and the laws of states with low wage exemptions, other than the exemptions themselves, our results would probably be little affected even if we could find a way to incorporate these differences into our analysis.

The peculiar way exemptions are expressed in Delaware and New Jersey raised special problems. The wage exemption in Delaware differs from county to county, so to arrive at a statewide exemption, we weighted the average of the county exemptions by the counties' 1960 populations.

The exemption in New Jersey was a minimum of $18 a week, or 90 percent of a man's earnings if his wage is not more than $2,500 a year. Apparently the court has authority to set a lower exemption when the earnings of higher-paid debtors are being garnisheed. We made the very conservative assumption that the court would always exempt at least an amount each week equal to 90 percent of the weekly earnings of a man earning $2,500 a year, or 0.90 $\times$ $48.08 = $43.27. Applying this to the actual average earnings of New Jersey's workers, which are $118.96 a week, we obtained an exemption of 36.4 percent. In practice, the New Jersey courts customarily exempt 90 percent of all employees' earnings. This practice, however, gives more support to the results of our statistical test, for New Jersey's bankruptcy rate is among the lowest in the nation.

5. BANKRUPTCY IN OTHER COUNTRIES

Further perspective on bankruptcy in the United States was provided by an inquiry into the laws and procedures of a few other Western countries. The results, although interesting to students and specialists in bankruptcy, revealed no general cure for the weaknesses of our system and few ideas for greater efficiency, lower cost, or more equitable treatment of debtors and creditors. We therefore offer only a few illustrative comments rather than a complete report of findings.[3]

Between the American system and European systems (and among the latter) there are great differences in attitudes, law, procedure, and numbers of cases. For example, wage earners cannot become bankrupt in Belgium, France, and Italy; only "tradesmen" have this privilege.

Bankruptcy in Europe is predominantly a creditors' remedy, intended to suppress and punish deception and fraud by debtors and to obtain equal shares in the assets for the creditors. Bankrupts are stigmatized, and limitations are imposed on their activities. There are no bankruptcy discharges

3. Bankruptcy laws and procedures of selected Western commercial countries were studied in several ways. The staff reviewed available literature in English, which is limited mainly to the British and Canadian systems. Meetings were held and proposals reviewed with Canadian officials making a survey of their own bankruptcy procedures. Victor G. Rosenblum visited bankruptcy courts in England, Belgium, the Netherlands, France, and West Germany, observing court procedure and interviewing officials. Stefan A. Riesenfeld of the University of California (Berkeley) School of Law prepared a paper comparing major features of the French, Italian, and West German systems with that of the United States. Von Ernst Mezger of the Sorbonne prepared a supple - mentary memorandum on certain aspects of French procedure. Pierre R. Loiseaux of the University of Texas School of Law wrote a memorandum on the bankruptcy system of Denmark. Finally, material from all these sources was consolidated and analyzed by Rosenblum.

For a presentation of related interest see the symposium on creditors' remedies in various countries in *American Journal of Comparative Law*, Vol. 17, No. 1 (1969).

in Belgium, France, the Netherlands, Germany, Italy, and Denmark. Discharges are possible in common law countries (England, Canada, Australia) but may be delayed for years or conditioned on certain actions by the debtor, or both.

Organization for bankruptcy differs too. France and Belgium, for instance, have "commerce courts" presided over by tradesmen elected to the bench by fellow businessmen—thus institutionalizing control by creditors. Officials called *syndics* do work like that of our trustees, and others called *agréés* represent creditors. Both must qualify through government examinations and must purchase their practices from their predecessors. British bankruptcy courts are presided over by "registrars," judicial officials appointed for life by the lord chancellor. Cases are administered by officials (somewhat like trustees) called "official receivers," who are civil servants paid by the government.

The other countries share the U.S. problem of finding an appropriate level for administrative costs; none has costs below 20 percent of assets realized. Belgium has the lowest published percentage cost, 21 percent, and England the highest, 34 percent in cases closed by nonofficial trustees and 40 percent in cases closed both by official trustees and by official receivers. Canadian costs are approximately 24 percent.[4] Yet, because of the widely varying circumstances, such comparisons have little validity. Comparison of yields to creditors would have even less because of differences in eligibility for bankruptcy, practices concerning secured debts, incentives for creditors to participate in the process, and many other factors.

6. BANKRUPTCY SYSTEM EXPENSES

Possible annual costs of the bankruptcy agency proposed in Chapter 10 are as follows:

	Millions of dollars
Headquarters salaries (250 professional and clerical personnel)	3.5
Field salaries (1,500 personnel)	16.0
Fringe benefits (8 percent of salaries)	1.6
Expenses of protection, insurance, storage, sales, other	7.5
Other expenses (travel, supplies, and so forth—25 percent of salaries)	4.9
Total	33.5

4. *Annuaire Statistique de la Belgique* (Brussels: Ministère des Affaires Economiques, 1966); *Bankruptcy Annual Report* (London: Board of Trade, 1967); *Canada* Yearbook (Ottawa: Dominion Bureau of Statistics, 1967).

Some $3.0 million of this could be paid for by filing fees (200,000 cases at $15).

Comparing this estimate with costs of the present system is difficult because of the complexity and variety of the present financing, but these expenses for fiscal 1968 are roughly comparable:[5]

	Millions of dollars
Bankruptcy Division	0.3
Referees' Salary and Expense (S&E) Fund	11.9
Clerks of court (198,000 cases at $3)	0.6
Trustees' compensation (198,000 cases at $10)	2.0
Expenses of administration, nominal-asset cases, less portions for S&E Fund and attorneys for bankrupts and creditors[6]	2.1
Expenses of administration, asset cases, less portions for S&E Fund, attorneys for bankrupts, and attorneys for creditors	16.4
Expenses of administration, Chapter XIII cases ($21.3 net realization at 17 percent median expense less portions for S&E Fund and debtors' attorneys)	1.5
Total	34.8

Added to this are the expenses of administration in Chapters X, XI, and XII cases, which are not given here because they may include business operating costs.

5. These figures are estimated from "Tables of Bankruptcy Statistics" (1968), supplemented by information from the Administrative Office.

6. A deduction is made for attorneys for debtors and creditors because they may still be used under the new system.

APPENDIX C

Supplementary Tables

TABLE C-1. *Occupations of Debtors*
In percent

| Occupation | Interviewees, straight bank-ruptcy and Chapter XIII | File cases[a] | |
		Straight bankruptcy	Chapter XIII
Semiskilled and unskilled workers	32	32	65
Craftsmen, other skilled workers	28	26	21
Clerical personnel	12	7	2
Service workers	7	1	3
Professionals and semiprofessionals	7	3[b]	3
Proprietors, managers; officials	5	10[b]	—[c]
Sales personnel	2	2	3
Farm workers	1	1	0
Military personnel	—[d]	1	1
Other workers	7	—[c]	1
Unemployed	—[d]	10	—[c]
Housewives	—[d]	6[e]	0

Source: Interviews and file sample of straight bankruptcy and Chapter XIII cases. Percentages may not add to 100 because of rounding.
a. Excluding Northern Ohio and Southern New York.
b. In straight bankruptcy cases with liabilities of $10,000 or more, the proportions in these categories were approximately doubled.
c. Less than 0.5 percent.
d. Not shown.
e. In spouse cases.

TABLE C-2. *Debtors by Type of Employment*
In percent

Type of employment	Interviewees, straight bankruptcy and Chapter XIII	File cases[a] Straight bankruptcy	Chapter XIII
Manufacturing and industrial	49	46	49
Business and trade	17	16	13
Services	15	28	23
Government	10	5	13
Military	9	3	1
Agriculture	—[b]	2	—[b]

Source: Interviews and file sample of straight bankruptcy and Chapter XIII cases. Percentages may not add to 100 because of rounding.
a. Excluding Northern Ohio and Southern New York and debtors who were interviewed.
b. Less than 0.5 percent.

TABLE C-3. *Distribution of Scheduled Liabilities in Former-Business and Nonbusiness Straight Bankruptcy Cases*
In percent

Scheduled liabilities (in dollars)	Total	Former business	Nonbusiness
Under 1,000	3	—	3
1,000–2,499	20	3	23
2,500–4,999	26	9	28
5,000–7,499	13	18	12
7,500–9,999	8	20	6
10,000–19,999	18	26	17
20,000–49,999	11	15	10
50,000–99,999	1	6	1
100,000 and over	—[a]	1	—
Median amount	$5,180	$9,849	$4,603

Source: File sample of personal bankruptcy cases. Percentages may not add to 100 because of rounding.
a. Less than 0.5 percent.

TABLE C-4. *Distribution of Scheduled Liabilities in Chapter XIII Cases*
In percent

Scheduled liabilities (in dollars)	Seven districts	Northern Alabama	Other districts
Under 500	25	33	—a
500–999	25	30	9
1,000–2,499	31	27	42
2,500–4,999	12	7	28
5,000–7,499	2	1	6
7,500–9,999	—a	—	2
10,000–19,999	4	1	10
20,000 and over	1	—	3
Median amount	$992	$779	$2,446

Source: File sample of Chapter XIII cases. Percentages may not add to 100 because of rounding.
a. Less than 0.5 percent.

TABLE C-5. *Percentage of Total Debt and Median Amount Owed in Personal Straight Bankruptcy and Chapter XIII Cases, by Type of Debt*[a]

Type of debt	Former business Percentage of total debt	Former business Median amount owed (dollars)	Nonbusiness Percentage of total debt	Nonbusiness Median amount owed (dollars)	Chapter XIII Percentage of total debt	Chapter XIII Median amount owed (dollars)
Personal						
Finance companies	3.5	889	17.3	983	33.8	470
Banks and lending institutions	—[b]	—[b]	14.9	849	9.4	362
Credit unions	0.2	395	1.6	490	3.9	446
Individual loans	9.1	1,792	8.0	464	3.3	255
Utilities	0.2	82	0.6	92	0.5	67
Medical services	1.9	342	6.1	365	5.4	231
Nonmedical services	1.5	392	2.3	109	2.2	90
Retail merchants	4.9	749	16.0	643	26.4	400
Cosigned notes	1.8	2,444	1.3	416	0.1	98
Judgments	1.6	1,191	5.4	1,321	1.2	250
Rent	0.2	581	0.8	244	0.3	138
Taxes	0.3	97	0.3	78	0.7	219
Other	5.0	676	25.1	684	10.1	72
Business						
Merchandise suppliers	15.9	2,332				
Lending institutions	18.7	2,093				
Services	5.2	483				
Utilities	0.2	227				
Rent	1.5	1,340				
Taxes	1.9	769				
Equipment	0.2	2,812				
Wages	0.05	258				
Other	26.1	4,387				

Source: File sample of personal bankruptcy and Chapter XIII cases.

a. For this calculation we attempted to eliminate overlapping spouses' liability. The table excludes secured debts in Northern Ohio, the pilot district.

An attempt was made to classify the debt in each sample according to its age. This failed to produce reliable data, because the petitioners' attorneys frequently ignored the requirement that such information be included in the schedules. Moreover, when the age of the debt was available, it was still impossible to tell how much of the recent debt represented a refinancing of older obligations.

b. Since it was impossible to distinguish between personal and business borrowings, figures for both are under "Business, Lending institutions."

TABLE C-6. *Proportions of Scheduled Liabilities in Personal Straight Bankruptcy and Chapter XIII Cases, by Class of Debt*
In percent

| | Straight bankruptcy | | | Chapter |
| | Total | Former business | Nonbusiness | XIII |
Class of debt				
Priority	2	3	1	1
Secured	51	27	60	56
Realty	34	17	41	27
Personalty[a]	17	10	19	29
Unsecured	48	70	39	43

Source: File sample of personal straight bankruptcy and Chapter XIII cases. Percentages may not add to 100 because of rounding.
a. Such as cars, furniture, and appliances.

TABLE C-7. *Median Number of Creditors in Personal Straight Bankruptcy and Chapter XIII Cases*

| | Straight bankruptcy | | |
| | Former business | Nonbusiness | Chapter XIII |
Class of debt			
Priority	1	0	0
Secured	2	2	1
Unsecured	23	10	6

Source: File sample of personal straight bankruptcy and Chapter XIII cases.

TABLE C-8. *Median Assets and Liabilities as Scheduled in Personal Straight Bankruptcy and Chapter XIII Cases*
In dollars

| | Assets | | | |
Type of bankruptcy	Secured liabilities deducted	Secured liabilities not deducted	Impossible to tell	Liabilities
Straight bankruptcy	388	602	576	5,180
Former business	938	1,945	683	9,849
Nonbusiness	350	544	542	4,603
Chapter XIII	406	482	405	992
Northern Alabama	385	315	371	779
Other districts	422	667	418	2,446

Source: File sample of personal straight bankruptcy and Chapter XIII cases.

TABLE C-9. *Median Values of Selected Types of Exempt Property Claimed Compared with Median Values Allowed, by District*[a]
In dollars

District	Clothing[b]		Household goods[b]		Clothing and household goods[b]		Automobile		Homestead	
	Claimed	Allowed	Claimed	Allowed	Claimed	Allowed	Claimed	Allowed	Claimed	Allowed
Northern Ohio	128	115	457	275	500e	500e	—	—	500d	500d
Northern Alabama	234	209	480	460	1,166	945	439	409	1,500	1,400
Maine	83	76	200e	200e	200e	200e	—	—	750f	—
Northern Illinois	71	71	186	211	162	158	80	77	3,145	3,045
Oregon	128	128	284	279	266	266	222	209	1,628	1,646
Western Texas	316	233	714	999	915	500	749	650	12,500	12,500
Southern California	228	96	374	380	595	560	168	162	7,026	8,198

Source: File sample of bankruptcy cases.

a. Values are grouped medians unless otherwise noted.
b. Some debtors' attorneys listed clothing and household goods separately; others combined them.
c. The statutory maximum ($500) for household goods was used with few exceptions.
d. Ohio petitioners almost invariably assigned the $500 statutory value to homestead exemption claims.
e. The statutory maximum ($200) for household goods was used with few exceptions.
f. Claimed in only one case.

TABLE C-10. *Mean Time between Filing, Discharge, and Closing for Former-Business and Nonbusiness Cases, by District*[a]

In months

District	Former business			Nonbusiness		
	Filing to discharge	Discharge to closing	Filing to closing	Filing to discharge	Discharge to closing	Filing to closing
Northern Alabama	15.6	6.2	21.8	9.2	0.6[b]	9.3
Maine	15.0	1.6	15.5	8.2	4.0	12.2
Northern Ohio	9.9	6.8	12.9	8.6	8.8	17.0
Oregon	9.8	0.5[b]	10.4	10.0	0.5[b]	10.5
Southern California	6.0	7.3	13.3	4.3	3.0	7.1
Western Texas	4.7	7.9	12.6	1.8	3.9	5.7
Northern Illinois	3.1	7.0	9.7	4.3	3.6	6.4
Seven districts	7.7	5.9	12.5	6.1	4.1	9.7

Source: File sample of personal bankruptcy cases.

a. Means in each column are based on cases in which both the relevant dates were available. Either the discharge or the closing date (or both) was sometimes missing from the file. This accounts for the fact that the "Filing to closing" column figures do not necessarily equal the sum of the figures in the other two columns.

b. Discharges in these categories were usually granted simultaneously with closing the case.

TABLE C-11. *Median Size of Estate in Chapter XIII Cases, by District*[a]

In dollars

District	All cases	Arranged	Dismissed
Southern California	955	2,318	499
Oregon	917	1,844	425
Western Texas	741	1,531	741
Maine	655	1,960	299
Northern Alabama	575	884	271
Northern Illinois	115	2,269	0[b]
Northern Ohio	50	1,000	26[b]
Median	580	984	253
Median, excluding Northern Alabama	599	2,129	195

Source: File sample of Chapter XIII cases.

a. Grouped medians, except in Western Texas, where actual figures were used because of the small sample size.

b. The low medians for dismissed cases in Northern Illinois and Northern Ohio reflect the high proportion of cases in which dismissal occurred *before* confirmation in those two districts.

TABLE C-12. *Distribution of Scheduled Liabilities in Business Straight Bankruptcy and Chapter XI Cases*
In percent

Scheduled liabilities (in dollars)	Straight bankruptcy		Chapter XI
	Involuntary	All cases	
Under 1,000	0	2	0
1,000–2,499	—a	1	0
2,500–4,999	0	6	0
5,000–7,499	0	2	1
7,500–9,999	0	3	1
10,000–19,999	15	15	1
20,000–49,999	35	33	9
50,000–99,999	24	23	11
100,000–249,999	16	9	28
250,000–499,999	2	4	23
500,000–999,999	5	3	15
1,000,000–1,999,999	0	0	9
2,000,000 and over	0	0	2
No data	2	—a	0

Source: File sample of business bankruptcy and Chapter XI cases. Percentages may not add to 100 because of rounding.
a. Less than 0.5 percent.

TABLE C-13. *Proportions of Scheduled Liabilities in Business Straight Bankruptcy and Chapter XI Cases, by Class of Debt*[a]

In percent

Class of debt	Straight bankruptcy	Chapter XI
Secured	33	29
Realty	13	12
Personality	20[b]	17[b]
Priority	7[b]	5
Wages	1	1
Taxes	5	4
Rent	1	—[c]
Other or unspecified	—[c]	—[c]
Unsecured	60	66

Source: File sample of business bankruptcy and Chapter XI cases.

a. Several caveats are in order. Claims scheduled as unsecured were not infrequently proved as secured. State and federal statutes giving liens for tax claims were generally ignored, and those claims were usually scheduled as priority rather than secured claims—and occasionally even as unsecured. The scheduling of rent claims for priority—which occurred in every district in our sample—is in all instances erroneous. Rent claims are entitled to priority in bankruptcy proceedings only if they are given priority by state law and no such priority was conferred by the applicable state law in any district in the sample. Wage claims were not infrequently scheduled for full priority, although only that part earned within three months of bankruptcy, not to exceed $600 a claimant, is entitled to priority. There was frequently an unavoidable imprecision as to the amount of tax claims—estimates had to be made where the tax had not yet been assessed or where interest and penalties on delinquent payments had not yet been computed. Finally, there were all-too-frequent instances where a tax incurred but not yet assessed, or interest and penalties for delinquency, were simply ignored in the schedules.

b. Pilot study in Northern Ohio did not make further breakdown of types of personal property securing debts or of basis for priority claims.

Personal property for the other districts breaks down to roughly the following proportions. In straight bankruptcy cases—equipment (including motor vehicles), 6 percent; accounts receivable, 3 percent; inventory, 2 percent; other or unspecified, 10 percent. In Chapter XI cases—equipment, 7 percent; accounts receivable, 4 percent; inventory, 1 percent; other, 5 percent.

c. Less than 0.5 percent.

TABLE C-14. *Percentage of Total Debt and Median Amount Owed in Business Straight Bankruptcy and Chapter XI Cases, by Type of Debt*

Type of debt	Straight bankruptcy		Chapter XI	
	Percentage of total debt	Median amount owed (dollars)	Percentage of total debt	Median amount owed (dollars)
Merchandise suppliers	28.3	11,077	30.4	84,500
Lending institutions	25.1	5,747	25.3	31,400
Rent	15.0	1,447	0.1	1,870
Individual loans	6.4	6,187	2.8	15,300
Taxes	4.8	2,196	4.4	7,650
Services	2.6	965	4.7	4,900
Equipment suppliers[a]	2.0	3,323	1.6	16,000
Wages	1.5	1,157	0.6	2,035
Cosigned notes	0.5	4,000	1.4	160,000[b]
Utilities	0.3	336	0.2	671
Judgments[b]	0.2	870	—	—
Other[c]	13.3	6,500	28.5	36,500

Source: File sample of business bankruptcy and Chapter XI cases.
a. Includes both purchases on credit and rentals.
b. Information on the nature of the underlying claim was usually not contained in the files.
c. Often it was impossible to distinguish between the personal and the business obligations of sole proprietors and partners, or to characterize the nature of business debts.

TABLE C-15. *Median Assets and Liabilities in Business Straight Bankruptcy and Chapter XI Cases*
In dollars

Item	Straight bankruptcy	Chapter XI
Assets		
Secured liabilities deducted	6,355	115,000
Secured liabilities not deducted	12,398	167,500
Impossible to tell	13,762	164,500
Liabilities	39,902	243,865

Source: File sample of business bankruptcy and Chapter XI cases.

TABLE C-16. *Details of Unsuccessful Chapter X Cases, by District*

District	Nature of business	Scheduled liabilities	Scheduled assets	Time to dismissal	Time to adjudication
Southern New York	Apartment house construction	$2,096,941	$1,600,000	6 months	—
Southern New York	Two diners, tourist home	82,937	—ᵃ	6 months	—
Northern Ohioᵇ	Motel	20,633	26,291	6 weeks	—
Northern Ohioᵇ	Motel	75,098	164,520	6 weeks	—
Southern New York	Printing	1,318,844	250,155	—	2 months
Western Texas	Steel fabrication	176,970	74,250	—	2 months
Southern California	Bowling alley	54,377	11,420	—	6 months to Chapter XI, then 2 weeks to dismissal

Source: Files of all Chapter X cases in the eight districts in the study.
a. No data. Plan disapproved when debtor was found solvent.
b. Consolidated case of two corporations with common sole stockholder.

TABLE C-17. *Cases in Which Petitions for Review Were Filed as a Percentage of Cases Closed, by District and Type of Case (Asset and Arranged Cases Only), Fiscal Years 1964 and 1965*

District and type of case	1964			1965		
	Peti-tions filed	Cases closed	Percent	Peti-tions filed	Cases closed	Percent
Northern Ohio						
Straight bankruptcy	8	1,138	0.7	8	2,511	0.3
Chapter XI	—	7	—	3	11	27.3
Chapter XIII	—	23	—	—	42	—
Northern Alabama						
Straight bankruptcy	7	101	6.9	2	120	1.7
Chapter XI	—	—	—	—	1	—
Chapter XII	—	2	—	—	—	—
Chapter XIII	—	3,094	—	2	3,092	0.1
Maine						
Straight bankruptcy	3	216	1.4	3	225	1.3
Chapter XI	3	2	—	1	1	100.0
Chapter XIII	4	135	3.0	6	320	1.9
Northern Illinois						
Straight bankruptcy	22	324	6.8	14	383	3.7
Chapter XI	1	22	4.5	3	25	12.0
Chapter XIII	—	81	—	—	144	—
Oregon						
Straight bankruptcy	4	961	0.4	6	1,006	0.6
Chapter XI	1	—	—	—	3	—
Chapter XIII	1	25	4.0	—	33	—
Western Texas						
Straight bankruptcy	4	36	11.1	2	67	3.0
Chapter XI	1	—	—	1	2	50.0
Chapter XIII	—	1	—	—	6	—
Southern New York						
Straight bankruptcy	20	146	13.7	21	207	10.1
Chapter X	1	1	100.0	1	—	—
Chapter XI	12	88	13.6	12	68	17.7
Chapter XIII	—	—	—	—	4	—
Southern California						
Straight bankruptcy	61	1,289	4.7	50	1,708	2.9
Chapter X	3	—	—	1	1	100.0
Chapter XI	28	21	—	27	39	69.2
Chapter XII	2	3	66.7	2	2	100.0
Chapter XIII	—	268	—	1	381	0.3
Chapter unknown	1	—	—	—	—	—

TABLE C-17 (*continued*)

District and type of case	1964			1965		
	Peti-tions filed	Cases closed	Percent	Peti-tions filed	Cases closed	Percent
Eight districts						
Straight bankruptcy	129	4,211	3.1	106	6,227	1.7
Chapter X	4	1	—	2	1	—
Chapter XI	46	140	32.9	47	150	31.3
Chapter XII	2	5	40.0	2	2	100.0
Chapter XIII	5	3,627	0.1	9	4,022	0.2
Chapter unknown	1	—	—	—	—	—

Sources: Data on petitions reported by clerks of district courts at the request of the Administrative Office of the U.S. Courts; tabulated by Brookings staff. Figures in the "cases closed" columns are from Administrative Office of the U.S. Courts, "Tables of Bankruptcy Statistics" (1964 and 1965), Tables F 4a and F 4b. This is a complete enumeration, not a sample.

Straight bankruptcy cases are asset cases only. Chapter cases are arranged cases only. If a case was filed under one chapter and later converted to another, it is counted under the latter. Thus adjudicated special relief cases are counted as straight bankruptcies.

A case in which petitions were filed in both fiscal years is counted in both years.

A consolidated spouse case (consolidated, that is, by the court) is counted as one case.

TABLE C-18. *Outcome of Petitions for Review in Fiscal Years 1964 and 1965, by District*

District	Outcome			Total petitions	Appealed to court of appeals
	Referee affirmed[a]	Referee reversed[b]	Withdrawn, settled		
Southern California	105	38	21	164	43
Southern New York	56	12	21	89	23
Northern Illinois	31	8	6	45	6
Northern Ohio	17	3	0	20	5
Maine	12	1	10	23	3
Western Texas	12	1	2	15	5
Northern Alabama	11	0	0	11	1
Oregon	8	4	0	12	2
Eight districts	252	67	60	379	88

Source: Data on petitions reported by clerks of district courts at the request of the Administrative Office of the U.S. Courts; tabulated by Brookings staff.

a. The colloquial term is "petition dismissed," which is without statutory basis.

b. The colloquial term is "petition granted," which is without statutory basis.

TABLE C-19. *Decisions by Court of Appeals in Petitions for Review in Fiscal Years 1964 and 1965, by District*

District	Petitions appealed	District court decision			Referee's decision		
		Affirmed	Reversed	Withdrawn, settled, pending	Upheld	Overruled	Other[a]
Southern California	43	17	7	19	19	5	19
Southern New York	23	11	4	8	10	5	8
Northern Illinois	6	3	2	1	3	2	1
Northern Ohio	5	3	0	2	3	0	2
Western Texas	5	1	1	3	1	1	3
Maine	3	3	0	0	3	0	0
Oregon	2	2	0	0	1	1	0
Northern Alabama	1	0	1	0	0	1	0
Eight districts	88	40	15	33	40	15	33

Source: Data on petitions reported by clerks of district courts at the request of the Administrative Office of the U.S. Courts; tabulated by Brookings staff.
a. Never perfected, withdrawn, dismissed by stipulation, outcome not clear, record incomplete, or dismissed for failure to comply with court rules.

TABLE C-20. *Years of Service of Referees in Office on June 30, 1969*
In percent

	All districts[a]		Eight districts in study[b]	
Years of service	Full-time referees	Part-time referees	Full-time referees	Part-time referees
Under 6	37	26	28	33
6–11	36	32	39	50
12–17	13	13	18	0
18–23	7	21	9	0
24–29	4	3	2	17
30–35	2	3	2	0
Over 35	1	3	2	0
Median	8.2 years	10.5 years	9.4 years	8.0 years

Source: Special study for this project made by the Administrative Office of the U.S. Courts.
Percentages may not add to 100 because of rounding.
a. There were 166 full-time and 38 part-time referees in all.
b. There were 46 full-time and 6 part-time referees in the eight districts studied.

TABLE C-21. *Reasons for Termination of Referees in Bankruptcy,*
July 1, 1947, to June 30, 1969
In percent

	All districts[a]		Eight districts in study[b]	
Reason	Full-time referees	Part-time referees	Full-time referees	Part-time referees
Retired	40	12	45	17
Died	25	21	28	28
Resigned	16	37	14	33
Not reappointed	14	22	7	0
Appointed federal judge	2	1	3	6
Other	2	7	3	17

Source: Special study made for this project by the Administrative Office of the U.S. Courts.
Percentages may not add to 100 because of rounding.
a. There were 109 full-time and 115 part-time referees in all.
b. There were 29 full-time and 18 part-time referees in the eight districts studied.

TABLE C-22. *Administrative Office Headquarters Bankruptcy Costs, Fiscal Years 1964–67*

In dollars

Category of costs	1964	1965	1966	1967[a]
Bankruptcy Division[b]	92,781	110,232	130,698	139,531
Bankruptcy Statistical Unit[b]	29,899	27,334	28,883	34,272
Support services[c]	68,000	73,000	75,000	82,000
Total	190,680	210,566	234,581	255,803
Cost per case terminated[d]	1.17	1.20	1.26	1.33

Source: Special compilation by the Administrative Office of the U.S. Courts.

a. Comparable figures for later years are not available. Assuming a 10 percent rate of inflation, the total for fiscal 1968 would have been $281,383 (or $1.42 per case closed). In fiscal 1969, the appropriations procedure was changed, so that charges for administration of bankruptcy cases were included in the total appropriation for the Administrative Office. In that process, Congress decided on a figure of $380,000 (or approximately $2 per case closed), which seems somewhat high.

b. The miscellaneous expenses component of this cost is estimated.

c. Estimated.

d. Computed from "Tables of Bankruptcy Statistics," Table F 1, for the respective years.

TABLE C-23. *Filing Fees and Amounts Kept by Referees' Salary and Expense Fund, and Percentage Charges, by Type of Case, Fiscal Year 1970*

Type of case	Filing fee	Charges
Straight bankruptcy	$50 (Fund keeps $37)	3.5% of first $50,000 of net realization in asset and nominal-asset cases, and 3% of the balance, $5 minimum charge, in cases filed on or after July 1, 1970
Chapter X	$70 if a bankruptcy proceeding is pending (Fund keeps $37) $120 if not pending	Reimbursement as allowed by judge on petition by referee
Chapter XI	$50 (Fund keeps $37)	3% of first $100,000 of total obligation paid or extended, and 1.5% of the balance, in cases filed on or after July 1, 1970
Chapter XII	$50 (Fund keeps $37)	Reimbursement as allowed by judge on petition by referee
Chapter XIII	$15, plus $15 when plan is submitted if liabilities exceed $200; plus $10 if under $200 (Fund keeps $25 of a $30 fee; $20 of a $25 fee)	1% of debtor's payments

Source: Administrative Office of the U.S. Courts, "Manual for Referees in Bankruptcy: Administrative Procedures and Regulations" (continually updated; processed), pp. 604.01–605.14.

TABLE C-24. *Salaries and Expenses of Referees' Offices, by District,*
Fiscal Years 1964 and 1969
In dollars

District	1964		1969	
	Total	Per case terminated	Total	Per case terminated
Southern California	876,971	46.79	1,305,279	47.42[a]
Northern Illinois	442,052	31.77	616,904	70.29
Northern Ohio	348,816	38.27	514,794	61.10
Northern Alabama	284,149	41.02	402,727	64.01
Southern New York	206,969	212.49	352,243	314.22
Oregon	191,187	48.07	286,291	60.86
Maine	99,444	73.23	141,959	86.77
Western Texas	48,552	315.27	62,707	176.64
Eight districts	2,498,140	45.29	3,682,904	62.60

Sources: Totals, special compilation by Administrative Office of the U.S. Courts; per case, "Tables of Bankruptcy Statistics" (1964 and 1969), Table F 1.

a. For this calculation (since California has been redistricted), one-half of the cases closed in the eastern district of California were added to those in the southern and central districts in an effort to provide comparability with caseload in the former southern district.

TABLE C-25. *Administrative Expenses Paid from Estates in Nominal-Asset Cases, by Category of Expense and District, Fiscal Year 1964*

In percent

Category of expense	Northern Ohio	Northern Alabama	Maine	Northern Illinois	Oregon	Western Texas	Southern New York	Southern California	Eight districts	All districts in U.S.
Trustee's commission[a]	58	44	75	22	15	45	19	43	40	44
Attorney for bankrupt	17	19	2	6	46	18	2	10	16	13
Attorney for trustee	7	10	3	30	3	6	26	3	8	10
"Trustee's and All Other Expenses"	1	6	4	5	5	9	7	17	9	8
Referees' Salary and Expense Fund[b]	9	7	8	4	8	7	6	6	7	7
Reporting testimony	—[c]	0	5	3	—[c]	0	6	8	4	3
Appraiser's fee and expenses	1	0	3	4	—[c]	1	3	3	2	3
Rental expense	2	0	0	5	0	7	7	2	2	2
Receiver's commission	—[c]	1	0	2	—[c]	—[c]	1	1	1	1
Attorney for receiver	—[c]	0	0	7	—[c]	0	2	—[c]	1	1
Auctioneer's fee and expenses	—[c]	—[c]	0	2	0	0	13	2	1	1
Receiver's expenses	—[c]	0	0	4	—[c]	0	—[c]	—[c]	1	1
Accountant's fee and expenses	0	0	0	—[c]	—[c]	0	0	—[c]	—[c]	—[c]
Attorney for creditors	—[c]	0	0	2	—[c]	4	2	—[c]	1	—[c]
Attorneys for others	—[c]	0	0	—[c]	0	0	4	—[c]	—[c]	—[c]
Total	97	86	100	96	78	96	98	95	93	95
Other distributions[d]	3	14	—[c]	4	22	4	2	5	7	5
Average administrative expense per case, in dollars[e]	$83	$116	$78	$240	$71	$190	$273	$166	$118	$110

Source: "Tables of Bankruptcy Statistics" (1964), Tables F 8 and F 9. Percentages may not add to totals because of rounding.

a. Calculated on a statutory percentage basis, subject to the referee's discretion to pay $150 without reference to such percentage.

b. Calculated on a statutory percentage basis, the percentage fixed by the Judicial Conference.

c. Less than 0.5 percent.

d. Payments included in total disbursements but not in expenses of administration: for example, expenses and obligations incurred in proceedings prior to adjudication; filing fees paid out of the estate; payments by the trustee in state court proceedings.

e. Does not include "Other distributions."

TABLE C-26. *Fees and Expenses Paid in Straight Bankruptcy Asset Cases as a Percentage of Estates, by Category of Expense and District, Fiscal Year 1964*

Category of expense	Northern Ohio	Northern Alabama	Maine	Northern Illinois	Oregon	Western Texas	Southern New York[a]	Southern California	Eight districts
Attorney for trustee	7.5	2.9	4.8	7.3	5.8	6.8	8.5	3.2	5.7
Trustee	6.3	6.0	9.7	2.7	6.7	2.5	3.8	4.0	4.1
Auctioneer	3.7	—	1.6	2.5	3.0	0.8	3.1	0.8	2.4
Referees' Salary and Expense Fund	3.1	2.8	2.8	2.3	3.4	2.5	1.6	1.9	2.1
Receiver	1.3	1.2	1.2	4.2	0.8	0.7	—	2.4	1.9
Attorney for debtor	2.7	1.9	1.9	1.7	4.2	1.5	1.0	1.2	1.4
Attorney for receiver	4.1	0.9	0.7	1.7	0.3	0.7	0.1	1.1	1.2
Accountant	2.8	—b	—	1.3	0.9	—	1.7	0.4	1.1
Appraiser	0.4	—	1.4	0.2	0.1	0.3	0.2	0.3	0.3
Shorthand reporter	0.4	—	0.3	0.2	—	—	0.1	0.4	0.3
Attorney for petitioning creditor	0.2	—	—	0.5 b	—	1.0	0.2	0.2	0.2
Adjuster	—	—	—	b	—	0.1	—	—	0.1
Attorney for creditors' committee	—	0.1	—	0.1	—	—	—	0.2	—b
Clerical and bookkeeping	—	—	—	—	—	—	—	0.1	—b

Source: File sample of business and personal bankruptcy cases.

a. Business cases only.

b. Less than 0.05 percent.

TABLE C-27. *Fees and Expenses Paid in Chapter XI Cases as a Percentage of Estates, by Category of Expense, Fiscal Year 1964*

Category of expense	Percentage of estates	Remarks
Attorney for debtor	10.2[a]	11.9% in Southern New York[b]
Referees' Salary and Expense Fund	3.8	
Attorney for creditors' committees	3.0	3.6% in Southern New York
Other	2.0	11.3% in Southern California[c]
Accountant	1.9	2.4% in Southern New York
Disbursing agent	1.2	
Special master	0.9[d]	Southern New York only
Attorney for receiver	0.4[e]	
Receiver	0.4[e]	
Secretary to creditors' committee	0.2	
Auctioneer	0.2	
Administrative rent	0.2	Southern New York only
Shorthand reporter	0.1	
Attorney for petitioning creditor	0.1[f]	
Appraiser	0.1	
Trustee	—[g]	
Clerical and bookkeeping	—[g]	Southern California only
Adjuster	—[g]	Southern California only

Source: File sample of Chapter XI cases.

a. 5.6 percent if Southern New York is excluded.

b. Debtors are generally left in possession in this district.

c. Where businesses are frequently operated until an attractive sale can be arranged.

d. Expenses in cases that started under other chapters but were later changed to Chapter XIs.

e. The low percentages that went to receivers and attorneys for receivers are accounted for by two factors. First, the figures are influenced by the large number of cases from Southern New York, where debtors-in-possession rather than receivers are the general rule. Second, there is the inclination of attorneys to waive compensation.

f. Attorneys who petitioned for a receiver's appointment in Chapter XI.

g. Less than 0.05 percent.

Index

Adjudicati[...] petitioner [...] bankruptcy [...] matically a[...] ... their p[...]

If an invol[...] is filed or if a petitioner und[...], XI, or XII fails to reach agreement with creditors, adjudication may occur either with the consent of the bankrupt or by order of the court after a hearing on the issue. A Chapter XIII petitioner who fails to reach agreement with creditors or to complete payments to creditors may be adjudicated only if he consents.

Arrangement An agreement between the petitioner and creditors for extended payment or reduction in amount, or both, of all or some of the debts affected by the proceeding.

Asset case A case in which the proceeds of nonexempt assets are sufficient to pay administrative expenses and make some distribution to creditors.

Assignment of wages An agreement giving a creditor the right to collect a portion of a debtor's wages if a default occurs without resorting to judicial procedures.

Attachment A process used at the initiation of a lawsuit by which a lien is placed on property as security for the payment of any judgment recovered.

Bankruptcy A term used generally to describe proceedings undertaken in a federal court when a debtor is unable to pay or to reach agreement with his creditors outside of court. Most bankruptcies are initiated voluntarily by the debtor, though occasionally creditors file an involuntary bankruptcy petition.

Bankruptcy court Technically, the United States District Court, which is the federal court of general trial jurisdiction. However, the term is generally used to describe proceedings held before a federal bankruptcy referee, to whom most of the district judge's responsibilities in bankruptcy matters are referred.

Business bankrupt A bankrupt whose financial problems result from a current business venture.

Chapter X A proceeding used very rarely by large corporations whose stock is widely held. A Chapter X plan, if approved, can affect the company's capital structure, and can include both secured and unsecured debts.

Chapter XI A proceeding used almost exclusively by businesses that wish to pay off all or part of their unsecured indebtedness over an extended period of time. Only unsecured debts can be included in the proposed payment plan; a majority of the creditors must consent before the plan can be approved.

Chapter XII A proceeding that allows unincorporated debtors to propose an arrangement of debts secured by real estate, as well as of unsecured claims. Rarely used.

Chapter XIII A proceeding in which a wage earner can propose to pay all or part of creditors' claims over an extended period of time. To have a plan approved, a majority of the unsecured creditors and all secured creditors whose claims are dealt with by the plan must consent.

Cognovit note A promissory note that includes a cognovit clause allowing the creditor to obtain a judgment without notice to the debtor.

Composition A plan that provides for full satisfaction of creditors' claims, by partial payments either in a lump sum or over an extended period of time.

Confession of judgment Process by which a creditor "confesses" the debtor's obligation, usually pursuant to the terms of a cognovit note, and thereby obtains a judgment.

Confirmation The referee's approval of the debtor's proposed payment plan, as accepted by the required creditors. The confirmation order often includes detailed instructions about how the payments are to be distributed.

Creditor control The theory on which the present Bankruptcy Act is based. It assumes that, because their claims may remain unpaid, creditors should have (and will use) the authority to choose the trustee and to insist on energetic collection of assets and investigation of the bankrupt's behavior.

Deficiency judgment A judgment that a creditor can obtain when the proceeds of collateral are insufficient to pay a secured debt.

Discharge An order entered in a bankruptcy proceeding relieving the debtor of paying balances remaining due after nonexempt assets are distributed. Only creditors who had notice of the bankruptcy proceeding are affected.

Estate The accumulated nonexempt assets in a bankruptcy case, which are distributed for payment of administrative expenses and creditors' claims.

Exempt assets Property which a bankrupt may keep. Such property is of a category or amount that is unavailable for satisfying creditors' claims because of federal or state laws applying to bankruptcy proceedings.